Selling Hospitality

Selling Hospitality

A Situational Approach

Richard G. McNeill Jr., Ed.D., CHME
John C. Crotts, Ph.D.

THOMSON
DELMAR LEARNING

Australia Canada Mexico Singapore Spain United Kingdom United States

THOMSON

DELMAR LEARNING

Selling Hospitality: A Situational Approach
by Richard G. McNeill and John C. Crotts

Vice President, Career Education Strategic Business Unit:
Dawn Gerrain

Director of Editorial:
Sherry Gomoll

Acquisitions Editor:
Matthew Hart

Developmental Editor:
Patricia Osborn

Director of Production:
Wendy A. Troeger

Production Editor:
Matthew J. Williams

Director of Marketing:
Wendy E. Mapstone

Channel Manager:
Kristin McNary

Marketing Coordinator:
David E. White

Cover Design:
TDB Publishing Services

Interior photographs:
Getty Images

For permission to use material from this text or product, contact us by
Tel   (800) 730-2214
Fax   (800) 730-2215
www.thomsonrights.com

Library of Congress Cataloging-in-Publication Data

McNeill, Richard G.
    Selling hospitality : a situational approach / Richard G. McNeill Jr., John C. Crotts.
        p. cm.
    Includes bibliographical references and index.
    ISBN: 1-4018-3281-4
    1. Selling. 2. Hospitality industry—Marketing. 3. Tourism. Career development. I. Crotts, John C. II. Title.

HF5438.25.M44 2006
910'.68'8—dc22

                                        2005050890

NOTICE TO THE READER

Contents

v

Preface

Welcome to the world of hospitality sales professionals. Hospitality sales is a dynamic and rewarding field that can stay exciting over a long career.

Selling Hospitality: A Situational Approach is designed to provide you with insights into the hospitality sales field as well as a realistic view of the knowledge and skills you will need to master in order to be successful in it. This framework provides a road map for your future that you can start using right away, but which also has the depth to be helpful throughout your career. In today's rapidly changing business environment, the shelf life of many aspects of your hospitality and business degree can be quite short. In this text we have drawn on the insights as to what is currently the state of the art as well as what factors are influencing the evolution of the sales profession to serve you well into the future.

We believe you will find this text is unique among hospitality and tourism management textbooks. Our intent is to stimulate interest among students in sales as a preferred career path. In addition, it is our hope that this text encourages faculty to develop courses in hospitality sales. Virtually all hospitality management and business degrees require courses in marketing, but seldom in personal selling. Sales, if covered at all, is limited to a chapter at most in most marketing textbooks—providing students little opportunity to evaluate the career option, let alone develop their personal selling skills.

This is unfortunate since the career opportunities for marketing-oriented students are more developed and promising in sales as compared to marketing.

Marketing versus Sales

People hold a variety of misconceptions about the fields of sales and marketing. Marketing includes product/service development, place (location and distribution), promotion, and pricing. It requires information about people, especially those interested in what you have to offer (your "target market"), such as what they like, where they buy, and how much they spend. Its role is to match the right product or service with the right market or audience. As such, marketing is a way of doing business, heavily based on the "marketing concept," which holds that businesses and organizations should: (1) design their products/services to meet customers' needs and wants; (2) focus on those people most likely to buy their product rather than the entire mass market; and (3) develop promotional efforts that will generate the awareness, interest, desire, and ultimately sales from customers in order to achieve a firm's business objectives.

Few enterprises employ full-time marketing professionals. Instead, marketing at the retail or business-to-consumer (B2C) level generally involves management developing its marketing plan in consultation with selected advertising and public relations agencies contracted to execute the promotional aspects of the plan. In the hotel industry, sales are generated from free and independent travelers through paid forms of advertising, sales promotions, and media supported by the hotel's reservation department.

In contrast, these same firms deploy a large and well-trained sales force. In the hotel industry, these sales professionals are focused on generating sales from corporations, associations, and leisure and education groups that routinely purchase large blocks of hotel rooms and meeting facilities. These organizational buyers require a more targeted direct sales approach to earn their business as compared to *retail* customers. Therefore, hospitality marketing operates in a business-to-business (B2B) context where the sales professional takes the lead in developing and maintaining accounts with organizational buyers.

Organization of This Text

This text is organized as follows. Chapters 1 and 2 will expose you to the many aspects of a hospitality sales career, as well as the knowledge and skills you need to develop to be successful. While no ideal set of characteristics has been found to guarantee success, several factors are strongly related to high performance: emotional maturity and the ability to set goals, communicate well, and present oneself professionally. Chapters 3 and 4 present sales as a value exchange process that must satisfy the needs of both buying and selling organizations. The professional salesperson must assume the role of the principle architect of these business-to-business relationships to achieve his/her firm's organizational objectives. The role of the sales professional should be focused on creating win-win relationships in which value for both parties can often be expanded by the salesperson.

Chapters 5 and 6 present buyers based on their perception of the value of the product or service and what the salesperson can add in the value-building equation. Value is defined by the buyer, and not all buyers will equally value either the product or the service in the same way, or the full range of knowledge and capabilities the sales professional has to offer. Therefore the salesperson should be flexible in matching the correct selling mode to the type of buyer in terms of what the buyer values.

Chapters 7 through 13 represent the heart of the text and present the sales process in three distinct phases. Chapter 7 is concerned with Phase One—Pre-Negotiation Strategy, in which the salesperson *prepares for* negotiation, much like a rock climber or sailor prepares before heading out into challenging circumstances. In preparation, the salesperson develops and selects the appropriate negotiation strategies and tactics in order to maximize the probability of making a sale and updates and examines his/her database of customers and prospects to correctly target the potential buyer being approached. Chapters 8 through 12 detail Phase Two, the steps in the actual sales presentation or face-to-face contact in a complex multi-call sales process. Steps in the process include the approach, identification of needs, presentation of benefits, closing, and negotiating concerns. Chapter 13 summarizes the Phase Three post-sale responsibilities of the sales professional.

Chapters 14 through 18 are focused on building the knowledge and skills necessary to advance up the career ladder as a hospitality sales professional. Chapter 14 is focused on the legal and ethical boundaries within which a sales professional should operate, and also addresses the manipulative tactics of others that a salesperson will face over time. Chapter 15 provides a detailed understanding of roles of a director of sales. This treatment will provide the future sales manager not only an understanding of what he/she can expect from his/her supervisor, but also a clear road map of the skills and leadership abilities that need to be mastered to assume a role as a director of sales.

Chapter 16 explains the theory and assumptions underlying the sweeping changes as to how firms are taking their products and services to the marketplace. Sales professionals are highly compensated individuals, and in an effort to control costs, firms are deploying their sales force in highly selective manners. Chapter 17 summarizes the capabilities and benefits of sales automation technologies. We contend that sales automation can enhance the effectiveness of the sales professional and should be fully understood and leveraged by the sales manager to advance his/her career. Chapter 18 summarizes what we believe the future holds for hospitality sales professionals. Emerging capabilities of the Internet as a sales tool in combination with companies' relentless efforts to control costs will no doubt have an impact on the profession, creating both winners and losers, that should be appreciated by the future sales manager when charting his/her career path.

Supplements

An **Instructor's Manual** is available to accompany this text providing instructors with a sample syllabus, test questions, classroom suggestions and a Travel Management (Sales) Game, which allows students to bid for new business in a competitive environment. In addition, an **Online Companion** is available at www.hospitalitytourism.delmar.com containing electric support slides for each chapter designed to supplement classroom lectures and facilitate discussion.

Acknowledgments

Quite a number of individuals contributed to our understanding of personal selling as applied to the hospitality and tourism industry. Chief among them are Robert A. Gilbert, president and CEO of the Hospitality Sales and Marketing Association International; Meade Atkinson of Marriott Hotels; Mike Cheatam, Hyatt Hotels; sales trainer Paula Miller; Peter Rogers, vice president of MICROS; Ken McGovern of Daylight Software; Ronald Marks, University of Wisconsin, Oshkosh; Dr. Bruce Money, Brigham Young University; Howard Fiertag, Virginia Tech; and Steve Litvin, the College of Charleston. Furthermore, we need to extend a special thank you to all our former sales students at Northern Arizona University and the College of Charleston who reviewed and we hope learned from initial drafts of our concepts and chapters as the book evolved. Last, we would be remiss if we did not extend a special thank you to Marilyn McDonald for her time and talent in editing two diverging writing styles into one final version of this text.

About the Authors

Richard G. McNeill, Ed.D. CMHE, joined the School of Hotel and Restaurant Management (SHRM) at Northern Arizona University in the fall of 1989 after a career in sales and marketing management with a premier conference resort and hotel management company. Additionally, he founded and operated a firm that represented several Fortune 500 companies in negotiating with hotel and transportation suppliers for large corporate meetings. In addition to his industry experience, he was dean at a propriety graduate business school serving working adults and taught graduate level marketing and international business courses.

At NAU he teaches hospitality sales management, hospitality marketing, and international hospitality operations. Dr. McNeill's doctorate work focuses on continuous quality improvement models as applied to undergraduate hospitality administration programs. He integrates quality process concepts into all of his business-related courses.

His research interests include hospitality marketing and sales with primary emphasis on consultative selling to the meetings and conventions markets. His publications, seminars, and consulting work primarily focus on strategy and tactical and practical implementation of sophisticated and complex selling in hospitality-related business-to-business markets. He has authored more than 30 articles, contributed chapters to five textbooks, and presented at numerous academic and professional conferences.

Dr. McNeill holds an MBA from Thunderbird, the American Graduate School of International Management and both a bachelor's degree in political science and a doctorate in higher education from Arizona State University. Additionally, Dr. McNeill holds a Certified Hospitality Marketing Executive (CHME) designation from Hospitality Sales and Marketing International (HSAI).

John C. Crotts, Ph.D., is a professor and chair of the Hospitality and Tourism Management program of the School of Business and Economics, at the College of Charleston. Prior to holding this position, he lectured in the Advanced Business Programme on tourism subjects at Otago University, Dunedin, New Zealand, and was director of the Center for Tourism Research and Development at the University of Florida. Dr. Crotts has authored more than 50 journal articles and five books encompassing the areas of economic psychology, tourism marketing strategy, and management of cooperative alliances. In 2000 the Travel and Tourism Research Association recognized him as one of five stars in tourism research worldwide. In 2004, the School of Hotel and Tourism Management of Hong Kong Polytechnic University ranked him in the top one percent of scholars worldwide for his published research productivity. In addition to serving as the founding editor of *International Journal of Hospitality and Tourism Administration,* he also serves on the editorial board of the *Journal of Travel and Tourism Marketing,* the *Journal of Hospitality and Tourism,* and the *Scandinavian Journal of Hospitality and Tourism Management.*

Dr. Crotts received his Ph.D. in leisure studies and services from the University of Oregon in 1981. He also holds a bachelor's degree in sociology from Appalachian State University, an M.S. in education from Mankato State University, and an Ed.S. in adult education from the Appalachian State University.

DEDICATION

This book is dedicated to our wives,
Grace and Crystal

Whose love, support, and
understanding make all possible

Section 1

The Big Picture

CHAPTER 1

Hospitality Sales: Foundations of Success

After reading this chapter you should be able to

- ◆ discuss the knowledge, skills, and attitude needed to be successful as a hospitality sales professional

- ◆ describe the skills and traits you currently possess and those that you need to develop

- ◆ explain the basic ways sales professionals are compensated and to what extent

AIDA
EQ (emotional quotient)
PONS Test
relationship selling

consultative selling (relationship selling)
compensation
motivation

Consider for a moment the association meeting planner who has just finished a successful convention, the restaurant manager of a fine Italian bistro who has just opened a new account with a food wholesaler, or the outbound tour operator who has just put together a package of tour products for a tropical destination resort. At some point, each of these three customers was no more than a lead or prospect. In each case, someone in the sales department of the convention hotel, the food wholesaler, and the convention and visitor bureau did something right—and in doing so, gained these persons' attention and won their business.

Someone once commented that nothing happens in the hospitality business until something is sold. If so, the absence of salespersons would be fatal to the hospitality and tourism industry—for who would be there to sell it? A high percentage of sales in the hospitality industry come through business-to-business marketing, the specialized niche of sales professionals. Selling to corporate buyers in our industry requires more than just advertising that you are open for business; it takes a trained sales force to make things click in the mind of the client—to convert *features* into *benefits*—to win the business.

Make no mistake: the hospitality and tourism industry is competitive and clients' have tremendous freedom of choice. Creating *a*wareness, *i*nterest, *d*esire, and ultimately *a*ction (**AIDA** for short) in organizational buyers requires that a professional salesperson probe for and understand client needs and provide solutions to those needs that are better than the competition's. Even more than that, it requires the ability to build trust in you, the seller, because professional buyers have a lot riding on their purchase decisions. Therefore, a fundamental trait that leads to sales success is the ability of the salesperson to create and sustain trust with profitable corporate buyers.

A Vital Role in Our Economy

Few professions are misunderstood more than sales. To many people, salespeople are smooth talkers adept at manipulating clients into buying things they do not need. The career has been denigrated as one made up of the sort of people that should never be trusted. But this stereotype applied to today's successful hospitality sales professionals is false. According to Ron Marks (1997), they are individuals of knowledge, **motivation**, dedication, and integrity who are vital to the functioning of our economic society.

The goal of all organizations is to create, develop, and retain satisfied profitable customers. This is true whether the organization is a tourism destination, a hotel property, a restaurant, or for that matter, a one-person enterprise. Bringing supply and demand together to make a profit is essential for any organization. For example, hotels, which have supply, want to sell rooms and other services to guests, who provide demand, at rates that produce a fair profit. Doing this in a way that creates satisfied, loyal customers is the key to long-term profitability. Throughout this book you'll see a framework that presents sales as an *active relationship development process.* This framework links hospitality supply and demand and shows ways to create repeat patronage, deepen account penetration, and, ultimately, forge long-term buyer-supplier relationships.

Why a Framework on Hospitality Selling?

Experience is a good teacher for salespersons, but what is often overlooked—and vital for experience to be useful—is a framework with which to assess performance. Some salespeople have learned to sell exclusively through observing others; some have learned by trial and error—either way is harder than it needs to be. Unless the new salesperson knows what he/she is looking for, mere observation of even a great salesperson will provide limited information. Frequently, even the best salespeople themselves do not know the reason for their success, which in turn makes it difficult to teach anyone else.

Our framework is designed to give you a realistic view of the knowledge and skills you need to be successful as a hospitality sales professional. The framework provides a road map for your future that you can start using right away, but which has the depth to be helpful throughout your career. In today's harried business environment, salespeople need to grow and evolve professionally. Using a framework, like using a road map, can help you get where you want to be.

Traits of Successful Salespersons

A leading personnel testing company believes that a successful salesperson is stable, self-confident, goal-directed, intellectually curious, and good at networking. Other researchers and educators describe top salespeople as being organized, persistent, presentable, generally optimistic, socially intuitive, and incredibly honest. Research has shown that people are seldom born with all these traits. However, if you have desire, attitude, and honesty, you can learn the rest over time through training, coaching, and sales experience.

Another personality trait that has drawn the spotlight because of its importance for sales success is emotional intelligence. Unlike IQ, **EQ** (or **emotional quotient**) can be developed and improved.

What Else Do We Know about Personality and Sales?

It turns out that psychologists can see the future by watching four-year-olds interact with marshmallows. Researchers Mischel, Shoda, and Peake performed a thirty-year study (Mischel, Shoda, and Smith 2005). At the opening of the study, they invited children, one by one, into a plain room and told them, "You can have this marshmallow right now. But if you wait while we run some errands, you can have two marshmallows when we return." And then they left.

Some children grabbed for the treat immediately. Some lasted a few minutes before they gave in. But others were determined to wait. They covered their eyes; they put their heads down; they sang to themselves; they tried to play games or even to fall asleep. When the researchers returned, they gave these children their hard-earned marshmallows. The researchers then followed the children's progress, as they aged.

By the time the children reached high school, something remarkable had happened. The researchers found that those who as four-year-olds had the fortitude to hold out for the second marshmallow generally grew up to be better adjusted and more popular, adventurous, confident, and dependable as teenagers. The children who gave in to temptation early on were more likely to be lonely, easily frustrated, and stubborn. They buckled under stress and shied away from challenges. And when some of the students in the two groups took the Scholastic Assessment Test (SAT), the kids who had held out longer scored an average of 210 points higher.

If there is a cornerstone to emotional intelligence on which most other emotional skills depend, it is a sense of self-awareness, of paying attention to what we are feeling. For example, a nonaware person whose day starts badly at home may be grouchy all day at work without ever wondering why. The self-aware person makes a mental note to himself/herself and makes an extra effort to stay pleasant and balanced.

Another example involves anxiety, which can be a difficult emotion to control. Worrying is not necessarily a bad thing. In fact it has practical advantages as a rehearsal for danger; the act of worrying focuses the mind on a problem so it can search efficiently for solutions. The danger comes when worrying blocks thinking, becoming an end in itself, or if it causes a person to freeze up instead of to persevere. Such overworrying about failing actually increases the likelihood of failure. The classic case is that of a salesman so concerned about his falling sales that he can't bring himself to pick up the phone—which just guarantees that his sales will fall even further.

But why are some people better able to snap out of it and get on with the task at hand? Again, the answer is EQ and self-awareness. With them, people develop coping mechanisms that help them buck up or chill out, depending on the circumstances. Sadness and discouragement, for instance, are low arousal states. A high-EQ salesperson who becomes temporarily dispirited may slip on some running shoes and go out for a run. The game plan here is to trigger a high arousal state that is incompatible with staying blue. Relaxation works better for high-energy moods like anger or anxiety. Either way, the idea is to shift to a state of arousal that breaks the destructive cycle of the dominant mood. EQ helps you know when and how to do this.

In the corporate world, according to personnel executives, IQ may get you hired, but EQ gets you promoted. Consider the tale of a manager at AT&T's Bell Labs (a think tank for brilliant engineers in New Jersey), who was asked to rank his top performers. These were all very bright people, but the top ones weren't those with the highest IQs— they were the ones who got prompt answers to their e-mails. What was the connection? Those engineers who were good collaborators and networkers were popular with their colleagues and thus were more likely to get the cooperation they needed to reach their goals. Their more socially awkward counterparts had an EQ disadvantage.

Predicting Success: More Corporate Research

The idea of being able to predict which salesmen are most likely to prosper was not an abstraction for Metropolitan Life, which in the mid-'80s was hiring 5,000 salespeople a year and training them at a cost of more than $30,000 each. Imagine how unhappy they were when they realized that half quit the first year, and four out of five within four years. The reason: selling life insurance involves having the door slammed in your face over and over again. MetLife needed to know if it was possible to identify which people would be better at handling frustration and taking each refusal as a challenge rather than a setback.

To find out, the head of the company approached psychologist Martin Seligman at the University of Pennsylvania and invited him to test some of his theories about the importance of optimism in people's success. Seligman found that when optimists fail, they attribute the failure to something they can change, not some innate weakness that they are helpless to overcome. And that confidence in their power to effect change is self-reinforcing. Seligman tracked 15,000 new workers who had taken two tests. One was the company's regular screening exam, the other Seligman's test measuring their levels of optimism. Among the new hires was a group who flunked the screening test but scored as "super-optimists" on Seligman's exam. And sure enough, this group did the best of all; they outsold the pessimists in the regular group by 21 percent in the first year and 57 percent in the second. For years after that, passing Seligman's test was one way to get hired as a MetLife salesperson.

The PONS Test. Perhaps the most visible emotional skills, the ones we recognize most readily, are people skills like empathy, graciousness, and the ability to read a social situation. Researchers believe that about 90 percent of emotional communication is nonverbal. Harvard psychologist Robert

Rosenthal (1979) developed the **PONS test** (Profile of Nonverbal Sensitivity) to measure people's ability to read emotional cues. He shows subjects a film of a young woman expressing feelings—anger, love, jealousy, gratitude, seduction—edited so that one or another nonverbal cue is blanked out. In some instances the face is visible but not the body, or the woman's eyes are hidden, so that viewers have to judge the feeling by subtle cues. Once again, people with higher PONS scores tend to be more successful in their work and relationships; children who score well are more popular and successful in school, even when their IQs are quite average.

Empathy. Like other emotional skills, empathy is an innate quality that can be shaped by experience. Infants as young as three months old exhibit empathy when they get upset at the sound of another baby crying. Even very young children learn by imitation; by watching how others act when they see someone in distress, these children acquire a repertoire of sensitive responses. If, on the other hand, the feelings they begin to express are not recognized and reinforced by the adults around them, they not only cease to express those feelings but they also become less able to recognize them in themselves or others.

Beware of Fatal Flaws

When David Campbell and others at the Center for Creative Leadership studied derailed executives, rising stars who had flamed out, they found that these executives failed most often because of an interpersonal flaw rather than a technical inability. Interviews with top executives in the United States and Europe turned up nine so-called fatal flaws, many of them classic emotional failings, such as "poor working relations," being "authoritarian" or "too ambitious," and having "conflict with upper management."

At the center's executive-leadership seminars across the country, managers come to get emotionally retooled. "This isn't sensitivity training or Sunday-supplement stuff," says Campbell. "One thing they know when they get through is what other people think of them."

And the executives have an incentive to listen. Says Karen Boylston, director of the center's team-leadership group: "Customers are telling businesses, 'I don't care if every member of your staff graduated with honors from Harvard, Stanford, and Wharton. I will take my business and go where I am understood and treated with respect.' "

The implications for you, as a future hospitality leader (and hopefully a hospitality sales professional), should be clear. There are some essential traits, skills, and talents common to most successful sales executives. Some of them are built into your personality already; others you can work to acquire. If you aren't sure how you stand in some of these areas, you may be able to find out through standardized testing. Ask at your campus testing and counseling center, or talk to your advisement officer. If you've got the right stuff and the motivation to grow further, hospitality sales may be the career niche you've been hoping to find.

The Rewards of a Hospitality Sales Career

Everyone sells every day. When you interact with customers (either internal or external ones) in any way, you are selling. So even if you're not looking for a business card with "sales" in the job title, don't think you won't be selling, in some sense. In fact, the route to a general manager position with Marriott requires trainees to spend time in sales. Marriott not only understands that sales training and experiences provide trainees with an understanding of what it takes to create a customer, it also believes that the communication, persuasion, and interpersonal skills trainees glean in sales will serve them well no matter what leadership position they later choose.

Two Big Advantages to Sales Careers

But if you do choose to focus your career in sales, you will be rewarded. First, no other profession in the hospitality industry affords a person the ability to work primarily 8:00 to 5:00 Monday through Friday. There will be exceptions; in hotel sales, when a group you've sold is in-house, you will want to maintain a presence to ensure that everything is running smoothly for your client. But such requirements are the exception and your typical workweek will require you to be available when your clients are at work—that is, the normal workweek.

Second, sales managers are highly compensated individuals since they are responsible for the lifeblood of their hospitality firm (that is, income). Keith Kefgen and Rosemary Mahoney of HVS Executive Search, a New York–based human-resources consulting firm, produce the *Hospitality Compensation Exchange Annual Report.* The survey is conducted every two years and includes data from nearly 2,400 North American hotels, regarding 27 managerial positions. Results of their most recent survey are summarized in Tables 1–1 through 1–5. Though hospitality sales encompasses more than hotel room sales, the results clearly indicate the average **compensation** packages of sales professionals.

The survey reveals that the second or third most highly compensated member of the executive team is the director of sales and marketing—behind the general manager. Compensations generally vary by the size and complexity of the property as well as to a certain extent the property's location (that is, downtown city, suburbs, and so forth) and geographic region.

Table 1–1 Average Compensation by Region
all numbers in $

Position	MOUNTAIN PACIFIC		NEW ENGLAND / MID ATLANTIC		NORTH CENTRAL		SOUTH ATLANTIC		SOUTH CENTRAL	
	Average Salary	Average Bonus	Average Salary	Average Bonus	Average Salary	Average Bonus	Average Salary	Average Bonus	Average Salary	Average Bonus
Controller	58,619	6,591	59,369	4,204	52,253	4,708	53,257	4,483	49,243	5,304
Director of HR	49,892	4,907	55,876	3,937	48,647	4,569	52,972	4,534	43,099	4,530
Director of MIS	50,207	554	48,974	1,005	43,916	117	44,149	1,513	40,114	0
Director Sales & Marketing	63,375	4,732	69,445	5,714	57,507	5,196	62,282	6,039	53,664	5,270
Director of F&B	70,907	5,489	61,492	3,323	56,835	4,907	54,689	4,103	53,525	4,693
Director of Rooms	57,878	2,411	60,680	2,449	55,825	3,066	50,325	1,358	49,003	2,354
General Manager	95,098	21,659	88,770	15,168	63,543	13,278	75,997	13,733	75,772	16,474

Table 1–2 Average Compensation by Class of Hotel
all numbers in $

Position			ECONOMY		MID-RATE		FIRST-CLASS		LUXURY	
	Average Salary	Average Bonus	Average Salary	Average Bonus	Average Salary	Average Bonus	Average Salary	Average Bonus	Average Salary	Average Bonus
Controller	39,005	198	40,296	2,149	48,185	3,950	56,559	3,822	70,516	11,177
Director of HR	n/a	n/a	n/a	n/a	45,345	2,899	47,399	3,341	65,924	7,907
Director of MIS	n/a	n/a	n/a	1,502	45,955	365	45,625	704	50,132	1,021
Director Sales & Marketing	36,046	6,128	41,830	3,049	52,285	1,876	66,430	4,618	86,383	13,801
Director of F&B	n/a	n/a	44,525	2,768	56,884	4,296	62,476	3,263	69,946	7,168
Director of Rooms	n/a	n/a	47,290	0	53,739	1,159	56,266	2,563	55,031	2,038
General Manager	40,839	3,742	48,242	5,547	66,486	12,192	106,605	20,402	129,356	31,848

Table 1-3   Average Compensation by Type of Hotel
all numbers in $

Position	COMMERCIAL		CONVENTION		RESORT		ALL-SUITE		EXTENDED STAY		CONFERENCE CENTER	
	Average Salary	Average Bonus	Average Salary	Average Bonus	Average Salary	Average Bonus	Average Salary	Average Bonus	Average Salary	Average Bonus	Average Salary	Average Bonus
Controller	56,177	5,295	68,407	7,485	65,458	6,385	32,044	2,844	31,717	834	54,118	3,217
Director of HR	50,748	4,087	58,804	5,240	58,293	5,446	33,067	3,973	n/a	n/a	47,944	3,747
Director of MIS	46,692	527	47,478	187	55,943	1,236	n/a	n/a	n/a	n/a	42,807	1,950
Director Sales & Marketing	64,398	4,968	74,081	7,342	74,840	8,988	48,061	2,577	39,764	3,497	65,452	4,963
Director of F&B	61,427	4,606	70,665	2,665	68,300	5,101	43,425	5,467	n/a	na	56,644	3,055
Director of Rooms	56,000	2,261	60,821	2,613	55,484	2,102	n/a	n/a	n/a	n/a	53,803	920
General Manager	73,305	15,212	120,569	20,005	100,111	19,484	70,214	13,213	42,996	4,548	98,909	13,468

Table 1–4 Average Compensation by Size of Hotel
all numbers in $

Position	UNDER 150 ROOMS		150–349 ROOMS		350–549 ROOMS		550–799 ROOMS		OVER 800 ROOMS	
	Average Salary	Average Bonus	Average Salary	Average Bonus	Average Salary	Average Bonus	Average Salary	Average Bonus	Average Salary	Average Bonus
Controller	40,100	3,030	61,821	4,549	50,286	6,255	76,313	8,865	82,118	5,618
Director of HR	40,442	3,071	53,728	4,185	43,705	4,430	66,369	5,900	68,147	3,560
Director of MIS	n/a	n/a	40,132	572	47,110	983	49,970	1,254	56,252	141
Director Sales & Marketing	39,499	1,023	74,155	4,489	58,235	8,599	84,808	10,233	101,133	6,769
Director of F&B	51,350	3,009	65,406	4,336	55,458	5,116	78,278	6,039	87,291	3,134
Director of Rooms	38,897	111	53,202	2,148	50,516	2,116	60,754	2,918	68,895	1,743
General Manager	41,261	5,482	114,500	17,223	89,695	27,850	135,526	30,444	149,826	36,065

Table 1–5 Average Compensation by Hotel Location
all numbers in $

Position	AIRPORT		HIGHWAY		CENTER CITY		SUBURBAN		RESORT	
	Average Salary	Average Bonus	Average Salary	Average Bonus	Average Salary	Average Bonus	Average Salary	Average Bonus	Average Salary	Average Bonus
Controller	50,280	4,160	41,991	4,713	62,468	5,746	49,667	4,809	60,960	5,523
Director of HR	42,123	2,932	37,310	4,281	56,582	4,347	45,510	4,294	55,034	5,075
Director of MIS	43,900	0	n/a	n/a	48,886	644	40,371	693	50,702	1,071
Director Sales & Marketing	56,130	4,846	48,562	1,654	69,597	6,840	58,761	4,482	73,007	6,683
Director of F&B	57,159	4,811	54,490	4,177	65,245	4,420	59,755	4,445	64,341	4,416
Director of Rooms	50,877	3,214	n/a	n/a	58,802	2,264	50,736	1,487	55,693	2,090
General Manager	77,170	13,401	41,519	5,399	105,862	20,707	68,228	14,184	96,890	17,910

The basic goals of any compensation system are to enhance a firm's performance and to attract and motivate personnel. Generally, there are three basic methods of compensation: straight salary, straight commission, and combination plans of salary plus commissions or bonuses. As indicated in the previous tables, hotels generally create some kind of salary/bonus package for all members of their executive team. Those in operations generally receive bonuses based on their abilities to control costs and achieve certain levels of customer satisfaction. By contrast, a hotel sales compensation package generally includes a base salary with bonuses designed to encourage one of the following:

◆ exceeding sales quota (in terms of dollar volume)
◆ increasing sales to more profitable customers
◆ increasing account penetration to existing accounts
◆ making sales in low seasons and/or low demand dates

Other fields in the hospitality and tourism industry may be salary only, straight commission, or, like hotels, a combination of both. For example, sales managers of a convention and visitor bureau (CVB) usually earn a straight salary since such entities normally pay little to no commissions in terms of group bookings; therefore CVB sales managers are compensated for performance of all their duties, both selling and nonselling.

By contrast, salespersons involved in real estate sales of vacation homes are often compensated on straight commission. This keeps the cost of sales for the resort developer in proportion to gross sales, is easy to understand and administer, and provides the maximum incentive to the most productive salespeople.

Wholesale suppliers such as SYSCO Food Systems generally start off their sales managers on a combination plan involving a high base salary and low commissions. Over time, the sales director reduces the salesperson's base salary and increases his/her commission rates to arrive at an ideal ratio that offers the salesperson income security and incentive.

Many forward-looking firms provide bonuses to their salespeople based on customer satisfaction. These leading firms recognize that profits hinge on the perceived level of customer satisfaction and the ability to generate repeat business by developing some level of consumer loyalty. By motivating salespeople to concentrate on customer satisfaction, these firms are implementing what we call **relationship selling** or **consultative selling** (which will be covered in greater detail later in this book). This new way of selling is creating a sense of freshness in the sales profession. After participating in a customer-service-based compensation plan, one hotel salesperson commented, "I've been liberated from selling rooms. Now I can really focus on understanding my clients' needs."

Getting Started in Your Sales Career

Your first job in hospitality sales will likely have little resemblance to your last. Figure 1–1 provides somewhat of a road map of a hotel sales career. One may begin one's first sales job as a sales associate in reservations or telemarketing, or as an administrative assistant in the sales department. Sales associates can be found at the individual property level or concentrated in regional sales centers, such as Hilton Direct. These positions are good proving grounds, and generally people who show promise will spend less than a year in such roles. From there, salespeople generally advance to catering sales or convention sales, first as a sales manager and later as a marketing and sales director. They may specialize in inbound sales, outbound sales, or a combination of both.

FIGURE 1–1

The Hospitality Career Ladder

Self-Service Technologies	Sales Associate	Professional Salesperson	Relationship Manager
Internet Reservations Telemarketer Sales Assistant	Internal Sales Outside Sales		

The most senior sales professionals are often now fulfilling the emerging role of relationship managers. They are responsible for long-term agreements between buyers and sellers that promote mutually beneficial ties between two firms. With *purchasing partnerships,* or *strategic alliances,* as they are often called, buyers receive a continual stream of quality products and services, whereas suppliers are assured of a significant portion of buyers' orders. The relationship enables the partners to plan requirements on a mutually beneficial time schedule with mutually satisfactory pricing. More will be discussed on this trend in Chapter 18 of this text.

◈ SUMMARY

Hospitality sales is a dynamic and rewarding field that can stay exciting over a long career. Although we have discussed many traits considered desirable for success in sales, no one has discovered a set of personality traits that is absolutely necessary for success in selling. To put it another way, research has yet to find the profile of a "born salesperson." If you are interested in sales, this should encourage you. Because of the wide diversity of selling positions and the adaptability of human beings, you may be able to "grow yourself" into an effective sales professional, even if you have only a minimum amount of skill to begin with. In other words, if you are mature and motivated and have good communication skills, you could become proficient in any type of sales. The process of becoming a good salesperson is dynamic, and the best professionals never stop trying to improve their skills.

Although no ideal set of characteristics has been found to guarantee success, some factors are strongly related to high performance: working hard and working smart. These two factors include the ability to set goals, communicate well, and present a professional appearance. To do so, you must also demonstrate maturity, dependability, honesty, and integrity. The good news is that these characteristics can be developed through thought and careful practice—and are useful not only professionally, but also personally.

References

Crotts, J., C. Coppage and A. Andiho. 2001. Trust-Committment model of buyer-supplier relationships. *Journal of hospitality & tourism research.* vol. 25(2), 195–208.

Dotlich, D. and P. Cairo. 2003. *Why CEOS fail: The 11 deadly sins and how not to commit them.* Jossey-Bass.

Marks, R. 1997. *Personal selling: A relationship approach.* Upper Saddle River, NJ: Prentice Hall.

Mischel, W., Y. Shoda, and R. Smith. 2005. *Introduction to personality;* 7th Edition. New York, NY: John Wiley and Sons.

Rotheenthal, R., J. A. Hall, M. A. Dimatteo, P. L. Rogers, and A. Archer. 1979. *Sensitivity to communications: The PONS test.* Baltimore, M.D.: Johns Hopkins University Press.

Seigman, M. 1990. *Learned optism.* New York: Pocket Books.

DISCUSSION QUESTIONS ◈

1. How is sales similar to but at the same time different from marketing?
2. Describe at least two personality traits you believe are associated with effective salespersons. Justify your selections.
3. What is EQ? Can it accurately be measured?
4. Describe the compensation methods used to reward and motivate salespersons. Which method would you prefer? Why?

CHAPTER 2

Buyers and Sellers in the Hospitality Industry

After reading this chapter you should have a better understanding of

- ◆ the variety of sectors in which you can focus a hospitality sales career
- ◆ the unique aspects of selling to organizational buyers as compared to consumers
- ◆ the stages of the organizational buying process

B2B
B2C
prospects
customers

yield
REVPAR

Virtually every organization that is directly or indirectly connected to the hospitality and tourism industry has a staff of sales professionals. Why? Much of an organization's revenue does not simply walk through the front door. It must be actively sought. Even in the best of conditions—even when a firm has a sufficient level of advertising and is receiving referrals through positive word of mouth—these are still only inquiries. It takes a professional salesperson to probe and determine the prospective buyer's underlying needs, show how his/her firm's features would translate into benefits, and then actually book the business.

Buying and selling make up a two-sided view of a single process—economic exchange. Buyers purchase from sellers and sellers sell to buyers. One cannot exist without the other. As we will later learn, most organizations operating in a market-based economy have both a buying department and a selling department. Salespeople of one business sell to the buying department of another organization or to an individual consumer. So, while salespeople are busy selling the product or service of their organization, their own company's buying department is often simultaneously making purchases from some other company.

Buying and selling take place in what has been referred to as a *value* or *supply chain*. Manufacturing firms purchase raw materials from organizations in order to make products. These manufacturing firms sell their finished products to other organizations which in turn sell them to another organization (business-to-business, or B2B, markets), which in turn sells them to the end user—usually the individual in the business-to-consumer, or B2C, markets. For example, the farmer buys seed and fertilizer to grow his/her crops. The farmer then sells agricultural produce to a food wholesaler, which sells to a hotel or free-standing restaurant, which in turn sells to a meeting planner for group meals or to individuals. All along the chain, and at each economic exchange interaction, there are sellers negotiating with buyers.

Interaction of Hospitality Industry Buyers and Sellers

Hospitality Salespeople Actively Manage the Economic Exchange Process

Although economic exchange takes place between both buyers and sellers, it is usually the responsibility of the seller to initiate and manage the exchange process. In other words, the seller is usually the one who must be proactive in seeking out the buyer and ensure that a sales transaction takes place.

Professional selling requires far more skills than order taking. Even when the prospective buyer (prospect) initiates the contact, it is likely that he/she is contacting several other firms in search of the best solution or value. Most firms cannot afford to wait for the prospect to come looking for them. More often, firms realize that to compete they must proactively go after new business and thereby create new demand. Typically, they will actually dedicate a percentage of their gross revenues to fund such sales efforts. In these instances, the sales professional wears the hat of a minimarketer and manages the economic exchange process with the prospective buyer by proactively doing the following:

◆ Identify a list of sources of prospects (leads) within his/her selling territory.
◆ Prioritize the leads according to the highest quantity and quality of prospects.
◆ Determine the best method(s) to make an initial personal contact with these prioritized prospects.
◆ Determine the best method to make an initial contact.
◆ Stimulate the contacted prospect to agree to a face-to-face or telephone interview meeting during which the prospect's *needs* are first investigated and later the salesperson's product or service *benefits* that satisfy the needs are communicated.
◆ Ask for the prospect's business, and if the prospect actually buys, transform the prospect into a **customer**.
◆ After the purchase or sale, maintain and develop the salesperson-customer relationship on a long-term basis to generate repeat and referral business.

These may seem like fairly simple steps, but they require a level of sophistication to be effective.

Types of Buyers and Sellers in the Hospitality Industry

If we again think of the value or supply chain briefly introduced previously, we can readily see that the hotel salesperson who has sold a meeting facility and services to an independent meeting planner has completed just one step in the buyer-supplier process that enables such an event to take place. The very same meeting planner has probably also bought related services from off-premise caterers, special events consultants, entertainment agents, and speaker bureaus. Looking backward one step will remind us that the meeting planner sold *his/her* services to the association's board of directors, which required using his/her own skills in prospecting, personal selling, and negotiating.

Hotels are not only sellers but also buyers. A study by PKF Consulting (2000) indicated that the hotel industry in the United States alone purchases over $18 billion in goods and services. These include furnishings, interior design services, computerized property management systems, back office accounting systems, landscape and golf greens maintenance—and on and on.

The same is true for the restaurant industry. Restaurants that sell to individuals and groups are just part of the final stage of a series of buyer-seller relationships. Between 25 and 35 percent of the revenue made from restaurant patrons goes to suppliers to pay for wholesale food costs. This is yet another example of a buyer-seller relationship. Explore even deeper and you will see that the restaurant owner or manager has been a buyer in another sense. He/she has purchased the real estate and building for the restaurant, as well as everything required to operate it efficiently, such as kitchen equipment, furnishings, linens, a point of sales system, and a host of services such as bookkeeping, time-and-attendance systems, grounds maintenance, contract services, and so on (see Figure 2–1). Economic models reveal that for every one job created in the hospitality and tourism industry, 1.8 additional jobs are directly and indirectly supported in the broader economy.

FIGURE 2–1

Buyers and Suppliers in
the Hospitality Industry

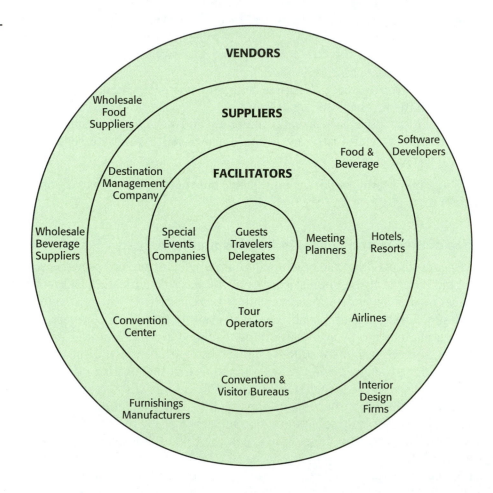

If you meet the salespersons of our industry's suppliers, you will find that the best have previous experience working directly with the final end user in the hospitality and tourism industry (that is, the guest). Why? One of the first truisms in sales is to know your product *and* your customer's industry better than your competitors. Who better to sell a new restaurant account for a food wholesaler than a salesperson with culinary or restaurant management experience? The same is true for virtually all other buyer-seller dyads in the hospitality and tourism industry.

Are you interested in becoming a salesperson for a supplier? Career sales opportunities as an industry supplier are extremely varied—with upstream suppliers (such as hotel designers and IT systems designers) to downstream suppliers (such as wholesale food suppliers). Upstream suppliers are most active at the beginning of a hotel project or renovation and get their business from hospitality companies that are investing in a project. Downstream suppliers depend more on guest or tourist demand. The busier the hotel or restaurant is, the more supplies it will need to buy.

According to the World Travel and Tourism Council (2001), the market for both upstream and downstream suppliers is expected to remain strong. Worldwide capital investment in hospitality and tourism infrastructure is expected to grow 9.4 percent annually from $701.3 billion in 2000 to $1.4 trillion by 2010. Travel and tourism demand is currently estimated at $4.5 trillion and is forecasted to grow to $8.5 trillion by 2010, a 4.2 percent annual growth rate.

Hospitality Sales Is Primarily Focused on B2B, Not B2C

Simple economics dictates that the involved and relatively expensive process of hospitality sales makes it unfeasible to focus on the final guest or consumer. That's why hotels have reservations and restaurants have wait staff to take the orders of individual customers (the B2C or "business-to-consumer" relationship). Hotel sales and catering sales are focused on selling blocks of rooms or catered functions to buyers who are typically other businesses, not individuals (the B2B or business-to-business relationship).

There are a few exceptions. Selling vacation homes or amenity communities generates enough revenue to warrant the expertise of a professional salesperson's time and effort. In addition, catering sales will focus on the SMERF (social, military, education, religious, and fraternal) markets that represent individuals planning events such as weddings, reunions, and the like. The point is that economics dictates the level of effort that should be dedicated to win the business.

It's Not *What* You Book but *When* You Book It

Another truism, particularly in hotel sales, is that most group business is sold at a discount. Reserve a room at any hotel as an individual and you will no doubt be offered the rack rate or highest rate available. Inquire at the same hotel to book 50 rooms for three nights with food and beverage and you will no doubt be offered rates that are discounted—especially if the business falls during a low-demand period.

The decision to accept or decline the business from a group is often made by the sales director, who will determine if the booking will displace higher-paying transient customers anticipated on the dates in question. The group sales department is often provided a *group ceiling,* defined as the number of rooms they are expected to sell as a part of the total rooms to be sold at the hotel. Group sales are responsible for bringing the property as close to sold-out status as possible without displacing higher-paying transient guests. Often sophisticated yield management software or sales management software is used to aid the process. Whether the process is manual or computerized, the sales manager will use one of two formulas to analyze the desirability of a potential group business: **yield** and revenue per available room (**REVPAR**). Calculating yield or REVPAR is relatively simple. For any given night at a hotel:

Revenue Realized ÷ Revenue Potential = Yield
Revenue Realized ÷ Rooms Available = REVPAR

Assume that a group was willing to book 50 rooms per night at the 'C' rate of $75, checking in on a Sunday afternoon and checking out on Wednesday morning. Further assume that Monday and Tuesday nights are particularly high demand days for higher-paying individual business travelers who normally pay the 'A' or 'B' rate of $110 and $95, respectively. The questions that must be answered are: would accepting the group business displace higher-paying customers, and, if so, what impact would it have on the yield or REVPAR? If the answer is negative, from a revenue standpoint it would not make sense to accept the booking. But psychologically, remember this: it is important for the salesperson never to decline this business but instead simply deny the *rate*. Experience shows that groups who cannot get the rate they'd like when they'd like will often respond to incentives—and adjust their dates to times in which the hotel needs the business and are therefore willing to book at the 'C' rate.

Selling to Organizational Buyers. As previously mentioned, selling to organizational buyers involves sales not to the ultimate guest or visitor, but to other businesses such as meeting and event planners, tour wholesalers, incentive travel houses, corporate travel offices, restaurant managers, hotel owners, and so forth. There are several dimensions that distinguish the marketplace of organizational buyers from the consumer marketplace.

Derived Demand. One major source of difference is that the ultimate demand for the goods and services comes not from the buying organization itself, but from the buying organization's consumers. If the meeting or event planners make a bad purchase decision, their organization may suffer financially, but so also will their personal reputation. So much rests on important meetings and events that a bad decision can undermine the buyer's job security. To minimize such risks, organizational buyers will rely on firms that have a positive reputation, and they often use elaborate search and selection processes.

The smart salesperson can take several measures to reduce the risk a buyer perceives in the purchase decision. First, the salesperson can make a point of presenting a credible image—either on the phone or in person. A friendly and attentive attitude is essential, as are appropriate dress and grooming. (Buyers look for symbolism: if the salesperson is inattentive or sloppy during the courtship process, wouldn't he/she be unreliable after the contract is signed?)

Researching the buyer's company and having testimonials from satisfied customers in his/her industry are also valuable. Research by Hospitality Sales Solutions has shown that meeting planners look for

- salespeople who are courteous, polite, and to the point
- salespeople with an in-depth knowledge of their own products
- salespeople with an in-depth knowledge of the customer's industry
- suppliers who can be trusted
- salespeople who are discreet
- salespeople who are honest
- salespeople who keep promises
- a product or service that is consistent in quality
- a product or service that performs as anticipated

The salesperson plays the pivotal role in winning new business. Sales is often described as the ability to create and sustain trust in a client or prospect. It can often be thought of as *giving and fulfilling promises*.

Size and Frequency of Orders. Organizational buyers place orders that are considerably larger than those of an individual consumer. A contract with a meeting planner may involve tens and even hundreds of thousands of dollars in revenues for the hotel, whereas a hotel's remodeling contract with a design and architectural firm may run into the millions of dollars. Patience plays a factor as well, since the period of time between orders from organizational buyers is typically longer. A national meeting planner may hold a meeting in a particular region of the country only every four to five years; a hotel may renovate its property only every three to six years. The savvy salesperson will continue the relationship during the off years so that when it comes time for another purchase decision, he/she will be in good standing with the client.

Sophistication of Organizational Buyers. Organizational buyers are considerably more sophisticated than buyers in the consumer marketplace. They have to be very careful in considering the costs and technical requirements of what is being purchased. Often the organizational buying decision involves more than one individual. The association's board of directors may have more influence than the meeting planner as to destination and site selections. The decision as to what vendor to use in renovating a hotel may be influenced by the hotel's owner(s), its management company, and the franchiser. Knowing who are the gatekeepers, decision influencers, and, ultimately, the decision makers is the responsibility of the salesperson.

Organizational Buyer View of the Economic Exchange Process. At the beginning of this chapter we stated that hospitality salespeople actively manage the economic exchange process. Although this is true, professional salespeople must not only view the economic exchange process through their own eyes, but also imagine how the prospective buyer sees the economic exchange process. Don't you think that this would greatly improve the salesperson's ability to meet the real needs of the prospective buyer? Although the view of the exchange process from the buyer's perspective is somewhat different from that of the salesperson, they are remarkably similar. In Chapter 4 we will expand upon this topic, but for now we introduce how organizational buyers view the economic exchange process and make decisions. There are five steps to the buying process.

1. Recognition of Needs—Here the potential buyer anticipates, recognizes, and outlines the specifications of his/her needs.
2. Evaluation of Options—Here the potential buyer searches for and assembles alternative sources and qualities of potential suppliers that might satisfy his/her needs.
3. Resolution of Concerns—Here the potential buyer analyzes the pros and cons of the alternative sources and suppliers that potentially can satisfy his/her needs.
4. Purchase—Here the potential buyer chooses from among the alternative sources and suppliers and makes a decision to buy from one of them.
5. Implementation—Here the now actual buyer becomes concerned about implementation of his/her purchase and seeks feedback and evaluation of the purchase's performance.

Recognition of Needs. This is the recognition on the part of the buyer that a need or problem exists and that a solution is available. Often it is thought that professional salespersons create needs and a call for action from a prospect. However, organizational buyers are sophisticated and do not respond well to such manipulative tactics. Leading salespersons concentrate their time and efforts on identifying prospects, understanding their needs, and proposing solutions. Communication skills are essential at each point in this process.

The more sophisticated organizational buyers will outline in detail specifications of what goods and services they require. A corporate meeting planner may require a meeting room that can accommodate 70 individuals in a classroom setting, teleconferencing capabilities, two adjacent breakout rooms, meals, an evening reception, and 70 guest rooms, for a check-in on June 21 and checkout on June 23. The specs may often cite rates that the group has previously paid as an indicator of what the group is prepared to pay.

Evaluation of Options. Once the specifications have been clearly outlined, the search for qualified suppliers begins. In the case of the corporate meeting, the meeting planner will telephone or mail to the hotel sales staff the dates and specifications. Sales professionals often prefer to receive specs by phone since it gives them a greater opportunity to explore more deeply the purpose of the meeting, who will be attending, and what the event is meant to accomplish. These insights help the salesperson present the property in the most favorable way. Seldom is it possible to close the sale during a single call, particularly with a new account. Instead the salesperson gathers information so he/she can prepare a proposal for the buyer.

At this stage, the buying organization receives and scrutinizes proposals from several vendors. In the case of a corporate meeting, the meeting planner may select the top proposals for further consideration.

Resolution of Concerns. In this phase, the buyer consults with management on a short list of proposals and awaits their decision. In the case of corporate meetings or conventions, the salesperson must remember that the meeting planner/buyer may not necessarily be the decision maker, but is, instead, the bridge to the ultimate decision maker(s)—and will be summarizing the features and benefits of the facility to people with whom the salesperson has no contact. The point here is to make sure the decision influencer has all the necessary information needed to support the proposal. It is also important to remember that even after a final selection has been made, negotiations may continue regarding such matters as price, terms, and schedules.

Purchase. The potential buyer decides among the alternative sources and suppliers that he/she has assembled. The potential buyer has now been transformed into a customer. In later chapters, we will learn that the decision to purchase from one supplier and not another is based on many factors. Buyers make decisions based on the total value or benefit that they will receive from a chosen supplier. And, value is not only found in the product or service itself.

Implementation. After a purchase, most customers experience what has been called *buyer's remorse* or *post-purchase concern.* This is especially true when the purchase is a service like a convention, conference, or a meeting. Why? Because services are performed by people, and people can have variable performance—good days and bad days. Regardless, the buyer becomes concerned with implementation immediately following his/her purchase. In Chapter 13, "After-Sale Implementation, Relationship Management, and Continual Improvement," we will learn that management of this buying step is extremely important to be able to build customer relationships and generate repeat and referral business.

The buyer evaluates the performance of the purchased product or service either formally or informally, but the salesperson has an evaluative responsibility, too. Professional salespeople know that they should monitor events they've sold to assure themselves that everything is running smoothly. This will increase the likelihood of favorable evaluations and the probability of repeat business and referrals.

What It Takes to Be a Success

Selling to professional buyers requires working hard and working smart. Necessary qualities include emotional maturity, initiative, persistence, and the ability to set goals. For those who work to develop these skills, the field of hospitality and tourism expands immeasurably and the rewards are high.

Suppose you are a salesperson with a firm that develops and markets property management systems for the hotel industry in North America. Further assume you are paid on straight commission and want to earn $65,000 this year. If your normal commission per installed unit is $500, you will need to sell 130 units per year, or an average of 11 per month. Let us suppose that you will be able to make one sale for every three presentations you make. That translates to 33 qualified prospects every month. Now, how do you get those prospects? Let's say that one out of every five phone calls generates one appointment. If so, you'll need to make 165 calls per month, or eight per workday. When you do the math, you'll see that eight calls every workday will produce at least 1.6 appointments . . . and one sale every two days—so initiative and persistence *will* pay off. If your account includes hotel chains, one sale to a moderate-sized chain could fill your quota for a month, a quarter, or even a year.

Thriving on "No"

Obviously, if you make 165 calls per month to capture 11 sales, you will be hearing the words "No thanks" on a regular basis—that is, rejection. It takes emotional maturity not to withdraw or become defensive in the face of rejection. Yet successful salespeople learn to accept "no" gracefully and continue on with their job. Looking at it as a sheer number of potential customers may help. For instance, if you are selling to hotels, you'll be pleased to know that the latest Census (2000) showed 48,619 hotel companies in the United States. If you disciplined yourself to contact 50 per week, it would take you 19.4 years to contact every business once. And, if it took you three calls to close a sale, you theoretically would be able to sell your product to every U.S. hotelier in 58 years.

The point is that people who are willing to handle rejection and take risks in order to reach their goals are the ones who succeed. In his book *Making Things Better by Making Things Worse,* psychiatrist Dr. Allan Fay relates how he treats shy men who are afraid to ask women for dates by instructing them to go out and collect as many rejections as possible over the course of several weeks. Before too long, the men realize the more rejections they receive, the less traumatic each rejection becomes. Not too much later, they no longer fear failure. The same principle is true for selling. Pursue failure! It's a matter of arithmetic: the more rejections you receive, the more success you will have. Baseball great Babe Ruth is not remembered for the 1,330 times he struck out; he is remembered for the 714 home runs he hit. Successful hospitality sales professionals make things happen; the unsuccessful sit waiting for success to come to them. If you ask the top sales professionals, you'll find that they perceive themselves as *powerful,* not passive. They thrive on the feeling of being active players—an invigorating feeling, indeed.

References

Fay, A. 1978. *Making things better by making things worse*. New York: Hawthorn Press.

PKF Consulting. 2000. *Dimensions of the U.S. hotel procurement market.* San Francisco, CA: PKF Consulting.

Pollack, A., and L. Benjamin. 2001. *Shifting anals: The tourism ecosystem in transformation.* London: Desticorp Ltd.

U.S. Bureau of the Census. 2000. *Economic census.* Washington, DC: U.S. Bureau of the Census.

DISCUSSION QUESTIONS ◈

1. Compare and contrast the value of the economic exchange on both a B2C and B2B basis.
2. Selling to organizational buyers differs from selling to consumers in what unique ways?
3. Yield and REVPAR are two metrics used in hotel sales to make what types of decisions?
4. What are the fives stages in the organizational buying process? Why is it important to view the relationship development process from this perspective?

CHAPTER 3

Creating Mutually Beneficial Value Exchanges

LEARNING OBJECTIVES

After reading this chapter you should be able to

- ◆ describe the relationship of sales to marketing in a business-to-business context
- ◆ identify selling as an economic exchange process between buyers and suppliers
- ◆ explain the similarities and differences between transactions and relationship exchanges
- ◆ understand how value can be created through the exchange process

KEY TERMS & CONCEPTS

micromarketing
value
transactions
relationship exchanges

It may surprise you to know that sales (and the theory and practice that surround it) is of great interest to academics and other thinkers. In the 1950s, academics began to look at the various forms of commercial exchange and to wonder if they could be unified into a comprehensive model. At that time, those who practiced advertising and public relations saw themselves as separate from practitioners of the art of personal selling. Once these areas were connected theoretically, the discipline of marketing was formally born. Personal selling was wrapped into the communications function of this marketing model. Today, traditional marketing literature characterizes personal sales within the Four Ps of marketing: product, price, place, and promotion. Usually, it is included in the category of promotion mix, along with other communication tools such as advertising, public relations, and sales promotion tools.

The Rise of Micromarketing

Selling has been defined in many different ways by various writers—and most of these definitions have been narrowly focused. To our minds, personal selling has been trapped within the traditional marketing model for too long. While theoreticians were looking the other way, sales "escaped" the limitations of that model and has reinvented itself into the specific form of **micromarketing**. This term means that the salesperson, on a one-to-one or team-to-team basis, performs all of the functions of traditional marketing. Traditional marketing now plays an overall supporting role for micromarketers. Instead of focusing on categories of customers traditionally called *market segments* by the marketing literature, micromarketers focus on very specific business-to-business (B2B) customers who desire customized products and services.

As we will see in Chapters 4, 5, and 6, salespeople are beginning to limit their selling activities to fewer numbers of large B2B customers who meet clearly defined specifications. Some of the simpler activities that used to occupy salespeople (such as airline or room reservations), are now being streamlined by technology and the Internet. In today's markets, a product or service has to be pretty complex and have long-term revenue potential to justify the use of a living salesperson. In those cases, the personal salesperson becomes a micromarketer.

Customers, however, continue to purchase noncomplex and inexpensive products. Companies must ensure that these customers are able to do this with ease and to their satisfaction. By using the less expensive alternatives of technology, companies can lower selling costs and still effectively reach many customers who previously required a live salesperson. The Internet provides interactivity between buyer and seller unlike any capability that we have had in the past—but these channels need to be reviewed regularly by professionals with a sales perspective to make sure they are meeting customer needs.

In summary, today salespeople and sales forces focus on customers desiring complex—and usually expensive—products and services. Generally, they sell only to B2B (business-to-business) markets. To be effective, they have adopted the tools of marketing and have become micromarketers. In this situation, traditional marketing becomes a *support* function for salespeople. Companies selling noncomplex and inexpensive products and services are reducing selling costs by phasing out living salespeople. In the situation of simple and noncomplex products and services, *traditional marketing* is the primary function used to complete a commercial exchange between buyer and seller. In the Information Age, computerized databases, global communications, and the interactivity of the Internet make possible eliminating the salesperson in noncomplex sales.

Selling Defined

This chapter introduces several important terms and the relationships between them. Many of the terms build on the ones directly before them. We recommend that you take the time to make the mental connections between terms and concepts because these are essential to course content. We'll start with our definition of today's selling—placing it within the micromarketing context:

> *Selling is a social and managerial process by which individuals and groups of individuals obtain what they need, want, and/or desire through creating and exchanging value with other individuals and groups of individuals (adaptation of Kotler 1988, 3).*

This definition hinges on two key concepts: *value and exchange*. **Value** is exchanged between two sets of individuals or groups of individuals. One of these sets of individuals is called the *seller* and one set is called the *buyer*. Value to the buyer is usually found in the product or service, but, as we will later learn, value to the buyer is increasingly found in the *ease of the acquisition process* itself. Value for the seller is usually found in the money or revenue received, but we will see that sellers today are increasingly placing more importance on the value of customer relationship potential and loyalty potential, especially for long-term repeat and referral business.

Exchange takes place if something of value transfers from the seller to the buyer and, simultaneously, something of value transfers from the buyer to the seller. Both sets of individuals must agree that the values transferring to each are what each need, want, or desire. We believe that as the perception of value changes so do selling approaches. *Situational selling*, as presented in this text, is the appropriate selling response to a changed perception of value—a changed situation. And, the change in the perception of value can come from either the buyer, the seller, or both.

Situational selling approaches arise in response to changes in value perceptions. Historically, these changes happened slowly. Today, the pace of change means situational selling must be increasingly adaptive and responsive. We will address this in detail in the next three chapters. For now, let's closely examine the underlying concepts that drive our definition of selling.

Exchange

Four Ways to Obtain Value

The fact that individuals and groups of individuals have needs, wants, and/or desires and can place a value on what they want does not fully describe our definition of selling. Selling requires exchange. People can satisfy needs, wants, and/or desires in four ways:

- ◆ Self-Production—They can hunt, grow, or make items themselves. They don't have to interact with anyone else. There is no selling here.
- ◆ Coercion—They can steal or coerce from others. There is no benefit offered to others for what they receive. There is no selling here.
- ◆ Begging—They can appeal to others' sense of charity and mercy. There is no tangible benefit to others. There is no selling here.
- ◆ Exchange—They can approach others and offer some resource in exchange, such as money, another good, or some service. Selling arises from this last approach.

What Is Exchange? Exchange is the act of obtaining a desired value (usually in the form of products and services) from someone by offering something in return. Exchange requires five conditions:

- ◆ There are at least two parties to the exchange.
- ◆ Each party has something that might be of value to the other party.
- ◆ Each party is capable of communication and delivery.
- ◆ Each party is free to accept or reject the offer.
- ◆ Each party believes it is appropriate or desirable to deal with the other party.

Even with these five conditions in effect, there is only *potential* for exchange—no guarantees. For the exchange to actually take place requires two or more parties to agree on *terms of exchange*. This means that values exchanged will leave both parties better off than before the exchange; each party receives what it needs, wants, and/or desires (Kotler 1988, 7).

Exchanges are *processes* as opposed to events. Seeing an exchange as an ongoing process helps us to distinguish between transactional exchanges and **relationship exchanges**. Essentially, two parties are said to be engaged in the process of exchange if they are currently negotiating and moving toward an agreement. Once the agreement has been reached, a transaction takes place. A transaction is characterized by a several dimensions: (1) a minimum of two things of value, (2) agreed-on conditions, (3) a time of agreement, and (4) a place of agreement.

Transactional Exchanges vs. Relationship Exchanges

Transactions are the basic event of exchanges. A single seller can conduct transactions with many different buyers. Or a single buyer can conduct transactions with many different sellers. But today, sellers and buyers increasingly want to exchange with fewer and trusted partners. They would rather do most of their transactions with favorite partners. This leads to *relationship exchanges* as distinguished from *transactional exchanges*. These distinctions are crucial to fully understand our Chapter's 5 and 6 discussions.

Relationship exchanges are a continual long-term process between buyers and sellers. Whereas a transactional exchange process ends when an agreement or transaction takes place, in relationship exchanges one transaction builds on and leads to others. In effect, the exchange process is continual and ongoing over time with a series of many interrelated transactions taking place between the same seller and the same buyer.

Relationship sellers try to establish and buildup long-term, trusting, win-win relationships with customers and with their chain of suppliers and distributors. This is accomplished by promising and delivering high-quality products and services and by strengthening the economic, technical, and social ties between the seller and buyer organizations. Over time, buyer and seller grow more trusting, knowledgeable, and interested in helping each other (Kotler 1988, p. 9). There are significant benefits to both buyer and seller, including lower buying/selling costs, since the relationship reduces the need for individual negotiations for every little transaction. Lower costs are a value for both buyer and seller.

This leads us to the next important selling concept: in an exchange, both parties must receive value that satisfies their needs, wants, and/or desires.

Value

What Is Value?

By its simplest definition, *Value = Benefits minus Costs*. This definition can be further complicated by asking if benefits are real, perceived, or a mixture of the two. Regardless of complicating factors, the basic definition is useful in suggesting that there are two distinct ways to create value. Either additional benefits are added while costs remain the same, or costs of the current benefits provided are reduced. (A third scenario could be both rising benefits and rising costs, but with costs rising more slowly [Rackham and De Vincentis 1998, 13].)

Whose Definition of Value Is Important? The answer is, "Both the buyer's and seller's definition are important." If you refer back to our earlier definition of selling, you'll see that for selling to take place, we must have an exchange. To have an exchange, both buyer and seller must each transfer to the other something that the other values. The buyer may see value as residing inside the product or service received and consider this value to be worth more than the money that they give up to receive it. The buyer may also find value residing outside the product or service. For example, value might be found in the acquisition process itself: the ease, convenience, and timeliness of how he/she makes a purchase. And, value for the buyer might also be found in the quality of the relationship he/she has with a particular seller.

The seller may see value in the exchange from a traditional view: the amount of money or revenue received in exchange for the product or service. Increasingly today, sellers are looking beyond specific exchanges to find value in establishing a long-term commitment with the buyer through relationship building. Sellers are hoping that the first exchange or sale will lead to repeat and referral business over a long period of time. In some cases, they are willing to make sacrifices on their first sale to win this long-term opportunity. Sellers are now seeing relationship building as the newest form of competitive advantage.

Value for Both the Buyer and Seller

Sellers value competitive advantage, and to get it they must give customers more value than competitors do. In this quest, both sellers and buyers get the value they desire and end up with a win-win exchange.

Competitive selling companies have traditionally competed (and still do) based on value as perceived by the customer. When Company A provides value to a customer that is perceived by the customer to be greater than competitor Company B or C, Company A usually will attain competitive advantage. Combining the *Value = Benefits minus Costs* formula with the concept of competitive advantage helps us understand the basic ways companies compete with one another. Competitive advantage is achieved in two basic customer perceptions of value: value through *differentiation* or value through *lowest price*.

A company succeeds at differentiation when its product exceeds its competitor's product in quality, features, or some other variable—including value not residing in the product itself. Customers perceive a company's product with the most differentiation as having the highest value. *Lowest price* competitive advantage is straightforward. It means that one company's selling price is lower than its competitor's selling price for a product of similar quality. Customers usually perceive products with the lowest price as having the highest value.

In the 1980s, companies focused on quality improvement as a strategy for gaining competitive advantage. Through Total Quality Management (TQM) and other methods, companies tried to improve their products, deliver them more quickly, and make them safer, sleeker, sexier, and so on—all to differentiate them. Their strategy was to offer higher-quality products and services than those offered by their competitors, so that customers would value their products more. This approach was thought to lead to business success. Of course, almost everyone began reengineering and lowering prices, so before long, no companies appeared to have distinct competitive advantage.

In the 1990s, companies tried another route to competitive advantage; they focused on making their production and operations more cost effective. Through *business process reengineering*, companies worked to produce quality products at the lowest price. By offering the same higher-quality products and services as their competitors but at a lower price, they expected to achieve business success. But after a while, most competitors began using the same quality-improvement strategies and again it was hard for products to stand out.

During the 1980s and 1990s, many hospitality firms tried the same TQM and reengineering processes to raise their product or service quality and cut operational costs. With lowered costs, selling prices could be lowered or maintained as product or service quality was maintained or increased. For a while, companies that did this successfully were rewarded with competitive advantage in their markets. But this competitive advantage proved to be short lived.

Why? Quality improvements turned out to be easily copied in the hospitality industry. Operational cost saving methods, like TQM and, later, revenue yield management, became widely known and spread to all major players. The result was that everybody was doing the same thing. Everybody had a quality product at the lowest price. Customers did not see any difference in value between the competitors. So, price wars resulted. Selling prices often dropped below profitable levels. The industry began asking itself: "How does a selling company regain competitive advantage and the customer gain more value?" We will learn practical answers to these questions in the coming chapters.

What Is a Product and/or Service and How Is It Related to Value Exchanges?

Revisiting our simple value formula, *Value = Benefits minus Costs*, we are now at a point where we can discuss products and services and value exchanges. Simply stated, the product or service and/or other attributes associated with it offer benefits to the buyer. The product or service can be viewed as a "bundle of benefits." After the buyer subtracts all costs (money paid, time to acquire, hassle, and so forth) to acquire these benefits, he/she arrives at a perception of value he/she will receive when the product or service is delivered. This perception of value becomes an *expectation*. If expectations are met when the buyer takes delivery of the product or service, then the customer is, at the minimum level, satisfied. If expectations are not met when the product is delivered or implemented, then the customer is dissatisfied. To ensure customer satisfaction, generally, expectations must be *exceeded*. Somewhere in the process, the seller must add value that goes beyond the buyer's expectations. Consistent delivery of customer satisfaction builds long-term relationships and repeat and referral business: these are often referred to as the Three Rs: relationships, repeats, and referrals. As we will learn in Chapter 5, the Three Rs are the cornerstone of the new-style seller. Let's look more closely at the logic of product and service in more detail.

What Is a Product or Service?

Products and services are "bundles of benefits." They are problem-solving tools—buyers have problems to solve (needs) and sellers have a product or service that can potentially solve the problem or satisfy the need. People will buy products and/or services if they solve a problem or satisfy a need. One way to view a product or service is as a bundle or cluster of benefits or satisfactions as viewed by the potential customer (see Figure 3–1). Not all of the levels are equally important to all customers. For example, a very sophisticated customer may demand all levels whereas a less sophisticated buyer may not be aware of, or expect more than the core product or service.

Theodore Levitt envisioned products and services as being composed of several levels:

Core—Product or service basics. Hotels sell beds and restaurants sell food.

Expected—This is the level that the customer expects to find. If the seller does not fulfill this expectation, the buyer simply will not consider the offering. In effect, expected levels are the "price of admission" for the buyer to allow a seller to even talk to him/her. For example, newspapers at the door used to be "value-added" but are now expected because most business hotels have copied the idea and now deliver this. Today, as mentioned earlier, most products are of high quality and offered at very efficient pricing. Thus, a seller is mistaken when he/she believes that quality is a value-added benefit—today quality is expected.

Relating Buyer Motivation to the Levels of Product or Service

Frederick Herzberg, a noted management philosopher and organizational psychologist, commented on buyer motivation as related to Levitt's Four-Level Product or Service Model (Figure 3–1).

Selling Motivators—Herzberg theorized that the four levels of products/services have differing power to motivate customers to select one company's product offering instead of a competitor's. He divided

FIGURE 3–1

Four-Level Model of Product or Service

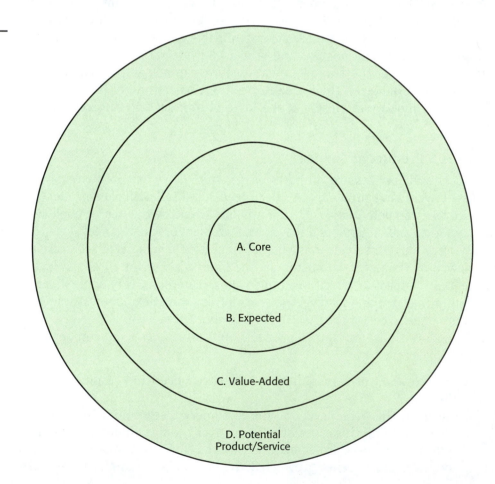

A. Core

B. Expected

C. Value-Added

D. Potential
Product/Service

the four levels into two categories depending on their power to motivate customers.

Hygiene Factors—these are the "core" and "expected" product levels of Levitt's model.

These are "must-have" variables: they don't motivate a buyer to buy, but a lack of them "demotivates" the buyer to buy.

Because customers' expectations tend to escalate continually, the magic buttons of quality, service, and price/value have lost their power and are now seen only as "hygiene factors"—that is, they function at the "expected" product level. A company that offers these levels can minimally satisfy customers, but it can't inspire or motivate them to choose its offerings over others. To motivate requires exceeding expectations.

Motivational Factors—these are the "value-added" and "potential product or service" levels of the model.

Motivators are those levels where the buyer sees the seller's offering as more valuable than a competitor's. Buyers use the value formula to compare the value of two company's offerings. They will calculate value and expect one company to give more value than another. Here is where the source of competitive advantage can be found.

Companies must continually search for new motivational factors since factors that once gave competitive advantage are rapidly lowered into hygiene factors as competitors copy one another and buyers' expectations continually rise.

So, what is a product or service? It is the buyers' perceived value of benefits offered minus the costs of acquiring those benefits. Now it is time to link value obtained in the exchange process with customer satisfaction—the driver of the Three Rs (relationships, repeats, and referrals).

Customer-Delivered Value Formula. Let's extend the simple value formula we've been working with along the way: *Value = Benefits minus Costs* now can look like:

Customer-Delivered Value (CDV) = Total Customer Value (TCV) minus Total Customer Costs (TCC).

Customers buy from the firm that they believe offers the highest CDV.

TCV is derived from the four levels of product or service shown in Figure 3–1. These value perceptions are really based on the customer's *judgment*—and judgments can be influenced by the salesperson or other marketing communication channels. Other influencers are word-of-mouth from friends and acquaintances as well as general reputation.

TCC comes from the costs of money, time, energy, and physical factors (worry, for example). Customers also perceive and judge costs.

CDV in effect is seen as "profit" by the customer. It is the excess of gain in *value* over *costs* to the customer. Based on judgments of value and costs, the customer decides whether or not he/she will obtain a profit. If a profit is determined, he/she will buy. These profit/loss calculations become the buyer's "expectations." Simply meeting expectations, as we have seen above, is no longer enough. Exceeding expectations is necessary to give a selling company competitive advantage.

Customer Satisfaction Formula Depends on *Expectations*. Once more, we take our simple value formula and give it a new look: *Value = Benefits minus Costs* now becomes:

Product Service Performance minus Customer Expectations
= Customer Satisfaction

Or

Customer Dissatisfaction
(PSP) minus (CE) = (CS) or (CD)

Customers are, at a minimum, *satisfied* with a performance that meets their expectations—and usually *ecstatic* with a performance that exceeds them. A high level of customer satisfaction can generate repeat business, customer referrals, and long-term relationships between buyer and seller. The key is in "expectations." The seller must set or influence the right level of expectation. Too low and there will be customers attracted and satisfied, but not in quantities large enough to maintain profitable revenue. Too high and buyers are likely to be disappointed and dissatisfied.

In the hospitality industry, customers buy services, so let's take a look at two models that attempt to explain value as perceived by buyers: (1) the Perceived Service Quality Model (Figure 3–2) and (2) the Gap Analysis Model of Service Quality (Figure 3–3). These models speak of quality. In these models, *quality* is a synonym for *customer satisfaction*.

The Quality/Customer Satisfaction Models

Models help us understand the complexity of hospitality service quality and its effect on customer satisfaction. First, we will discuss an early foundational model: the Perceived Service Quality Model developed by Christian Gronroos in 1982. Second, we will discuss an evolutionary form of the Gronroos model, the Gap Analysis Model developed by V. A. Zeithaml, A. Parasuraman, and L. L. Berry in 1988. The last model, currently packaged as the SERVQUAL

Model, is widely used in the hospitality industry to understand and improve the quality of hospitality service.

Perceived Service Quality Model

In 1982, Christian Gronroos, a Scandinavian economist, introduced the Perceived Service Quality Model (see Figure 3–2). According to Gronroos, service quality studies and models have always been based on what customers perceive as quality. In other words, service quality is an outgrowth of the marketing concept; its focus is on the customer. From this viewpoint, what is important is what the customer perceives as quality or value and not what designers or operations people feel is good or bad quality.

Theories based on customer buying behavior have strongly influenced many service quality models. Many are tied to the notion that the customer's postpurchase perception is a function of his/her prepurchase expectations and thus serves to confirm/disconfirm his/her concept of service quality. The confirmation/disconfirmation concept is the foundation concept of both the Gronroos and SERVQUAL models.

FIGURE 3–2

The Perceived Service Quality Model

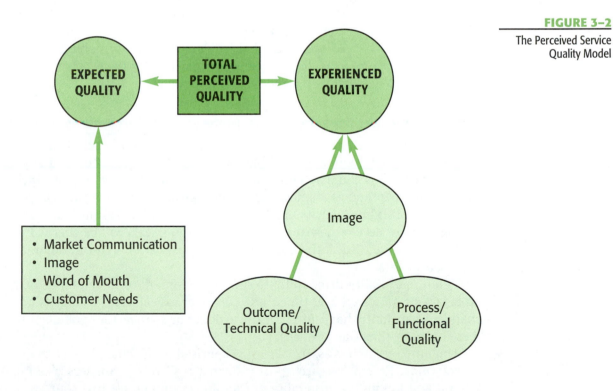

Source: Adapted from Gronroos, C. 1991. Quality comes to service. In Scheuing, E. E., and Christopher, W. F., eds. *The service quality handbook*. New York: American Management Association.

According to the Perceived Service Quality Model, the quality of a service, as perceived by the customer, is the result of a comparison between the expectations of the customer and his/her real-life experiences. If the "experienced quality" exceeds "expected quality," the "total perceived quality" and customer satisfaction are positive. If expectations are not met by performance or the actual experience, the perceived quality is low and customer satisfaction is negative. Success in satisfying the customer is dependent on initial expectations compared to actual performance.

The Five-Gap Model of Service Quality

Another widely used model of service quality is known as the Five-Gap Model (Kotler, Bowen, and Makens 1996, 357–361). Knowing what customers expect is the first and possibly the most critical step in *selling* . . . and then *delivering* service quality. Thus, the organization and its marketing/sales staff must know what their customers expect so they can work to provide services that their customers will perceive as excellent. This an extension of the marketing concept and consultative selling approach that requires, first, that sellers use thorough questioning to understand what the customer needs and wants and, second, that sellers successfully deliver the product or service benefits that will satisfy those customer needs and wants.

An awareness of the five gaps can help sales professionals troubleshoot the source of service problems. In some ways, the gap model serves as a diagnostic guide, much like that used by doctors or mechanics.

Gap 1: Consumer Expectations vs. Management Perceptions

Often hospitality sellers and the operational managers whose job it is to deliver services fail to understand what customers expect in the offered product or service. This could be something as basic as not understanding which features (of the product) are necessary to deliver high-quality service. *Gap 1* occurs when this breakdown of understanding occurs. For example, a hotel's manager might develop a system to ensure that all guests will be checked in within 15 minutes. But if the hotel guest gets upset after a 10-minute wait, then Gap 1 exists.

Often, hospitality firms initially survey customers to understand their expectations. However, over time these customer expectations change (since change is constantly happening). If the product or service does not adapt to these changes, then Gap 1 widens.

Ongoing research is essential to stay apprised of the changing customer expectations. Formal research plus informal research (managers walking around and talking to hospitality guests, for example) are two sources of information. The sales force, especially for complex group business, is a vital resource for tracking changing customer expectations.

FIGURE 3–3

The Gap Analysis Model
of Service Quality

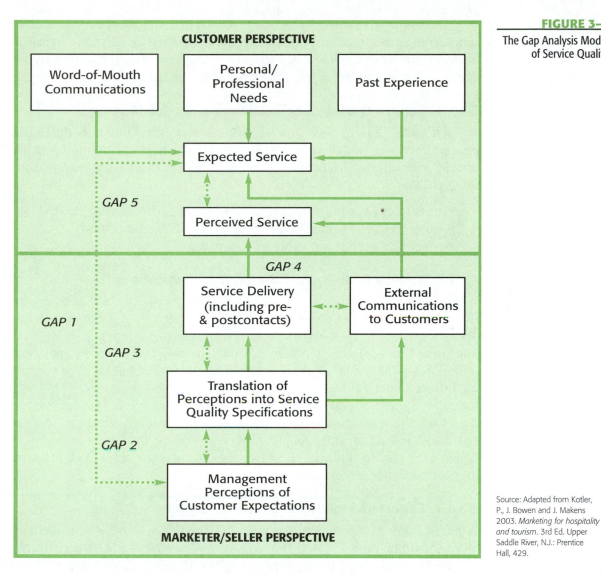

Source: Adapted from Kotler,
P., J. Bowen and J. Makens
2003. *Marketing for hospitality
and tourism*. 3rd Ed. Upper
Saddle River, N.J.: Prentice
Hall, 429.

Gap 2: Management Perception vs. Service Quality Specifications

When hospitality managers know what customers expect, *but* cannot or will
not develop products/services and systems to deliver it, then *Gap 2* occurs.
Several reasons for Gap 2 are:

- inadequate commitment to service quality
- seeing the feasibility of addressing customer expectations as unrealistic
- inadequate task standardization (within the hospitality organization)
- absence of goal setting by management and inability to get employee
  "buy-in"

The hospitality industry has been accused of being short-term oriented. When companies focus on short-term profits and are unwilling to invest in human resources, technological tools, and equipment, they will almost always develop service quality delivery problems. This brings us to Gap 3.

Gap 3: Service Quality Specifications vs. Service Delivery

When hospitality managers know what customers expect *and* have developed products/services, systems, and specifications to deliver it *but* employees are unable or unwilling to deliver the service, then *Gap 3* occurs. Several reasons for Gap 3 are:

- employees are not given the tools and working conditions to do the job
- employees are not correctly selected, trained, and motivated
- employees are not properly "led" by managers

Gap 4: Service Delivery vs. External Communications

When hospitality management (represented by marketing and sales executives) promises more in its external communications than it can deliver (via operations), then *Gap 4* occurs. External communications include, but are not limited to, advertising, public relations, pricing messages, and personal selling. Hospitality marketers/sellers must be sure that what they are promising buyers is "doable" by their operations team. You may be surprised to know that, sometimes, general managers unintentionally contribute to Gap 4, when they treat the marketing/selling process and operations/delivery process as separate—and set separate goals for them. Everyone, from top management down, must understand that these two areas must seamlessly work together to meet customer expectations.

Gap 5: Expected Service vs. Perceived Service

Gap 5 is where "the rubber meets the road." The size of Gap 5 is dependent on all of the other gaps. If you'll recall: *expected service* is what the customer expects to receive from the hospitality organization. *Perceived service* is what the customer believes or perceives that he/she has actually received from the hospitality organization (after the service experience).

Gap 5 is the difference between expected service and perceived service. Customer satisfaction and quality are dependent on this gap being reduced or eliminated. Hospitality management is responsible for reducing this gap—and ideally, getting rid of it entirely.

The Gronroos and SERVQUAL models are useful for understanding how buyers' perceptions of value impact the exchange process. Like a long train of dominoes, value perceptions affect expectations, which affect the level of customer satisfaction or dissatisfaction. Levels of satisfaction affect the Three Rs: relationships, repeats, and referrals.

SUMMARY ◆

Today, both buyers and sellers perceive value differently than in the past. Situational selling approaches reflect value changes and offer practical tactics and strategies to create successful selling exchanges. In Chapter 4 we will learn more about the new buyers and their perceptions of value. In Chapter 5, we will learn how the new sellers have modified selling approaches in response to value shifts from the buyer's perspective and how they themselves have changed in the way they view value. In Chapter 6, we will explore the various situational selling tactics and strategies available to address different buyer/seller perceptions of value. In latter chapters discussing the buying/selling process, we will stress the seller's requirement to understand the buyer's problems to be solved and needs to be satisfied and then to match these needs with product "bundles of benefits" that are valued by the customer.

References

Gronroos, C. 1990. *Service management and marketing: Managing moments of truth in service competition*. Lexington, MA: Free Press.

Gronroos, C. 1991. Quality comes to service. In Scheuing, E. E., and W. F. Christopher, eds. *The service quality handbook*. New York: American Management Association.

Kotler, P. 1988. *Marketing management: Analysis, planning, implementation, and control*. Englewood Cliffs, NJ: Prentice Hall.

Kotler, P., J. Bowen, and J. Makens. 1996. *Marketing for hospitality and tourism*. 3rd ed. Upper Saddle River, NJ: Prentice Hall.

Levitt, T. 1975. Marketing myopia. *Harvard business review*, Vol 53 (5), 26-41.

Rackham, N., and J. De Vincentis. 1998. *Rethinking the sales force: Redefining selling to create and capture customer value*. New York: McGraw-Hill.

DISCUSSION QUESTIONS ◆

1. In a B2B setting, is sales a part of marketing or marketing a part of sales? Discuss.
2. Compare and contrast transactional selling and consultative selling. Is a focus on long-term high-valued business always necessary to achieve one's organizational sales goals?
3. How can the salesperson add value to the buyer in the exchange process?

Section 2

Understanding the New World of Buyer-Seller Relationships

CHAPTER 4

The New World of Buying:

Changing Perceived Value has Reshaped Buying Decisions

After reading this chapter you should be able to

- ◆ explain the forces that influence the commoditization of goods and services
- ◆ identify the types of buyers in terms of their perception of value

- ◆ describe how competitive advantages can be achieved by the seller in correctly matching the selling technique to the customer's perception of value

intrinsic value
extrinsic value

strategic value
buying motives

After 25 years of a deep sleep, corporate meeting planner Rip Van Winkle awoke. As he walked around his company to find old friends, he rubbed his eyes in disbelief at the changes that he found. Down on the manufacturing floor, the legions of workers and supervisors had virtually disappeared. The noisy machinery smelling of oil had been replaced by quietly moving robotic arms attended by a few hygienically dressed attendants calmly moving to check strangely glowing television screens. "This looks more like a laboratory than the factory I remember," he thought. Rip moved to the second floor to visit the area where secretaries gathered in a central area to provide typing services to all the corporate managers, but this, too, had disappeared. He moved from department to department and couldn't find anything that looked familiar. There were fewer employees, and people were working differently. Everything had changed.

Rip had been a top meeting planner for the company and they decided to hire him back. His first assignment was a 250-person national meeting. So he did what he had always done: placed a few calls around to various hotels to see if they could supply him the dates and rates needed. It had taken him a while to get around to placing these calls as he had been feeling depressed and anxious, given experiences in this strange new world. On his first call, to a salesperson at a five-star resort, Rip felt a sudden surge of excitement. He was home. He was on familiar ground.

The salesperson began, "Mr. Van Winkle, let me ask you a few questions about your needs." This was followed by a few open- and closed-ended questions. Rip thought, "This is familiar and has been around for a long time." Then the salesperson began a presentation of the features and benefits of the hotel. When Rip disagreed with one of the salesperson's proposals, the salesperson quickly responded with an old technique called "handling the objection." Rip was surprised at himself. He wasn't angry at this obviously manipulative technique; he was just happy to be in a familiar situation. "Everything else has changed, but at least sellers talk to buyers in the same way." He whispered to himself, "It's great to be back."

Rip Van Winkle fully recognized the selling approach he had just encountered. He had experienced it over and over again 25 years ago before he had fallen asleep. In fact, that same approach had been practiced since 1922 when Edward Kellogg Strong Jr. authored *The Psychology of Selling Life Insurance*. The selling approach was very familiar and comforting. "Yet," he wondered, "if everything else has changed, why is this still the same?"

Good question. As we discussed in Chapter 3, achieving competitive advantage requires a company to match its selling and exchange process to its buyers' perception of value. Buyers' perceptions of value continually evolve, and selling approaches must also evolve or they will not be appropriately responsive. As the following brief history will demonstrate, buyers have historically changed and modified the way they perceive value. Today's buyers are no exception. They no longer perceive value the way they did in the recent past. Yet, as evidenced by the way that they approach selling, sellers seem to believe that buyers have not changed at all.

Before we get into the discussion of today's situation, let's briefly review how we came to live in a world where everything from product and services to ideas and political influence seem to be *for sale*. Your first reaction may be that in a book on the most modern methods of selling, history is not very relevant. The fact is, you will still find organizations that ask their salespeople to live in a "time warp." Understanding the roots of their behavior will help you as a consumer . . . and it may prevent you from accepting employment with a firm that has not joined the twenty-first century.

A Historical Perspective of Exchange
The Emergence of *The New Buyer*

Prehistory, the Beginning of Cities, and Early Trade

The *prehistory* period of man refers to the period before written accounts of the history of humans. Up until about 10,000 years ago, people were hunter/gatherers. Even during prehistoric times, humans engaged in trade. Stone and pottery objects discovered in locations far from their origins show us that our most ancient ancestors traded/exchanged items across amazing distances.

We trace the emergence of large-scale agriculture to the Mesopotamian valley. The process of caring for crops caused people to begin to settle in one place, which led to the development of villages and towns about 8000 BC. As civilizations became more complex, towns became cities, and people began to specialize as crop growers, object makers, bakers, weavers, and so on. We can surmise that variations in weather and resources caused shortages and excesses of crops and local products. The desire to acquire something of useful value and to obtain it in exchange for something of less useful value produced the conditions for exchange and trade—which was accomplished through *barter*. Barter is a form of exchange in which a buyer swaps goods, such as agricultural products, for other goods offered by a seller. Every town or city featured a market or trading center where locals displayed surplus goods. Periodically, traders from other regions would bring an influx of new or "exotic" goods (Peeler 1996).

In such simpler times, buyers' perception of value resided in the simple availability of products. Often the relevant question was: Are there any products available for barter? In situational selling terms, *availability* was the key. From the buyers' perception availability was value.

The Last 2,000 Years

It may be hard for you to picture a time when people did not believe they had a right to choose their destinies—to "be all that they could be"—but this is a recent development, historically. In a pattern that was accepted thought for thousands of years, people had fixed niches within the social order. A segment of life called *economic* had not yet been conceived. Then, around 1450, during the *Age of Discovery* and the *Renaissance* people began to see more options opening up.

In the fifteenth and sixteenth centuries, as Columbus and others "discovered" and began trading with the New World, economic growth accelerated in Europe. Europe now needed craftspeople to build and make items for trade. People began to be paid in wages. The great feudal domains of the earlier medieval period were broken up. Serfs became "free" laborers, which led to increases in production and improved standards of living. A greater variety of products became accessible. The combination of more wage-earning customers and more products available meant that markets (aka buying–selling situations) dramatically grew.

As the financial status of larger segments of the population improved, so grew opportunities for education, political power, and entrepreneurship. A broadening of education encouraged developments in literature and the arts and sciences. The growing middle class responded to the instinctive human urge to improve one's life and comfort through the acquisition of things.

In short, humans dramatically changed in the way that they viewed their existence and daily lives. Humankind had begun the journey toward the consumer society of today. We became a world of exchanging value between buyers and sellers. What is important to remember about this exchange process is that people value different things at different times. Salespeople must stay alert for changes in the dynamics of the exchange process.

For example, with the Industrial Revolution, products were being massively produced in factories. At the same time, settlers, especially in the American Colonies, were pushing further into the frontiers. Products would land at major harbors such as Boston and New York, but a poor road infrastructure made it difficult for these products to be distributed throughout the land. The dynamics of the exchange process changed. Buyers' perception of value shifted from availability of products in central locations to having products brought to their frontier locations. *Distribution* by traveling peddler was the situational selling approach to address the buyers' perception of value.

Today's Buyer

The birth of what we can legitimately call *customers* or *buyers* took place about 500 years ago. These buyers have always wanted value, but they keep redefining their definitions and perceptions of value. This is not to say that each new shift in the perception of value replaces the old; it merely means that new forms of value must be addressed by the selling organization. Today's sellers must fully understand that the buyer commands the power position within the *exchange process* (buying/selling process) and that the selling company must focus on giving the buyer the value he/she wants.

Most selling organizations are just now waking up to this fact! Value has migrated away from a single focus on product or service itself. Today's new buyers have new perceptions of value. When buyers perceive value in a new way, we can say that the *situation* has changed. Successful sellers modify their behavior and selling approaches to these changed situations. In this text, we focus on *situational selling*. You can't select the appropriate situational selling approach if you do not understand how the customer perceives value.

The New World of Buying and Perceived Value

Forces That Have Changed Today's Customer Perception of Value

What has changed the old definition of value into the new definition of value? Let's take a systematic look at the changing variables that have caused buyers to redefine value . . . and caused sellers to adapt the way they respond.

1.   Products and services are becoming *commoditized*. A commodity is a product that is indistinguishable from other competitive products. From the buyers' perspective, all these products look alike and can be substituted for one another without any difference being noticed. Simply providing quality products and services at a low price is the "price of admission" for sellers to be invited to do business with buyers. Educated buyers correctly understand that they don't need to deal with a salesperson to purchase commodities.

2.   Quality of products and services quickly rises to meet rising buyer expectations. As we discussed in Chapter 3, buyers learned something from the 1980s' "quality era." Trying to achieve competitive advantage through a product differentiation strategy of offering more quality than competitors quickly erodes. Rising buyer expectations simply demanded that all sellers provide quality products and services. Then they demanded lower pricing! In the '90s, most companies did everything they could to lower their costs, so they could then lower their prices. Yet, buyers continued to expect more value. Their battle cry was: "Either give us a value-added product or service with more benefits than your competitors or give us acceptable quality at still lower prices."

3.   Technology advances allow communication and coordination throughout the sales process. There once was a time when the linkages or *channels* from selling organizations to buyers depended on a system of humans dealing with other humans. At that time, having salespeople negotiating directly throughout these channels was necessary. Today, computerization and especially the Internet have changed all of this. Buyers want "what, when, why, from whom, and how" on their own terms. They don't want to be limited to

dealing only with a salesperson. As a result, sellers have created many new 'go-to-market' channels to meet the new buyers' perception of value. That is because value has again evolved. It now includes providing the buyer with many ways to acquire products and services. Technology has enabled sellers to set up selling systems composed of multiple channels and linkages to reach the buyer.

4.   The customer is barraged and short of time. While computerization and the Information Age were predicted to free more time for people, it had the effect of creating more work. Neither buyers nor sellers seem to have enough hours in the day to handle everything that is placed on their "plate." To save time, the buyer wants to work with a few dependable and trustworthy suppliers. The buying wisdom of the past dictated that every purchase decision should be bid out to a large number of potential sellers to stimulate a bidding war. Now that most quality sellers already have the lowest price, buyers are beginning to place value on trust and relationships—and the time saved by sticking with a circle of favored suppliers. This also reduces both parties' need for large staffs of purchasing agents, who rank fairly high on the payroll food chain. Thus, if buyers can gain value by dealing with only a few sellers, everybody wins: both buyers and sellers.

Consequences of Value Shifts

What happens when most products begin to look alike, when the customer perceives them to be interchangeable? You would think, from our discussions in Chapter 3, that companies that offer the lowest price would have the competitive advantage. Since products *look* alike and actually *are* alike you might think that the strategy of *differentiation* would fall down before the strategy of *lowest price*. But, sometimes sellers have to draw the line; sometimes the lowest price is a price that is simply not profitable. It doesn't do a company any good to sell more product than its competitors, but at unprofitable prices.

But a light shines at the end of this tunnel. What if customers again shifted their perception of value? What if the customer begins to see value and benefits in new ways? What if their new concept of value differentiation did not reside solely inside the product or service itself, but was found in the buying/selling *process,* for example in the convenience of acquiring the product or service? What if selling companies found new ways to reduce costs? Revisiting the value formula, *Value = Benefits minus Costs,* reminds us that a company that finds and delivers increased benefits while simultaneously reducing costs will dramatically increase value. This is exactly what progressive companies are doing.

We will now discuss some of the factors that have caused buyers to perceive the meaning of value in new ways. In Chapter 5, we will discuss how the new sellers have responded to these changes by adopting new and situational selling approaches.

Three Types of Value Buyers

The type of value that they seek in any exchange process can distinguish buyers as: **intrinsic value** buyers, **extrinsic value** buyers, and **strategic value** buyers (Rackham and De Vincentis 1998, 16).

Intrinsic Value Buyers

Value, for intrinsic value buyers, resides inside the product or service itself. They focus on the cost side of the value equation *(Value = Benefits minus Costs).* These buyers are usually well educated about the product or service. They are familiar with the various alternative competitive products and are convinced that any one of them will satisfy their needs and/or desires. When they need additional information about these products, they know exactly how to find it. Increasingly, they seek this information from the Internet.

Because they see the product as *commoditized,* they generally make their product choice based on price. The lowest priced product will be the one they select, so the selling company that offers the lowest price has the competitive advantage. Since these buyers understand the product or service very well, they don't need a salesperson to communicate with them or attempt to differentiate their now commoditized product. In fact, using a salesperson in this situation only *adds* costs, which is counterproductive for price-driven buyers. An example will help clarify the concept of an intrinsic value buyer.

Suppose a meeting planner or corporate trainer is looking for a hotel at which to hold a training meeting. A training meeting is a relatively simple and basic type of meeting. Most meeting planners and trainers know exactly how they want this to be conducted. Basic specification requirements for a two-day meeting are sleeping rooms and a meeting room for about 30 people, set up classroom style, with an overhead projector and screen, two refreshment breaks per day, and one lunch per day. Most limited-service hotels can handle such a meeting with the same quality level.

Let's suppose that Hotel A employs a salesperson and a conference coordinator. The salesperson sells the meeting and the conference coordinator works with the meeting planner or trainer during the time of the meeting. Now suppose Hotel B, a competitor of equal quality, can provide the same basic meeting but employs only a conference coordinator. Which hotel can offer the same (commoditized) meeting at a lower price and win the business?

Hotel B, of course. Eliminating the salesperson in this case was a smart move. The intrinsic value buyer was very knowledgeable about the details of training meetings and familiar with all of the competitive hotels capable of handling the specifications. What value could a salesperson provide that would justify adding additional costs (from the salesperson's salary and bonus)? Competitive advantage of lowest price went to Hotel B in this example. The buyer received intrinsic value; a high-quality product or service at the lowest price.

Extrinsic Value Buyers

Extrinsic value buyers focus almost exclusively on the benefit side of the value equation. Cost is not as important to them as is how the product or service is used or delivered. These buyers are interested in solutions. They are continually concerned with how the product will solve their problems, needs, and/or desires.

While it's true that even a commodity-like product or service can solve a buyer's problem, such products will not excite an extrinsic value buyer. The solutions are usually complex and relatively expensive solutions.

Value for extrinsic value buyers is found in the importance they place in the seller's ability to help them. They put a premium on advice and assistance. They want help in understanding the options available. They want the complex solution to be customized for their specific problem or need. Often they look at the seller as an expert partner in the exchange process.

Unlike the intrinsic value buyer, who sees no value in spending time with a salesperson, the extrinsic value buyer *expects* more quality time. These buyers are willing to invest time, effort, and costs in working with salespeople who can help them solve buying problems. Why? Extrinsic value buyers generally are considering the purchase of complex and expensive products or services and they expect the exchange to take place through a joint decision process. They want to work with a partner who serves as a trustworthy consultant. An example will help illustrate the extrinsic value buyer.

Corporate meetings and conferences come in various sizes, complexity, and expense. Earlier we discussed a commodity-like corporate training meeting to illustrate the intrinsic value buyer. The training meeting was relatively small in size and very straightforward in its specifications; it was not complex. Compared to our next example, it did not cost very much. Let's look at an example of a national sales meeting for a large U.S. corporation at a major resort.

The basic specifications for this meeting are: (1) 250 attendees, (2) single sleeping rooms for four nights, (3) three meals each day per person, (4) meetings going on three of the four days with a general session in the morning, (5) invited speakers and facilitators needing sophisticated high-tech audiovisual support, (6) special events such as theme parties, (7) opening ceremonies and closing ceremonies, (8) several optional events like a golf tournament and/or a tennis tournament, and (9) various off-property options such as hot air ballooning and horseback riding. Their budget for this meeting, exclusive of airfare for attendees, is $300,000.

When the salesperson asks the buyer what he/she needs, of course the buyer lists many of the items above. When the buyer is more closely questioned, he/she states, "I really want this to be a success. I don't want anything to go wrong. I have never met at your resort before and I'm not completely familiar with all the things that you can do here to make this meeting a success. Can you help?"

Let's look closely at this buyer's needs. What is the solution that he/she seeks? What will satisfy the buyer that they will have a successful meeting?

First, the buyer has narrowed down a list of high-quality and similarly priced resort properties. The buyer is trying to decide which of these similar properties can achieve his/her real need: a successful meeting. The buyer knows that a successful meeting is not solely found in the brick and mortar; it's found in the way that a staff of people can be orchestrated to plan and deliver all of many functions that come together to create an overall whole. So, the buyer is looking for thoughtful customization of the resort's unique offerings that will create a memorable experience.

Second, the buyer asked a seemingly innocent question, "Can you help?" The buyer was asking the salesperson to think along with him/her to jointly create a solution that would answer the basic problem: the need for a successful meeting. This request for the salesperson to adopt a consultant role also implied that the buyer needed to have trust in the salesperson. Additionally, the buyer stated, "I don't want anything to go wrong." This statement indicates that the need for trust in the salesperson is also extended to the need for trust in the entire resort.

In summary, the buyer is looking for a solution to a complex problem, "I need a successful meeting and I want to feel comfortable with my decision." Since the resort already meets specifications of quality and rates, value for the buyer is now found in the way the salesperson expertly partners with the buyer and how they jointly work together to reach a customized meeting program.

For extrinsic value buyers, real value can be created by the salesperson. These buyers frequently reject competitive sellers who have attractively priced and quality products or services, but haven't taken the time to deeply understand the buyer's real needs. These buyers value the process itself. They look for value from the sales effort that reaches beyond the product or service. A quality product or service is, of course, the beginning basis for all sales, but extrinsic value buyers require such things as advice and customization. They demand a salesperson whose help and advice creates extra value and will often pay additional costs to obtain this added value.

Strategic Value Buyers

Strategic value buyers want a level of value that greatly exceeds the product for sale *or* the consultative relationship they have with the salesperson. They want to have access to the seller's total organizational resources and competencies. They are looking to form an alliance or partnership with the selling organization and are willing to radically restructure themselves to accomplish this. They are looking for a strategic alliance, where both the buyer company and the seller company recognize key complementary competencies about each other. They want to fit together the way the two pieces of the yin and yang symbol fit . . . complementarily. Strategically, they both hope to reduce costs and to gain other operational efficiencies. A strategic alliance is a relationship between business equals who are working together to create an extraordinary level of new value that neither could create alone.

Strategic value buyers usually get involved in very intense relationships that are highly selective and usually confined to a few very large suppliers. Strategic value sellers that normally would sell to many buyers enter partnerships with a few buying companies—and sell all of their output just to them. In very rare cases you might have one selling company and one buying company.

Successful strategic alliances can be formed only when top management gets behind them. CEOs conceive and initiate the partnerships and then delegate to their selling teams and buying teams to bring the partnership to reality. Let's briefly look at an example.

Major hotel chains have many different types of hotels that are segmented: resort, convention, commercial, airport, limited service, long-term stay, all-suites, and so forth. Many such hotel chains have a wide national and international presence; their hotels are in most major cities. Suppose that the CEO of XYZ Hotels met with the CEO of ABC Corporation and made the following proposal: ABC Corporation will promise to use XYZ Hotels for at least 90 percent of business travel and 80 percent of its corporate meeting business each year. In return, XYZ Hotels will reduce all rates for ABC by 30 percent.

Why would XYZ Hotels be willing to do this? First, they would be able to eliminate most normal sales and marketing expenses that had formerly been committed to obtaining the equivalent ABC revenue. Second, they would have a predictable source of revenue. These benefits would more than cover the 30 percent discount.

Why would ABC Corporation agree to this? First, they would have a major cost savings on travel and meeting expenses. They would also save costs by reducing purchasing costs associated with the buying/selling process. Second, over time, they would have increased familiarity with the hotel chain's operations and procedures, which would reduce paperwork costs and streamline meeting planning and booking business travel. They might even integrate their computerized accounting systems.

Are there any downsides to these arrangements? Certainly. When two different people or corporate entities are brought into a very close relationship, the very closeness is often a source of discord. These relationships (often considered analogous to marriages) must be actively nurtured and maintained. Generally, each company in the partnership assigns a specific person or team to manage the new partnership culture. We will look more carefully at the pros and cons of and barriers to alliance-type relationships later in Chapters 14 and 18.

In summary, for successful exchanges to take place, both buyers and sellers must receive value in the exchange. The buyers' perceptions of value are the factor that determines the sellers' response. We have discussed three types of buyers based on how they perceive value:

◆ Intrinsic value buyers see products as a commodity and therefore place value on the lowest price. They don't see value in salespeople since they add unnecessary costs.
◆ Extrinsic value buyers see quality products as a foundation for value, but see value in the consultative advice, customization, and problem-solving attributes brought by the salesperson.
◆ Strategic value buyers see value in the synergies that a partnership or alliance between two or more companies can bring.

The preceding discussion has made a strong and definitive point. Value perceptions by both buyers and sellers will determine whether an exchange is successful. Buyers will not complete an exchange if they do not perceive that they will receive something of value for what they give. The same is true for the seller. We have attempted to categorize buyers by the value that they see as their *dominant buying motive* (DBM).

In the following discussion, we outline the process through which buyers acquire this DBM. In this discussion, keep in mind that the concept *value* is a substituted word for anything that the buyer perceives as a want or need.

How Buyers Make Buying Decisions

People are influenced by internal (individual psychological or physiological) and external (social) forces. These forces cause people to *perceive* that they need or want or *value* something. Internal forces are those that arise primarily due to the individual person responding to his/her own personal perceptions of conditions affecting him/her; external forces are those that arise from society. These include culture, social class, reference groups, roles, and general social influences. For business buyers, these external forces are found within their company's organization.

Buyers may not be aware of how their needs have been shaped by influencing forces. They may hold them dormant until something arouses or activates them. Then, when a *motive* arises, the buyer exhibits those needs as *behavior*. This behavior is intended to *satisfy* that aroused need.

How Customer Needs Shape Perceptions

Perception can be defined as the process that people use to receive information (stimuli) through the five senses and then assign meaning to this information. Perception is shaped by internal psychological and physiological conditions and external social influences. What is seen and felt and the meaning that we assign to it is filtered through our perception, which explains why different people may describe seemingly same objects or occurrences good, evil, sexy, boring, and so forth. *Selective perception* is the term given to this dynamic.

Buyers may screen out or modify information presented by a salesperson if it conflicts with their previously learned attitudes or beliefs. Salespeople need to learn as much background information about the buyer as possible before they make a sales presentation. Additionally, during the first and subsequent meetings with the customer, the salesperson should try to build a strong relationship so that there will be open dialogue and free discussion about personal perceptions. Salespeople should also review their own perceptions about various customer types (segments) to ensure that they are accurate.

In summary, buyers' needs are initially shaped and formed by both internal and external influencing forces. They remain dormant until they are activated by *motives*.

How Customer Needs Are Activated—Buying Motives

A buying motive can be seen as an aroused need, drive, or desire. The buying motive acts as a force that stimulates behavior. This behavior (buying decision) is intended to satisfy the aroused need. Salespeople need to understand buying motives to understand the reasons why customers buy or initiate behavior in the form of a buying decision. Buying decisions are often influenced by more than one buying motive. Within several buying motives, there is usually one *dominant buying motive* (DBM). Earlier in this chapter, we made a case that what is seen as the greatest value is usually the DBM. The DBM will have the greatest influence on the buying decision. Successful salespeople work hard to discover the buying motives that influence the customer's buying decision. There are three major types of buying motives:

    emotional buying motives
    rational buying motives
    hybrid buying motives

Buyers simultaneously base their buying decisions on emotional and rational motives. One or the other may be dominant . . . or they may be operating in balance (aka hybrid).

Emotional Buying Motive. An emotional buying motive prompts the prospect to act because of an appeal to some sentiment or passion. However, the most powerful of emotional motives are associated with our most basic human drives: fear and gain. Emotional motives can generally be seen as those of the heart as opposed to the head and come from a desire to satisfy a wish for pleasure, comfort, or social approval. However, the emotional motives of fear or gain can be accompanied by good solid rationality. For example, the fear motive might make someone decide to buy a life insurance policy so that his/her spouse and children won't be without support, and the gain motive might make someone decide to buy a stock or bond because of the potential (real or imagined) that it will increase in value.

Emotional motives are very powerful and often are the underlying basis of the dominant buying motive. Successful salespeople ask "feel-finding" questions during the "recognition of needs" phase of the buying process to uncover these powerful motives.

Rational Buying Motive. A rational buying motive usually appeals to the customer's reason or logical judgment. A buying decision based on rational buying motives is generally the result of an objective review of available information. Some examples include: (1) profit potential or enhancement, (2) quality of service, and (3) availability of technical assistance. Successful salespeople ask "fact-finding" questions during the "recognition of needs" phase of the buying process to uncover rational buying motives.

Hybrid Buying Motives. There are two types of motives that combine both the emotional and the rational and are thus hybrids: (1) patronage buying motives and (2) product or service buying motives. Both of these are learned motives rather than motives that spring forth from the individual primally or unconsciously. They are learned from prior experience with the selling company and/or reputation.

A patronage buying motive is one that causes the customer to buy products and services from one particular business (customer loyalty). The customer's prior experience with the firm has been judged beneficial; thus, the customer wishes to repeat the experience (repeat business). When competitive products are more or less the same, the patronage motive can be a very powerful plus for the seller. In a commoditized world the patronage motive can provide competitive advantage to a seller who has done well by the customer on other occasions.

Buyers may exhibit patronage buying motives if: (1) they've been pleased with the competence of the salesperson and the development of the relationship, (2) if they've received superior service and see this as added value, and (3) if they like the range of choice and variety offered by the seller.

A product or service buying motive is one that influences the customer to purchase one product or service over another. In a way, this is an emotional decision, since the customer may not directly compare the competitive products or services, but may instead have an intuitive feeling that one product is better than the other. Of course, these feelings may not be based on reality. They can be triggered by marketing stimuli designed to create that impression.

Some examples of product or service buying motives are: (1) brand preference, (2) quality preference, (3) price preference, and (4) design or engineering preference.

In summary, buyers of low-priced and noncomplex consumer products generally tend to rely heavily on emotional buying motives, whereas buyers of higher priced and complex products or services tend to rely on rational buying motives. However, always remember that both sets of motives, emotional and rational, are being considered by all buyers—just in different proportions. Thus, one might say that all buying motives are hybrids (Manning and Reece 1997).

How Buyers Buy—*Their* View of the Exchange Process

The Need-Satisfaction Buying Process Theory

The need-satisfaction buying process is a process of exchange that is buyer centered. This process looks at exchanges through the buyer's eyes. As we will learn in Chapters 5 and 6, smart sellers today make sure that they view the world from the buyer's perspective. Doing so makes them more effective and successful.

In the buying process, buyers select one product over another based on the value that they perceive will satisfy their needs. They arrive at this acquisition decision through a series of steps. Each of these steps is a miniproblem for the buyer to solve before he/she can proceed to the next step.

Previously we discussed three types of value buyers. Given that buyers perceive value differently, is there any acquisition process that they have in common? Rackham and De Vincentis (1998, 67) inform us that these buyers proceed through the *exchange process,* or as we label it, the *buying process*. Salespeople have traditionally viewed the exchange process through their eyes and have called it the *selling process*. As we will later learn, the smarter way to look at the exchange process is to integrate these viewpoints to better satisfy both parties. We call this more holistic viewpoint *the buying/selling process*. Before we describe this, let's first take a look at the traditional one-sided viewpoints. We'll look first at how buyers see the exchange process—and what sellers can do if their clients are coming from this direction.

Chapter 5 will follow with the seller's paradigm. In Chapter 6, we will reconcile the buyer's perspective of the process with the seller's perspective.

The Buying Process

Although they are not always consciously doing so, buyers typically buy products or services (especially complex products or services) in the following stages:

> Recognition of Needs—Buyers, especially extrinsic value buyers, are not always clear about their needs or the problems they seek to solve. The value that a salesperson can add at this stage is to help buyers recognize and define problems and needs in a new or different way.
>
> Evaluation of Options—With complex products, alternative and customized solutions are not always clear. The value that a salesperson can add here is to show superior solutions, options, and approaches that buyers may not have understood or considered.
>
> Resolution of Concerns (buyer decides on one of the competing products)—Value here is created by the salesperson in helping customers to overcome and remove obstacles so they can make their decision.
>
> Purchase (logistics of acquisition)—The value a salesperson can contribute here is to make the purchase painless, convenient, and hassle-free.
>
> Implementation—The salesperson adds value by showing customers how to install and use the product or service.

This is a typical buying process (sequence of steps en route to acquiring the product or service) that buyers in business-to-business (B2B) markets use. It is the view of the exchange process through the buyers' eyes.

SUMMARY ◆

There was a time when there were no economic buyers as we know them today. People did not engage in a world of monetary exchange. As agricultural producers, they did barter but for the most part were not engaged in monetary trade. Around the mid-1400s and accelerating with the Industrial Revolution, people were working in cities and earning salaries. We had entered a world of trade.

Whether bartering or buying and selling goods for money, people have always decided whether they would exchange with another person based on the concept of value (benefits received minus costs). How people perceive value determines the dynamics of the exchange process. Smart sellers attempt to understand the buyer's perception to be able to properly adjust their selling approach. In this text we refer to *situational selling* as the appropriate adjustment of the selling approach in response to the buyer's perceived value.

Today, buyers' perceptions of value are undergoing dramatic change and evolution. We identified three types of business value buyers: intrinsic, extrinsic, and strategic. In Chapter 5 we will see how sellers have adjusted their situational selling approaches to address these changes.

In this chapter, we also presented a primer on buying needs and motives. These concepts are important whether we are discussing exchange of products, services, ideas, or the broader term, *value*. In all exchanges, ultimately a value is being exchanged.

Sellers have historically viewed the exchange process through their eyes. They call it the *selling process*. Buyers, on the other hand, see the exchange process through their eyes. They call it the *buying process*. We introduced this process in this chapter. After discussing the sellers' view of the exchange process, in Chapter 5, we will reconcile both of these perspectives into an integrated and more effective approach (the buying/selling process) in Chapter 6.

References

Manning, G. L., and B. L. Reece. 1997. *Selling today.* 7th ed. Upper Saddle River, NJ: Prentice Hall.

Peeler, G. H. 1996. *Selling in the quality era.* Oxford, UK: Blackwell Publishers, Ltd.

Rackham, N. and J. De Vincentis. 1998. Rethinking the sales force: Redefining selling to create and capture customer value. New York: McGraw-Hill.

Strong, E. K., Jr. 1922. *The psychology of selling life insurance.* New York and London: Harper & Brothers Publishers.

◆ DISCUSSION QUESTIONS

1. Provide examples of how hotels produce superior benefits for their customers that distinguish or differentiate them from the competition. Can these attributes or services be copied or duplicated by the competition? How long will they provide competitive advantage?
2. Define value as discussed in this chapter. What are the two means in which value can be increased from the perception of the customer?
3. Do emotions ever become a dominant buying motive of an organizational buyer? Discuss an example.
4. Organizational buyers involved in a complex purchase decision go through a deliberate series of stages. What are they? What implication does this process have for the salesperson?

CHAPTER 5

The New World of Selling:

Responding to Changing Buyer Perceptions of Value

After reading this chapter you should be able to

- ◆ understand and articulate the three selling modes
- ◆ explain the importance of matching the appropriate selling mode or strategy to the right type of buyer based on the buyer's perception of value

- ◆ list the steps in the traditional sales process
- ◆ describe the evolution of sales as a profession both historically and into the foreseeable future

micromarketing
situational selling
transactional selling

consultative selling
alliance selling

The story of Cinderella is an ancient fable of victory, recognition of inherent merit, and rightful restoration. The heroine is mistreated by a malevolent stepfamily but achieves happiness and status through the benevolent intervention of a fairy godmother. Cinderella is the embodiment of a person or thing of merit, undeservedly neglected and forced into an obscure existence, who suddenly or unexpectedly arises to recognition and success.

In relation to its sexier stepsister *marketing, sales* has been perceived as the soot-covered and dirty Cinderella. Yet, the fairy godmother of *change* has created circumstances that have taken this Cinderella to the ball and eventual marriage to the prince.

Today's business-to-business (B2B) salespeople sell complex and customized products and services. They interact with buyers who are seeking solutions to complex challenges and needs. They are the point persons in their organization charged with building and developing relations with other firms faced with complex challenges and needs their firms can satisfy. *Marketing,* which previously treated salespeople as menial Cinderellas, now finds itself as the background support vehicle for those very salespeople. *Sales* is now the princess in a land where large complex product or service sales are important. No one else comes close to fitting the glass slipper.

Selling complex products today requires sophisticated salespeople who are savvy enough to practice all the principles of marketing, but who do so on the front lines of exchange—directly with their sophisticated B2B buyers. Today's new sellers can be thought of as *micromarketers*. They practice at a micro level what marketing does at a macro level. We call what they do **consultative selling.** If you were to examine the history of selling and economic systems (see sidebar), you would see that this is an evolutionary change based on a shift from product orientation to customer orientation.

In Chapter 1 we talked about why simply observing a top salesperson will not make a beginning salesperson an instant expert. Mere observation of even a great salesperson will provide limited information. Have you ever watched a four-year-old pretend to drive a car? Based on their limited observation, children turn the wheel dramatically from side to side. They don't understand that most of steering is done with small, subtle movements in response to relationships with other cars, the road, and traffic signals. They have no idea of the underlying principles of driving and how much of it depends on other people. Our framework for understanding the *new seller* is based on his/her appropriate response to changing perceptions of value by customers. We call this approach **situational selling.**

Emergence of the New Seller
A Historical Perspective of Exchange and the Changing Status of Those Who Sell

From Antiquity to the Industrial Revolution
◆ salespeople and merchants seen as despicable characters
◆ pirates had better reputation than peddlers and traders
◆ wealth and status lay in land holdings and livestock
◆ bartering and trading considered lowly

1300s through mid-1700s
◆ peddlers sell goods while traveling from town to town
◆ peddlers acquire inventory and set up shops, becoming merchants
◆ peddlers/merchants still societal underdogs
◆ unfairly taxed or begrudgingly given licenses
◆ commerce grew anyway; standard of living improved across all classes
◆ people question being frozen in society with no hope for advancement
◆ personal motivation for betterment increases
◆ availability of products spurs people to find ways to acquire them
◆ creativity and innovation flourish; new ways are found to produce goods
◆ workers begin to specialize; production increases
◆ prices drop and all classes have access to creature comforts and objects of beauty (Peeler 1996)

The Industrial Revolution begins circa 1760
◆ powerful changes in economics and social organization
◆ hand tools replaced by power-driven machines such as power looms and steam engines
◆ industry moves from small operations to large establishments
◆ previously expensive and scarce products become available and affordable
◆ England controls colonies (like United States) by forbidding them to manufacture goods; they must buy goods from England
◆ English goods imported to eastern seaboard (New York, Boston, etc.) need ways to reach pioneers moving westward
◆ *Yankee peddlers* emerge, carrying needed goods on horseback or wagon along routes with regular customers desperate for essential items
◆ Yankee peddlers need a reputation of honesty and responsiveness in order to get repeat business; they build relationships and begin to listen to customer needs

Essentially, the new seller is defined by the situational selling approach that he/she takes. Today's new seller practices a very different selling approach based on very different situations. Appropriate selling approaches change over time in response to changes in the meaning of value. The emphasis is on how value is perceived by the buyer, but the seller's perspective plays a role, too. First, the buyer's perception of value shifts, which causes a corresponding shift in the seller's approach to the exchange. Sellers have to assess whether they can respond to this new perception of value in a cost-effective way. If they can't, they might not pursue this buyer. It they can, they adjust their selling approach based on the new situation. This is the practice of situational selling. It's a seller's strategically thoughtful and appropriate adaptation to the buyer's changed value needs. Let's see how these new sellers evolved.

A Rapid Evolutionary Time Line Leading to Today's New Sellers

The old-time peddlers focused on selling products along a regular route. If they wanted to be welcome on return trips, they had to deal honestly with their customers. In order to develop repeat customers, they listened to their needs and noticed what items seemed in short supply. They didn't have room on their wagons to carry items that didn't sell—and they didn't try to sell their customers items they did not want. These were simple times and the buyer-seller relationship was pretty simple.

Peddlers Become Representatives of Manufacturers

Things started to change in the early 1800s. We have written records of the first paid sales force around 1816 when manufacturers started paying peddlers to "push products." With this competitive pushing of products, buyers began to perceive salespeople as less than honest.

Sales Forces and Sales Agents

By the 1920s, books were being written to train salespeople. Unlike today, when salespeople are best employed selling to B2B markets, these salespeople sold to consumers—business-to-consumer (B2C) markets. In 1922, E. K. Strong wrote *The Psychology of Selling Life Insurance,* the first book on how to sell using the then revolutionary psychological techniques that had just been made popular by Freud, Adler, Jung, and other early psychologists. The philosophy underlying these new techniques was still pushing products—this time by appealing to the customers' psychological needs. In essence, Strong taught that fear and greed were the main motivators found in all buyers.

He also taught that through a series of logical steps, a salesperson could lead the buyer to the sale. He cast a long shadow, eventually becoming a professor of psychology at the Stanford University School of Business, and wrote influential books, including *The Psychology of Selling and Advertising* (1925) and *The Psychological Aspects of Business* (1938).

Strong set the mold for most of today's selling-process training programs. For almost 80 years his influence produced sellers who were product oriented. They believed that newer, improved products promoted by advertising and personal sales would achieve profits. They concentrated on traditional selling (explained later in this chapter), which advocated finding many new prospects and concentrating on selling techniques that psychologically influence the buyer. We will later demonstrate why today's new seller must abandon these techniques.

Rise of Sales Engineers: A Transition toward the Marketing Concept

Around 1940, articles on selling and sales books began to speak of *sales engineers*. Technical graduates were wondering: "What is sales engineering?" "What possibilities does it offer and what does it take to be successful in it?" Bernard Lester, an electrical engineer at Westinghouse and a member of the newly formed American Marketing Association, responded with his 1940 book, *Sales Engineering.* Hitting the nail firmly on the head, Lester noted:

> *In the drama of industrial progress, the spotlight of public attention which has been centered upon the creators of technical products is now being directed upon those who are responsible for the distribution of those products (1940, v).*

Sales engineers were the predecessors of today's B2B market salespeople. They were different from typical salespeople selling inexpensive consumer products. Their task was to sell major equipment *to other businesses*. Sales engineers had to have a combination of technical knowledge about their products *and* be masters of the art of selling. They represented the beginning of customization of B2B selling.

At this point, marketing became a new concept, and the earliest marketing principles were set forth. Marketers liked the look of what sales engineers were doing, particularly their strategies of customizing products and focusing on the customer. In effect, marketing took over the role of customer customization and maintained that role for the next 40-plus years. (For a more detailed look at the birth of marketing, see the sidebar.)

The Birth of Marketing in America

1915 National Association of Teachers of Advertising founded from the annual convention of the Association of Advertising Clubs of the World in Chicago, June 1915

1931 American Marketing Society made up of practitioners in the field of marketing and marketing research, formed in New York

1933 NATA becomes NAMT, National Association of Marketing Teachers

1936 National Association of Teachers of Marketing and the American Marketing Society work together to publish the first issue of the *Journal of Marketing*

1937 AMA created from merger of National Association of Teachers of Marketing and the American Marketing Society

1938 Census Bureau asks AMA to participate in unifying the marketing definitions used by all government agencies

1940 AMA has 817 members and 11 chapters

Source: American Marketing Association (2001), American Marketing Association home page [online], http://www.ama.org.

The rallying cry of the science/art of marketing became *customer orientation,* with an emphasis on customer focus, not product focus. Marketing's big idea was to sell to targeted groups of customers categorized by group characteristics. Expansion of the new marketing philosophy took place in four phases, each of which caused changes in personal selling approaches.

a. **1950 to 1965—The Basic Marketing Concept**—The idea of customer orientation versus product orientation infiltrates the practices of *traditional selling* salespeople (discussed in depth later). They realize that it is important to learn more about the customer's needs *prior* to attempting to sell them a product or service, so they start to collect data on their prospective buyers.

b. **1966 to 1980—First Expansion of the Basic Marketing Concept**—Large customer market segments begin to be reduced to smaller market segments or niches. Consultative selling (discussed in depth later) in a basic form begins to appear. Salespeople are becoming diagnosticians of customers' needs as well as consultants offering well-considered recommendations. They identify buyer needs through a two-way communications process.

c. **1981 to 1990—Second Expansion of the Marketing Concept**—Marketing gains respect and is seen as important to the well-being of the total organization. A greater emphasis on market niches means that marketing practices and departments need more structure and start putting more emphasis on planning.

With the advent of more complex selling environments, basic consultative selling becomes more refined and the consultative salesperson becomes more important. Traditional B2C salespeople begin to be replaced by new distribution channels such as self-service, toll-free numbers, and Internet purchasing. The new hotshots are the indispensable B2B salespeople who have the right combination of skills for selling complex service products in the hospitality industry, such as major conventions.

d. **1991 to Present**—Third Expansion of the Marketing Concept—This is the beginning of the era of alliances between preferred suppliers and preferred customers who are committed to permanent relationships. Consultative selling again refines itself by adopting alliance thinking. Salespeople are encouraged to think of everything they say or do in the context of their long-term, high-quality partnerships with the goal of repeat business and referrals from their most profitable buyers. Sales force automation (SFA) and customer relationship management (CRM) software provides more targeted customer information.

Consultative sellers became micromarketers. **Micromarketing** means that today's sellers practice the principles taught in marketing but at the level of the single buyer. Whereas marketing is still a primary player in B2C selling, in B2B sales marketing is supportive of (rather than primary in) the relationship development process.

The New World of Selling in Response to Buyers' Perceived Value

Forces That Have Changed Selling Approaches

In Chapter 4, we discussed how and why buyers have changed the way they perceive value in products and services offered by selling organizations. Essentially, customers seek value. You should now be familiar with the simple value formula *Value = Benefits minus Costs*. Customers generally want more benefits at lower costs. You should also remember that benefits are not always found in the product or service itself. Benefits can be seen as doing business in a professional manner, dealing with those that one trusts, or conducting business in a convenient and hassle-free manner. Similarly, costs are not always monetary. Costs such as delay in delivery, errors, and so forth are real costs. The world of selling has responded to the customers' changed perception of value. Selling organizations have responded to both external and internal variables, which are related to customer value perception.

External Variables.   These variables are external to and uncontrollable by the sales organization. External variables continually and independently evolve, so selling organizations must constantly pay attention to them and develop responses that work. These variables were reported by Hartley and Starkey in an original study by Abberton and Associates in 1991 (Hartley and Starkey 1996, 20).

1.   **Changing Customer Needs**—Today, buyer-perceived value is not intrinsically found or built into the product or service but is found in the acquisition process or the way the buying/selling process is conducted. Buyers, like everyone else today, are overworked and value time, ease, reliability, and trust. Any seller who meets these needs creates value. Buyers today need and value being able to acquire a product or service, when, where, and how they want it.

2.   **Increasing Customer Sophistication**—Buyers are very aware of what's available in the product or service marketplace. The Internet and other communication avenues make this knowledge widespread, so salespeople can't compete solely on providing information or educating these customers.

3.   **New Customer/Supplier Relationships**—Trust and reliability were discussed earlier as "new customer needs." These needs have evolved because buyers no longer stockpile expensive inventories just in case they might need them. Instead they have embraced the Japanese strategy of "just in time" (JIT) inventories, which means that supplies do not arrive (at a factory, for example) until just when they are needed. JIT requires buyers to have very close relationships with a few very trustworthy suppliers. The hospitality industry has embraced this idea.

4.   **Internationalization Increases the Demands Suppliers Made on Salespeople**—Internationalization has increased the number of suppliers competing for both domestic and foreign business at the same time that buyers want to deal with fewer suppliers. Competition for these buyers has caused a redefinition of how to compete or gain competitive advantage.

Internal Variables. These variables are internal to and controllable by the selling organization. Here the selling organization can take a proactive approach in order to enhance sales and increase profitability by reducing selling costs. Selling costs can be reduced by making the buying/selling process more effective and efficient. From the 1996 Hartley and Starkey study, the most important areas of achieving this are the following:

1.   **Sales Force Effectiveness**—Effectiveness means working on the right things and spending energy where it will do the most good. Today, selling organizations increasingly place emphasis on profits, not sales potential. The operating phrase today is *lifetime value of the customer*. And this lifetime value is viewed not only in terms of top-line revenue, but also in terms of the

bottom-line cost, therefore profitability, of attaining this revenue. Not all customer accounts are worthy of having a sales force try to attain them. For example, in terms of the bottom line, which would be more preferable: to sell a $100,000 piece of business that costs $60,000 to deliver (profit = $40,000), or to sell a $70,000 piece of business that costs $15,000 to deliver (profit = $55,000)? Although the $100,000 figure sounds more impressive, it can actually be less profitable.

2.   **Sales Force Efficiency**—This means doing things right or very well and with the least cost. Sales force costs have been rising rapidly. The selling organization must continue to support the sales force, but seek savings through efficiencies. Some of these efficiencies include handing off buyer accounts to new salespeople who are paid less than seasoned veterans. Other efficiencies include using nonpersonal means, such as the Internet, to sell.

3.   **Multiple Channels and New Methods of Customer Contact**—This is related to sales force efficiencies mentioned above. Face-to-face selling by the company's field sales force is being supplemented and supported by: (1) direct mail, (2) telephone sales, (3) merchandisers, (4) third-party sales-support companies, (5) the Internet, and so on. Accounts are ranked by potential and loyalty. Top accounts receive the most intense "relationship" attention by the account executive. Lesser accounts are relegated to the supporting, or less expensive, methods. The way sales forces are organized is shifting to reflect this. Marriott and Hilton now use methods like cluster selling and event booking centers, for example (more on this later, in Chapter 16).

4.   **New Technology Is a Catalyst for Change**—Technology in all of its forms is driving change in the buying/selling process. As we will see in later chapters, the human relationship can be a competitive advantage given technology's creation of an impersonal world. We will further discuss the role of technology in Chapter 17. Sales force automation (SFA), database management (DBM), customer relationship management (CRM), and other technological tools applied to the new world of buying/selling are detailed.

Sellers' Responses to External and Internal Forces

Old-Style Selling–*Communicate* Product or Service Features. Up until now, the sales forces of companies have been content to *communicate* value that was created by others. In the past, this value was built into the product or service itself. Value in the past was seen as a product or service that had features that made it different, better, and faster, and intrinsically had more quality built into it than the competitive product. Essentially this was a sales-centric view.

New-Style Selling–Add Value as Demanded by Customer. Today, sellers need to add new responses to the forces driving the new world of buying decisions. To achieve competitive advantage, they need to: (1) respond to new definitions and buyer perceptions of value and (2) lower selling costs. As mentioned earlier, sellers don't throw out old tools or approaches; they add to their toolkit and respond appropriately to each situation as they find it. Competitive advantage is found in giving the buyer the value that he/she wants. In the process, the seller distinguishes itself from its competitors. To prosper, sellers must find new ways to *create* value during and after the process of selling itself.

Three Types of Sellers

The old saying that "selling is selling" comes from a widely accepted but outdated myth that there is a single set of basic sales principles that applies to all selling situations. The new economic and technological environment has dramatically changed this notion.

The three emerging selling modes are situational and correspond with the three new value buyers we presented in Chapter 4. To review, those types are intrinsic value buyers, extrinsic value buyers, and strategic value buyers. The three modes are transactional sales, consultative sales, and alliance sales. They pair up as follows:

intrinsic value buyers	transactional sales
extrinsic value buyers	consultative sales
strategic value buyers	alliance sales

Which selling mode to use depends on: (1) whether a product or service is simple or complex, (2) whether this is a "single-call" selling (salesperson initially meets the buyer and attempts to close the sale in one appointment) or "multiple-call" selling, (3) the number of people involved in the purchase decision, and (4) the sophistication level of the buyer.

Transactional Sales

Corresponding with the intrinsic value buyer (see Chapter 4), transactional sales is the oldest form of selling. These salespeople sell simple and low-to medium-priced products or services. Long-term relationships with customers are a costly luxury since the salesperson relies on many sales transactions to achieve his/her revenue goals. These salespeople attempt to sell in "single calls" in a single appointment with the buyer.

Today, many products and services are becoming commoditized. Simultaneously, buyers are becoming more sophisticated and have easy access to product or service specifications. Because these buyers know what they want, know where to get it, and have access to many product suppliers, they are primarily interested in one thing—price. What value can the salesperson add to the buying process? Not much! In fact, the salesperson in transactional sales is a cost that raises price. So, a competitor that sells without salespeople (over the Internet, for example) has a lower price.

In a transactional sale, the customer is interested in the lowest price and will choose the supplier offering the lowest price. An example of this is new car sales. Buyers don't need salespeople to tell them the features or benefits of a new car; you can find these on the Internet. Salespeople are not needed to negotiate prices; many dealerships have listed and nonnegotiable prices. Also, buyers shop the Internet to learn invoice costs and then shop further for the lowest prices. Couldn't this same thing happen in limited-service hotels with small meeting rooms as they seek to sell noncomplex training meetings? Yes! Many of these limited-service hotels are very similar—just like commodities.

What will happen to today's salespeople selling in transactional situations? They will be downsized or transformed. Sophisticated transactional customers don't need a salesperson.

Consultative Sales

Corresponding with the extrinsic value buyer, consultative sales is the second oldest of the three basic forms. It theoretically evolved by the mid-1980s but only today is being put into full practice. These salespeople sell high-priced and complex products or services. They must build long-term relationships with customers. They sell in multiple calls over a lengthy time period and usually need to influence buying committees. Fortunately, large conferences and conventions are complex products and services.

Here salespeople add value through *all* stages of the buying process. Their primary function is to build relationships with primary buyers—meeting planners and their meeting-buying committee—and learn how each company works through the meeting planning and buying process.

What will happen to today's salespeople selling in consultative situations? They will become more valuable to the selling company. The company will invest more resources in these people. Pay will rise and they will be increasingly supported by technology and continual training and development. Employers will support these "lead" consultative salespeople with a staff, and this staff will simultaneously be in training to eventually become consultative salespeople. This career niche should have a strong future.

Alliance Sales

Corresponding with the strategic value buyer, alliance sales is at the cutting edge of the three selling modes. As the newest form, it is also the rarest. In its most complete form, it is hard to see a distinction between the seller and the buyer. In fact, the selling company forms a selling team that exactly matches the buying team. Teams are represented by cross-functional areas: for example, both teams include a technology person and/or financial person as the situation dictates. These teams are as permanent as the partnership is. These strategic alliances are characterized by such things as the buyer and seller sharing information and expertise as well as physical resources such as a warehouse or computer purchasing system. The seller may even have a permanent office located at the buyer's facility. The vendor/buyer distinction found in both the transactional sale and the consultative sale is blurred.

In *Getting Partnering Right* (Rackham, Friedman, and Ruff 1996, 13) several dramatic examples of the blurring of sellers and buyers are presented, including:

◆ McDonnell Douglas cut almost $300 million from the development cost of its MD-95 by partnering with a number of suppliers, including Dalfort Aviation—who will actually assemble the new plane.
◆ FedEx has partnered with Intel to take over part of Intel's delivery logistics. As a result, guaranteed delivery time has improved from four business days to three—and delivery errors have been substantially reduced.

What will happen to today's salespeople in light of the growing "partnering" selling situations? It's logical to expect that consultative salespeople will be the initiators of new partnering arrangements. While partnering sales requires a strategic commitment from each organization's top executives, consultative salespeople who currently have solid relationships with major accounts should be able to perform a key brokerage role to these strategic alliances. Additionally, these salespeople will retain an important long-term role in the partnering teams. This is indeed a career goal to work toward.

How Sellers Traditionally Sell—Their View of the Exchange Process

The Traditional *Presentation* Process Theory

The traditional presentation process is a process of exchange that is seller-centric. This process looks at exchanges through the seller's eyes. Is this the approach we want you to learn? No, but it is the common approach that you will often see, so let us show you how it works. Traditionally, salespeople are taught to control the exchange process. This control ranges from predetermined and memorized scripts to a set agenda of steps that the seller is expected to enforce. We call this the *traditional selling process*.

The Traditional Selling Process

Traditionally, sellers are trained to sell in a series of steps. We present the most common terminology used in most sales texts and training courses.

These stages generally correspond with the buying process that we discussed in Chapter 4, but are clearly seller-centric and imply that the seller is doing something to the buyer. Whether this is outright manipulation or tightly controlled guidance of the exchange process remains for you to decide. Note that this traditional selling process is almost exclusively tied to the product. It does not have a spirit of joint decision making that we will lay out completely in Chapter 6 as we show you the integrated buying/selling exchange process.

Previously we discussed three new types of sellers. The following traditional selling process reflects transactional sales.

1. **Need Discovery**—This is classic and basic fact-finding inquiry and concerned with product needs. The seller asks open- and closed-ended questions. (A closed-ended question is usually a "yes" or "no" question or one with a brief answer, such as "You need classroom seating for how many?" An open-ended question may ask "Why do you feel that way ?" or "How would you describe a successful meeting?" Although the salesperson does try to learn what the customer needs, he/she is doing so only at the *core product level* you read about in Chapter 3.)

2. **Presentation of Features and Benefits**—This is a proposal consisting of matching product features and benefits with buyer needs learned in step 1. As we discussed earlier, benefits and value do not always reside in the core product.

3. **Overcoming Objections**—A focus here is on counterarguments or techniques designed to quash customer concerns about the presentation proposal in step 2. This is adversarial, not joint decision making.

4. **Closing**—The finality of the word *close* would indicate that all selling discussions or presentations are meant to end with a signed contract and sale conducted at a single sales presentation. In reality, most sales, especially complex sales, are conducted as a series of meetings and the ending step is really a joint decision, not to buy but to continue the process itself. One selling meeting leads to another until the exchange is culminated. And, as mentioned in Chapter 3, one sale may be seen as only one step in a series of sales throughout a long-term relationship.

5. **Follow-up**—Most traditional sales training advocates that once the sale is closed, then the seller should, at a minimum, give a call to check in: "Did you receive your shipment as promised?" This superficial treatment of after-sale follow-up is an indicator that the traditional selling process is aimed at **transactional selling** alone. By contrast, consultative sellers actively cultivate

the long-term relationship in the after-sale stage. They know this is the key to winning repeat and referral business.

The selling process just described does not teach you how to build long-term relationships—or even suggest that you should. Since it is a transactional selling model, costly relationship building is not a part of its strategy. It is aimed at making many transactions or single-event sales. Your future will lie in the new world of consultative selling, home of the ongoing relationship.

◈ SUMMARY

The new profession of selling is upon us. Cinderella is being transformed into the princess that she is. Unlike in the fairy tale, she will not return to the role of underappreciated stepdaughter. The new profession of selling is one of micromarketing of customized products and services. It is being redefined and balanced as it focuses on creating value in the buying process as opposed to solely focusing on the selling part of the equation.

The heyday of transactional sales is over, and transactional sellers will either transform themselves or be phased out of their jobs. If you choose to enter the sales field, you will have the advantage of not having to unlearn a dying approach to sales. Instead, you can begin with the current paradigm: consultative sales. Consultative salespeople of the future will be fewer in number but more technologically educated and supported by their companies. They will continue to grow in importance to selling companies. Additionally, the consultative sales accounts with intensely developed relationships will become the probable candidates to evolve into alliances.

Alliance selling (the newest and rarest niche) will continue to grow, though it is unlikely it will overtake consultative selling. Consultative salespeople will be the lead people in solution to these partnership sales alliances. They will avoid the traps of seller-centric exchange processes and, in doing so, will gain more freedom and respect within their organizations and within society.

References

American Marketing Association. Home page, http://www.ama.org.

Hartley, R. A., and M. W. Starkey, eds. 1996. *The management of sales & customer relationships.* Boston: International Thomson Business Press.

Lester, B. 1940. *Sales engineering.* New York: John Wiley & Sons, Inc.

Peeler, G. H. 1996. *Selling in the quality era.* Oxford, UK: Blackwell Publishers, Ltd.

Rackham, N., L. Friedman, and R. Ruff. 1996. *Getting partnering right: How market leaders are creating long-term competitive advantage.* New York: McGraw-Hill.

Strong, E. K., Jr. 1922. *The psychology of selling life insurance.* New York and London: Harper & Brothers Publishers.

DISCUSSION QUESTIONS ◇

1. Discuss the relationship between sales and marketing in both B2B and B2C environments. What factors influence one to be the dominant force in developing the customer over the other?
2. How are low-value accounts delegated in a sales organization?
3. Comment on the three types of buyers. Should a firm exclude one type of buyer for another?
4. Comment on which selling mode is appropriate for what type of buyer. Why add such complexity to a selling process?
5. List and describe the steps in the traditional selling process.

CHAPTER 6

Situational Selling:

Selling Approaches Depend on Value Perceptions of Both Buyer and Seller

LEARNING OBJECTIVES

After reading this chapter you should be able to

◆ understand the competitive forces in the marketplace that influence the selling strategies that should be applied

◆ apply the appropriate selling technique to the life cycle stage of the company

KEY TERMS & CONCEPTS

monopoly

oligopoly

imperfect competition

perfect competition

simple versus complex goods and services

competitive differentiation

BGC (business growth cycle)

PLC (product life cycle)

multiple channel selling strategy

Goldilocks came upon the house of the three bears. Being very hungry, her mouth began to water when she saw on the table three bowls of porridge. Tasting the first bowl and scalding her lips, she screamed, "This is too hot!" Picking up the second bowl, she dipped her spoon in only to find lumps clinging to it. "This is too cold." When she dug into the last bowl, the wonderfully warm cereal glided over her tongue. "Ahh . . . this is just right."

Each of the three bears was a unique individual. Each liked porridge at a different temperature: very hot, very cold, or medium warm. On the other hand, only one bowl was just right for Goldilocks. The same concept applies to buyers and sellers. Quite naturally, they have differing perceptions about the value they seek in various buying/selling exchange processes. This means that sellers must use different selling strategies and tactics and be able to tell which ones will be appropriate in different buying situations. This is what we mean by *situational selling*.

Situations

The situation to be addressed reflects value as perceived by both buyer and seller. As explained in earlier chapters, the factors affecting the shifts in these value perceptions include (1) *external changes* to the selling and/or buying organization, which are primarily driven by changing customer requirements, and (2) *internal changes* to the selling and/or buying organization, which are primarily driven by both the purchasing and selling companies' need to reduce the costs of exchanges (buying and selling costs). Essentially, changes in buying/selling approaches keep occurring because both the buyers and suppliers keep reengineering the exchange process to reduce these costs and, therefore, become more competitive.

Both the buyer and the seller must answer the following questions to arrive at an assessment of value related to the exchange process. The answers help them choose appropriate and effective exchange strategies and tactics *for each situation*.

Is the industry in a state of imperfect or perfect competition?
Is the seller's product or service of high quality, but so are the products of competitors?
Does the exchange involve complex or simple products?
In what stage of the **business growth cycle (BGC)** and **product life cycle (PLC)** are the selling company and its product or service?

Both the buyers' and sellers' perceptions of value are influenced by how they answer questions. These perceptions create different situations, which are best handled by a few basic strategies and tactics. Notice that we distinguish between strategies and tactics. A strategy is an overall plan designed to help you reach a goal. A tactic is something you do that works toward that goal. The strategy is the "big picture." The tactic is a puzzle piece that helps you make that picture a reality. You may want to remember this by noting that *S* precedes *T*, alphabetically. It is important to develop your strategy first and then look at what tactics will help you get to your goal.

Okay. Now let's look at appropriate exchange strategies and tactics for each of the common situations you'll encounter in situational selling.

Situation One—Perfect Competition

The study of economics teaches us that there are several categories of competition: (1) **monopoly** (one supplier), (2) **oligopoly** (a few suppliers in *unofficial* alliance), (3) **imperfect competition** (many suppliers of a product or service but the customer has limited information of these offerings), and (4) **perfect competition** (many suppliers of a product or service *and* the customer has wide access to information about these offerings). Salespeople have traditionally thrived in a world of imperfect competition. Since potential customers did not have full knowledge of all the offerings of products and services in the marketplace, they relied on salespeople to bring the newest products to their attention. Therefore, a salesperson who could get in front of a customer better than his/her competitor had an advantage. Salespeople were often treated simply as communication tools. While competition is still imperfect, even today, technology advancements are moving some products and services toward perfect competition because it is easier to communicate large amounts of information to potential customers conveniently, especially via the Internet. Potential customers don't need salespeople to provide them with information, and may actually feel slowed down when they have to work with one. They perceive face-to-face sales calls, especially just to receive basic product information, as a waste of time.

Thus, in the situation where the marketplace is moving toward a state of perfect competition, using salespeople only as *communicators* of products and services is a losing exchange strategy.

Situation Two—Competitive Differentiation

Potential customers buy products that they believe are favorably different from competitive offerings. Product differentiation is generally based on two general strategies: price and product quality. Given two competitive products of *similar* quality, most potential customers will usually choose the one with a lower price. Given two competitive products of *different* quality (measured by features and benefits), a higher-quality product will usually command a higher price and, conversely, a lower-quality product will command a lower price. Selling companies have traditionally competed using either a price or a product quality differentiation strategy.

As you now know, many products and services (including those in hospitality) are becoming commoditized. Customers don't see any meaningful difference in them, so salespeople cannot differentiate their products from competitive products except by price. This means the traditional sales presentations based on presenting superior features or benefits (quality) have lost most of their power to persuade. Competition based on price is the norm.

Many companies have attempted to add features and benefits to their products and services in an effort to avoid having to compete on price, but even these added features and benefits quickly lose their power because competitors are quick to copy these improvements. So quality differentiation strategies don't work for very long, and very soon price rules again as the **competitive differentiation.**

In this situation, salespeople who are selling commodity-like products and services based on a price differentiation strategy add unnecessary costs and will eventually be replaced by low-cost "go-to-market" selling channels such as the Internet. Reducing selling costs enables companies to compete more effectively, because lowest price rules in a commoditized market.

Situation Three—Simple versus Complex Products or Services

The dimension of **simplicity versus complexity of products and services** affects both Situation One and Situation Two discussed previously. Think of our earlier example of a simple product or service: a training meeting, which has relatively basic requirements and a relatively low budget. A complex product or service might be a multiple-day Association's International Annual Convention of 10,000 people with multiple events and a big budget.

Regarding Situation One (imperfect and perfect competition), *simple* products or services can be easily communicated through impersonal means such as the Internet. On the other hand, *complex* products have many subtle characteristics that can't be made clear without much discussion between the customer and the salesperson, so communications need to be on a personal basis, which requires live salespeople.

Regarding Situation Two (competitive differentiation), *simple* products are easily commoditized and therefore tend to compete based on price. On the other hand, complex products are individually tailored for each customer, which requires the special abilities of highly trained salespeople referred to as *micromarketers* in the preceding chapter. Customization means that unique customer needs must be addressed by unique product or service characteristics, and this means *individually and personally* shaping the product or service to solve the customers' needs or problems.

In this situation, we conclude that companies that now sell simple commoditized products should be shifting away from using an expensive direct sales force. They can do this by selling entirely through impersonal means such as the Internet or by using the salesperson in combination with a telephone call center and other means. By contrast, we conclude that complex products can avoid price competition and be differentiated by the value added by the salesperson himself/herself and through relationships and customized product or service solutions.

Situation Four—Business Growth Cycle (BGC)/Product Life Cycle (PLC)

The study of marketing informs us that a product goes through a life cycle similar to that of a human being: birth and early childhood, adolescence, adulthood, and old age/death. The goal of human beings should be to maintain their health and live as long as possible in an unimpaired state. Similarly, the introduction of and growth of a company's mix of products and services goes through a cycle called the business growth cycle (BGC) or product life cycle (PLC): introduction, rapid growth, maturity, and decline (Colletti and Fiss 1999). Again, the company, like the human being, wants to extend the maturity stage as long as possible by optimizing its performance and delaying decline and death.

Situational selling roles depend on what BGC and PLC stage the company is in. Most companies start their business with a single product or service, then grow a portfolio of multiple products or services, and finally optimize how they are using their resources to support only the most profitable products. The main idea is to recognize that each stage requires the company to adjust the way it "goes to market" and to adjust its selling roles to match its BGC and PLC stage.

1. **Introduction Stage**—In this stage and with a single product, all product sales are seen as "good" sales. The approach is simple: the focus is on selling volume and providing service to ensure that volume levels are maintained or increased. Typically, the direct sales force is the only go-to-market channel. The company battle cry is, "Any business is good business! Let's go after it before the competitors surface."

    a. The strategies used in this stage are
        - business strategy: Any and all business sales are sought.
        - marketing strategy: One product is produced and marketed. Energy is focused on this one item.
        - sales strategy: Survival of the company and getting the product established in the marketplace.

    b. The major business challenge is
        - how to achieve sufficient customer coverage by contacting more potential buyers

2.   **Growth Stage**—To move to this stage, the company must find ways to increase customer coverage. The typical approach is to hire more salespeople to sell the single core product. Product sales grow rapidly and so do profits. At this stage, the company is experiencing the flush of high sales volume and pays little attention to customer segmentation, customer sales strategies, or considering any go-to-market selling channels other than the use of a direct sales force. The battle cry is, "All business is good business! Let's own the market!"

   a.   The strategies used in this stage are
   - business strategy: Get more business. Build on levels already achieved. Increase volume.
   - marketing strategy: Still one product, but now focusing on a single market segment. Goal is to achieve increased market segment penetration and to expand market share within that single market segment. Note that the company is still producing the same single product.
   - sales strategy: Lower costs by using the direct sales force more efficiently. Becoming more efficient makes more funds available for hiring additional salespeople.

   b.   The major business challenges are
   - overcoming capacity limitations in manufacturing and sales so that you can produce enough or hire and train salespeople fast enough as the market is penetrated
   - struggling to hold your market share of the segment as competitors are attracted to the visibly growing market segment

3.   **Maturity Stage**—With increasing competition and slowing market segment share growth, the company begins to launch new products in addition to the single product previously produced. This is often unsuccessful as the existing sales force has lost its ability to sell new products; it has only been selling the single product to a single market segment. Companies often respond to slowing market share growth by discounting prices, which tends to cause profit margin deterioration. This deterioration gets management's attention.

First, management begins to strategically allocate resources by limiting sales to select groups of customers within its single targeted market segment. Management realizes that not all customers within the market segment are good customers. For example, selling costs to low-volume and/or high-maintenance accounts is not profitable business. Additionally, management begins to rethink the exclusive use of an expensive direct sales force as their sole go-to-market channel. The battle cry is, "*What* business is good business?"

a.   The strategies used in this stage are
  ◆ business strategy: What business should be pursued? Which customers are worthwhile?
  ◆ marketing strategy: Multiple products are produced to be sold to its single market segment.
  ◆ sales strategy: Hold market share and avoid slippage. Fight off competitors that are pursuing the company's single market segment.

b.   The major business challenges are
  ◆ price erosion as competitors are fought off
  ◆ admitting that some customer segments are not good business to pursue because they are unprofitable to sell to
  ◆ how to prevent the obsolescence (the decline or death stage of the BGC/PLC) of an existing and previously successful sales organization

4.   **Optimization Stage**—Normally, the stage that follows the maturity stage is the decline stage. Fortunately, there is often an alternative to falling into decline: the optimization stage. It reinvigorates a company and gives it a boost of energy and growth above the maturity stage.

All companies will eventually decline. Some (such as dot-coms) may live only months, whereas others thrive for centuries. The goal is to live as long as possible and this requires *optimization* or smart interaction with the marketplace, especially when growth slows down in the maturity stage. In the maturity stage, either the company must redesign its strategy so that it can stay alive (and even grow!) or it will enter a death spiral and eventually disappear from the economic landscape. Optimization requires a rethinking of strategies used in the maturity stage.

First, the company firmly knows that it can no longer be all things to all customers. It understands that only certain customers are worth the investment of direct sales coverage and allocation of superior customer service. In the preceding stage, the company began to realize this but did not act. Now, the company actively begins to redeploy resources toward those select customers who offer the best opportunities for sustainable growth. They refuse to chase all customers. In fact, they *fire* some of their customers.

Second, to replace the unworthwhile customers they have fired or have knowingly let slip away, the company looks for new profitable market segments and worthwhile groups of customers within those segments. The company battle cry is, "Only certain business is good business!"

a. The strategies used in this stage are
    ◆ business strategy: Pursue only certain business.
    ◆ marketing strategy: Define and manage worthwhile market segments.
    ◆ sales strategy: Optimize returns and create lifetime customers by building relationships with select customer accounts. These select accounts will provide increased business through repeat and referral business.

b. The major business challenges are
    ◆ how to develop and implement sales strategies that deliver value-added solutions to targeted customers
    ◆ how to apply multiple go-to-market selling channels to reach selected customers with appropriate resources
    ◆ how to build the processes and programs to support changes in the now reengineered sales force
    ◆ how to avoid obsolescence or the decline stage

We conclude that the BGC/PLC stages are appropriately addressed by using different exchange strategies and tactics. Most texts would have you believe that a particular selling approach is appropriate in all situations. Nothing could be further from the truth. No single selling strategy or tactic should ever be presented as a universal approach. Changing perceptions of value by both the buyer and seller require appropriately tailored exchange strategies and tactics. This clearly calls for a *situational selling* approach.

Very shortly, we will discuss strategies and tactics in more depth. As an introduction, let's summarize situational selling related to BGC/PLC by matching the stages just discussed with appropriate exchange strategies and tactics.

◆ Introduction Stage—transactional selling strategy using a prospecting tactic
◆ Growth Stage—transactional selling strategy using *both* a prospecting and negotiation tactic
◆ Maturity Stage—transactional selling strategy and negotiation tactic transitioning into a consultative selling strategy using a relationship tactic
◆ Optimization Stage—consultative selling strategy and multiple channel selling strategy with a relationship tactic. With a few highly select customer accounts, a transition would be made to an alliance selling strategy and multiple channel selling strategy coupled with a partnership tactic.

This may seem like a complex thinking process to go through—and initially it will be. But when you have practiced looking at situations in terms of stages, strategies, and tactics, much of this will become as natural as scoping out people at a party, deciding which one you'd like to date, and then figuring out the best way to persuade him or her to go out with you.

In summary, the situation in which a buying or selling organization finds itself and how that organization perceives value will dramatically alter the way that the exchange process is approached. Let's look more deeply at the problem of selecting the right exchange strategies and tactics for the right situation.

Different Situations Require Different Exchange Strategies and Tactics

Selling is an exchange process between a supplier and a customer. The interface (or place where the interaction takes place) between the two parties to this exchange varies by: (1) strategies—or the overall approach to the exchange interface and (2) tactics—or the face-to-face behavior between seller and buyer. Each individual company must customize its strategies and tactics based on its own industry and situation.

The three strategic selling approaches discussed in earlier chapters are the three basic strategies: transactional, consultative, and alliance. We now add a fourth *combination* strategy: **multiple channel selling strategy.** These strategies are implemented through four selling *tactics,* used singly or together: *prospecting, negotiation, relationship,* and *partnership tactics.* These strategies and tactics can be used by individual salespeople or by selling teams.

The Strategies

Three Basic Selling Strategies. In Chapter 5, we introduced and discussed three basic selling strategies: transactional, consultative, and alliance selling. These selling strategies are applied in situations where the *seller* sees the most value to be gained in the buying/selling exchange process. We've already matched these three selling strategies to the three types of value buyers introduced in Chapter 4: intrinsic value buyer, extrinsic value buyer, and strategic value buyer. These three selling and value buying approaches are *strategic* in nature. The strategies are fulfilled through various *tactics.*

Using the Three Basics in Combination. This is called a *multiple channel selling strategy.* Although we have devoted a long discussion to the three basic selling strategies, organizations today don't simply pick one of these and then use it exclusively. Essentially, they mix and match—doing a little dance to see how the supplier's and customer's perceptions of value fit together. This combination approach is especially common when the business growth cycle is factored into selling strategies and tactics.

A multiple channel selling strategy means that the buying/selling exchange process is disaggregated and its various *steps* are completed by different (aka multiple) salespeople or *channels*. For example, the organization might be approaching a specific buyer using a consultative selling strategy. Instead of using a single consultative salesperson to complete all steps of the buying/selling exchange process, a company might use multiple selling channels, as follows:

A lead is generated when the potential buyer responds to a request for proposal (RFP) . . . triggering a sales opportunity.

- ◆ A telemarketing support salesperson schedules the face-to-face initial appointment.
- ◆ A consultative salesperson then makes a personal sales call to the buyer and makes the sale.
- ◆ A team of technical support people (under the direction of the consultative salesperson) handles the after-sale service.

A multiple channel approach is becoming more common today. It still follows the basic buying/selling exchange process steps, but assigns different people and electronic channels working as a team to complete the process.

Four Selling Tactics

You will choose your *strategy* based on the given situation. Then you can pick the *tactics* that will help you accomplish your strategy. Tactics are the face-to-face actions taken in the buying/selling exchange process.

Prospecting Tactic. This is a traditional approach that seeks to bring in a lot of revenue through the "law of large numbers." Prospecting is often used by salespeople when the product or service is new, relatively unknown by the customer, and/or simple and low-priced. Today, prospecting is often assigned to sales support salespeople, who are usually new to sales. They prospect for customers by combing through databases or collecting inquiries from other channels, such as the Internet, surveys, or requests for more information—and then follow up on these using telesales techniques. Some large properties may hire a specialist to do outbound telesales. At smaller properties, where there is no support staff, *all* salespeople will spend some time prospecting. As you will see, prospecting is a building block necessary in all of the following tactics.

Negotiation Tactic. This tactic is used to emphasize small advantages over a competitor's product. The customer usually is a current purchaser of the product or service and is currently buying from a competitor. In this case, the task is not to locate the customer and introduce him/her to the advantages of your product or service. Instead, the goal of a negotiation tactic is to convince that buyer to use the seller's (your) product *in addition to* or *to replace* the competitor's product. In essence, the seller is selling *against a competitor* and not necessarily selling the product or service itself.

These products or services are usually commodity-like and compete on price. Examples include wholesale food or hotel supplies and equipment. Small advantages over the competitor can be enough to make the customer switch suppliers since the customer is loyal to the *commoditized* product or service rather than the supplying company.

The negotiating tactic, like the prospecting tactic, is closely associated with the transactional selling strategy, but when used to achieve a *win-win* outcome during a specific exchange, it can be part of a consultative selling strategy.

Note: According to Roy Lewicki, David Saunders, and John Minton in their 2001 book, *Essentials of Negotiations,* the words *bargaining* and *negotiations* are sometimes confused and carry different connotations. For example, *bargaining* is like the competitive haggling over price that happens on a used car lot. Here one gets a sense of a *win-lose* exchange in the making. The term *negotiations,* on the other hand, creates visions of formal events such as international treaties or labor union and management discussions. Here one gets a sense of a *win-win* exchange in the making.

The negotiation tactic can be either win-lose or win-win. When this tactic is used with the transactional selling strategy, we unfortunately encounter a predominance of win-lose outcomes. When the negotiation tactic is used with the consultative selling strategy, it needs to work toward a win-win outcome because the consultative selling strategy depends on a *relationship tactic*. Consultative sellers depend on long-term business relationships for generating repeat and referral business. They do not want to leave a customer feeling he/she has lost in an exchange.

Relationship Tactic. This is a problem-solving approach that seeks to bring in a lot of revenue by "penetrating" large accounts. These selected accounts usually have the potential for a "lifetime" of business.

When using this tactic, the seller must rely on trust and relationships because the product or service is complex or new and must be customized. This complexity causes a feeling of uncertainty or risk within the buyer. A foundation of trust and relationships establishes an environment that allows the seller to operate as a problem-solving consultant who deeply probes the underlying needs of the customer.

A seller cannot design a customized product or service solution without gaining an in-depth understanding of the buyer's needs and problems. This *in-depth* understanding distinguishes the consultative seller from the transactional seller who sells to more *surface* buyer needs.

This tactic is closely associated with the consultative selling strategy, but obviously a very intense relationship tactic is also used with the alliance selling strategy.

Partnership Tactic. This is a "let's grow and change together" approach used to facilitate the acceptance of change within the partner organizations that are agreeing to the alliance. When a customer company enters an exclusive (or near exclusive, aka primary) agreement with a supplier company, this agreement is very different from a traditional supplier/buyer relationship. Traditionally, there are many suppliers selling to a customer. So, exclusive or primary supplier relationships are a major *change* for both the supplier and the customer. Change does not occur overnight. Change must be sold. Thus, alliance sellers (or alliance managers) must be able to influence (sell the idea to) multiple stakeholders in both the selling and buying organizations. Additionally, and like a long-term marriage, the relationship must be actively maintained and continually nourished.

This tactic is primarily associated with an alliance selling strategy, however alliances are usually an evolutionary refinement of consultative selling strategies, so partnership tactics are also appropriately used in consultative selling, especially as relationships between buyer and seller become more intense.

How to Implement Selling Strategies and Tactics

The *Individual* Approach to Selling Strategies and Tactics

When we think of salespeople and customers, we usually have a vision of two individuals negotiating over the terms of exchange. There's a salesperson sitting in front of a buyer's desk trying to convince him/her to make a purchase. This one-on-one interaction works best in the transactional situation and can apply in the consultative and alliance situations. However, when we reach the more sophisticated strategies of consultative and alliance selling (and the tactics that work best with them), we most likely will encounter buying and selling exchanges conducted by *teams*. We will see not only selling teams, but also *buying* teams.

The *Team* Approach to Selling Strategies and Tactics

There are two basic team approaches: *ad hoc teams* (informally assembled for the specific task at hand) and *formalized teams* (formal and semipermanent arrangements).

Ad Hoc Team Strategy. Because of the complexity of the product or service, both selling teams and buying teams are assembled as needed and on a temporary (ad hoc) basis to make the exchange. The salesperson acts as a manager of the selling team. The principal buyer (meeting planner) coordinates his/her corresponding buying team. Essentially, there are two types of ad hoc teams.

◆ bilateral teams—In this arrangement, one team has multiple players, whereas the other side has just one. For example, a selling team could sell to a single buyer, or an individual salesperson could sell to a buying team.

◆ multilateral teams—In this arrangement, both teams have multiple players. Multilateral teams are most often used by consultative salespeople selling very complex products.

In today's complex world of sales, teams can be internal to the organization . . . or external to it! An *internal* team might be composed of functional experts within the selling organization; for example, a catering department salesperson might be a player on a hotel's sales team.

In an *external* team situation, a salesperson from a hotel might team up with a salesperson from a local golf course, so that jointly, they can offer needed benefits to a customer.

Formalized Team Strategy. By "formal teams" we mean that agreements, contracts, or operating policies *formalize* these arrangements. They differ from ad hoc teams, which are formed for specific (and usually temporary) purposes. These formal arrangements are found in several circumstances:

1.   **Reengineered "Multiple Channel" Teams**—These are used to execute the buying/selling process in a more cost-effective manner, which means the selling team may use different people for different tasks. For example, lower-cost supporting sales salespeople (telemarketers) might be used to generate prospects and leads for the higher-cost and experienced salespeople who do the face-to-face negotiations. Later, these telemarketers may assist in after-sale service.

This team format is used primarily by consultative salespeople selling very complex products with additional strategic direction and support by top management who have begun to "reengineer" the buying/selling process to reduce costs.

2.   **Partnership Teams**—These are used when formal alliances have been built. Functional teams on the side of the selling/supplying company are coordinated with functional teams on the side of the buying company. Both

teams are coordinated by an *alliance manager,* who works for the benefit of both the seller and buyer—the alliance itself. The formal role of alliance manager is a new one for salespeople. In most cases, an alliance salesperson gets tapped to grow into the new role of coordinating two or more functional teams . . . and logistics for the alliance partners.

In a Complex Situational World, How Does a New Salesperson Begin?

Situational selling approaches are complex (see Table 6–1). When either the buyer's or seller's perception of value shifts, situational sellers must be ready to apply an appropriate selling strategy and selling tactic. It's only logical that the amateur salesperson becomes a little confused. As you can see in Table 6–1, a career as a salesperson will probably begin at the simplest selling strategy level: multiple channel support selling or transactional selling. The important message of Table 6–1 is that all strategies and tactics build on one another. Once an amateur salesperson has mastered the basic buying/selling exchange process he/she will likely move upward to the more sophisticated selling strategies: consultative and alliance. Regardless of the strategy, the basic steps of the buying/selling exchange process remain constant.

The Buying/Selling Exchange Process

Synthesis of Buying and Selling Processes

We've already discussed the exchange process from a buyer-centric perspective and then from a seller-centric perspective. We now integrate and synthesize these two views into what we will label the *buying/selling exchange process,* which reflects *both* the perspective of the buyer and that of the seller. It is the generic process seen in the left column of Table 6–1.

Across the top of Table 6–1, we have labeled the columns with the important strategies discussed earlier in this chapter. Each of these strategies interprets the generic buying/selling exchange process (in the left-hand column of the table) in different ways. As the exchange strategy becomes more sophisticated, each of the steps in the process will be implemented in a different way. These differences are listed in the table.

This table is complicated and complex—and you may wonder which of the paths you would follow. Well that, too, is *situational!* If you are just beginning as a salesperson, you will probably work with a *multiple channel strategies* (support sales) approach at a regional or chain level—or at a property level with a transactional selling strategy. Table 6–1 can help you through the steps of the *buying/selling exchange process* for each appropriate strategy.

TABLE 6–1a Buying/Selling Exchange Process Part One–Strategy Characteristics		
Salesperson Experience and Sophistication	**Beginning Salespeople**	**Beginning Salespeople**
BUYING/SELLING EXCHANGE PROCESS	**MULTIPLE CHANNEL STRATEGY** Sales Support Individuals	**TRANSACTIONAL SELLING STRATEGY** Individuals or Teams
LENGTH OF PROCESS (Measured by number of Buyer/Seller meetings throughout the exchange process)	*SHORT* Usually one meeting and done electronically	*SHORT TO MEDIUM* Single or very few personal meetings
GOALS	**Sales Associates/Channels Outbound Telesales** – generate "prospects" (qualified leads) working from "cold leads"). **OR** work in team giving after-sale service assistance to outside salesforce. **Inbound Telesales** – respond to incoming inquires ("warm leads"). They attempt to close these sales (usually in a single call).	**Sell** to New Buyer **Then rapidly move** to another Buyer
INTENSITY OF RELATIONSHIP BUILDING BETWEEN BUYER AND SELLER	**Non-existent** – Supporting "channels" assist other sales people. They are used where and when needed. The assisted sales person is the primary actor.	**Very low** – too expensive when strategy and tactics require many transactions to be completed.
TYPES OF PRODUCTS/SERVICES	**Commodity-Like Products** **Outbound Telemarketers** – Selling "qualification" or general "interest" in further contact by another experienced *outside salesperson*. **Inbound Telemarketers** – Receive inquiries from "warm leads" then attempt to sell the product to them.	**Commodity-Like Products** (Simple – Product/Services) *(Sell Features/Benefits)*
SELLING TACTICS	**Prospecting Tactic** **Outbound Telemarketers** – Generate "prospects" for other salespeople using a "cold lead" source. **Inbound Telemarketers** - Receive "warm leads" that are inquiries generated by other marketing actvities. They make an attempt to sell "simple" accounts. They refer "complex" accounts to the appropriate salesperson (more experienced).	**Prospecting & Negotiation Tactics** (win/win best but win/lose is unfortunately common) "It is not a matter of IF the buyer will buy, but FROM WHOM will he/she buy." The salesperson here is looking to present a product advantage compared to competitors. Even a slight advantage may motivate the buyer to buy. Negotiation often centers on price and terms since the quality of products are more or less the same (thus, commodity-like).

Experienced & Sophisticated Salespeople	Experienced & Sophisticated Salespeople With Managerial Skills
CONSULTATIVE SELLING STRATEGY Individuals or Teams	**ALLIANCE MANAGING STRATEGY** Individuals or Teams
LONG Many personal meetings	*VERY LONG* Continuous personal meetings to establish "acceptance" of the alliance and ongoing "sustaining" the alliance
Open Major Organizational Accounts with high purchase potentials (within many divisions of the account) **Then Penetrate** these accounts - by the Consultative Seller and/or his assisting Team	**Facilitate or Implement "change"** within and for acceptance of the Alliance. **NOTE:** At the point that a seller decides to pursue an "Alliance," the role of "Salesperson" has been transformed into "manager" of implementing or "selling" the change process to the alliance partners. After change is Implemented, an Alliance Manager vs. Seller may begin to focus on sustaining activities and managing and coordinating practical logistics.
High – Account penetration is dependent on repeat business and referrals. Trust in the relationship facilitates the joint problem-solving approach.	**Highest** – Alliances are partnerships who agree to exchange with one another on an almost exclusive basis. This, like a marriage, requires the highest intensity of relationship.
Problem-Solutions (Complex Products/Services) *(Sell Solutions)* **BELOW** the discussion of "consultative seller" will simultaneously discuss two selling processes: for the first buyer and then for developing the account.	**Change and Cooperation** Implementing the Alliance and Sustaining the Alliance *(Sell Mutual Alliance Synergies that are beneficial to Personal and Organizational Interests)*
Negotiation Tactic (win/win) & Relationship Tactics **First Buyer** – Obtain a first sale in the account through a more refined and sophisticated sales process than "transactonal selling." **Then** Strengthen and build a strong relationship with this "gateway" person through superior product *implementation* and ongoing *maintenance* (leads to repeat business from this first buyer). **Then** **Development Activities:** Seller looks for creative solutions for other divisions of the account and asks his "gatekeeper" for referrals within the account.	**Alliance Tactics** "Exists as long as both parties to the alliance see that it is mutually beneficial to each and is trustworthy." "Change (acceptance and acting) must be achieved through a systematic and ongoing *change/sustain campaign.*

(continues)

TABLE 6–1a Buying/Selling Exchange Process (continued)
Part One–Strategy Characteristics

SOURCE OF NEW POTENTIAL BUYERS (Database Building)	Database for Basic Prospect Qualifications: "Suspects" qualified into "prospects"	Database for Basic Prospect Qualifications: "Suspects" qualified into "prospects"
		NOTE: This prospecting or lead activity can be disaggreated and accomplished by in and out-bound telemarketers.
	Outbound Telemarketers – Extensive activity management generating "cold leads" and qualifying them into "prospects."	OR The transactional salesperson must do the "prospecting" himself or herself.
	Inbound Telemarketers – Responding to "warm leads" ("suspects"). Qualifying into "prospects" and then selling process begins.	

TABLE 6–1b Buying/Selling Exchange Process and Selling Strategies
Part Two–Matching the Generic Buying/Selling Exchange Process with Strategies

Salesperson Experience and Sophistication	Beginning Salespeople	Beginning Salespeople
BUYING/SELLING EXCHANGE PROCESS	**MULTIPLE CHANNEL STRATEGY** Sales Support Individuals	**TRANSACTIONAL SELLING STRATEGY** Individuals or Teams
GENERIC BUYING/SELLING EXCHANGE PROCESS	**FEATURE/BENEFIT EXCHANGE PROCESS**	**FEATURE/BENEFIT EXCHANGE PROCESS**
PHASE 1–PLANNING FOR NEGOTIATION (Chapter 7)	Pre-Approach: Prospect **Inbound** = basic "script" guidelines **Outbound** = "list" management	Pre-Approach: Prospect
PHASE 2–THE BUYER/SELLER MEETING **Step 1:** APPROACHING THE BUYER (Chapter 8)	Approach: Basic introduction	Approach: Prospect
Step 2: INVESTIGATING NEEDS (Chapter 9)	**Need Discovery** – Individual buyer Very basic (rates and dates) since buyer is familiar with this commodity-like product and wants "price"	**Need Discovery** – Individual buyer Basic Questioning Skills

Database for Detailed Account "Champion" Power Sources and Interests:	Database for Detailed Alliance
	"Buyer & Seller" Power Sources and Interests:
Primary Contact in account (first buyer and/or significant relationship) is the "base"	**Interested Persons with Varying "Buying Perspectives"** within the Alliance
Seller generates new problem-solving ideas then seeks "champions" of a new problem-solving idea and uses as proxies to sell the *idea* within their organizations.	**Performance Buyers** (users) **Policy Buyers** (technical, purchasing, and other policy-driven functions)
	Profit Buyers (those with access to company assets)
Seller must be aware of various power sources of "champions."	Systematically sell "change" and "acceptance" to the above set division by division.

Experienced & Sophisticated Salespeople	Experienced & Sophisticated Salespeople with Managerial Skills
CONSULTATIVE SELLING STRATEGY Individuals or Teams	**ALLIANCE MANAGING STRATEGY** Individuals or Teams
PROBLEM/SOLVING EXCHANGE PROCESS	**ORGANIZATIONAL CULTURAL "CHANGE" PROCESS**
First Buyer: Prospect: Pre-Approach Planning **Development Activities:** Strategic Account Penetration Plan	Strategic plan for systematic "change" toward an alliance or toward a reduction of resistance to the alliance
First Buyer: Approach Prospect **Development Activities:** Approach – "Champion"	Approach – Pre-selected divisions and individuals, and other designees according to the contracted alliance agreement.
Problem Discovery – First buyer Advanced questioning skills **Development Activities:** Research specific Company Problems— then the specific interests and power positions of individuals involved with the problem/solution	Alliance Research – Who are the people on both sides of the alliance and what are their individual interests related to maintaining and sustaining the alliance?

(continues)

| **TABLE 6–1b** **Buying/Selling Exchange Process and Selling Strategies** *(continued)* | | |
Part Two—Matching the Generic Buying/Selling Exchange Process with Strategies		
Step 3: DEMONSTRATING CAPABILITY (Chapter 10)	Feature presentation (Simple "benefits" added) Remember that incoming inquiry wants basics (rates and dates) and already know needs well	Match product features/benefits with custtomer needs. Objections or resistance to the above "matching" or other objections are "answered."
Step 4: NEGOTIATING CONCERNS (Chapter 11)	Handling objections	Handling objections and negotiating positions
Step 5: GAINING COMMITMENT (Chapter 12)	**Inbound** = ask for the order or refer to outside sales **Outbound** = hand off prospect to outside sales	Ask for the order
Step 6: AFTER-SALE IMPLEMENTATION AND RELATIONSHIP MANAGEMENT (Chapter 13)	"Hand off" to next level in process: A salespeson or CSM (convention service manager)	Short-term follow-up perhaps done by outbound telemarketers Due to "law of large numbers" relationship building is not cost efficient

Definitions. In this text, we assume that the new salesperson will begin his/her career in an environment that uses the transactional selling strategy. With experience, he/she will begin to learn the more sophisticated consultative selling strategy. Thus, we will teach the buying/selling exchange process in a hybrid form:

In Chapter 7, we will connect the principles of negotiation with the buying/selling exchange process and teach the buying/selling exchange process from a blended viewpoint of two selling *strategy* positions: we will blend the best of the transactional selling strategy with that of the consultative selling strategy, but refer to this blended strategy as the *consultative selling strategy* because its distinguishing characteristics are those of relationship tactics. We will adopt a blended negotiation and relationship tactic, but refer to our tactic as a *win-win negotiation tactic*.

The examples we will use to illustrate these strategies and tactics will be a full-service-property-level hotel with a resident sales force that sells meetings and conventions. As Table 6–1 illustrates, you could apply the same general buying/selling exchange process in several situations, but we are focusing on the full-service property because it is the most common and most easily grasped situation.

First Buyer – This is a face-to-face presentation that is a matching of "solutions" with "problems."	Capability is demonstrated on a continual basis. In an alliance, each partner must deliver as promised and be ready to openly communicate and rectify any problems that arise.
Answering buyer questions	Discussing and alleviating concerns
First Buyer – Ask for the commitment to solution. This "prospect" now becomes a "customer" and "gatekeeper" to pivot into account development. **Development Activities:** Sales process is repeated to "close" as the account is penetrated division by division.	Ask to "advance" the commitment to the alliance or openly support. Advancement might simply be having them agree not to resist. Ideally, they would become supporters.
First Buyer—Implement and maintain—assemble implementation teams (from selling company) and actively stay involved with implementation. **Development Activities:** First Buyer "gatekeeper" and pivotal point to start penetration of account. **Continual** development of account with goal for penetration.	With the support of one group of people in place, leverage growing support and systematically move through the organization. *Alliance seller* (selling "change") systematically intensifies the commitment of allied organizations to continued cooperation. In addition to or replacing the alliance seller, an *alliance manager* may be added, who coordinates logistics and cross-functional teams (versus selling "change").

To summarize definitions used in this text:

buying/selling exchange process—A synthesis of the perspective of both the buyer and the seller as they view the process of exchange. This synthesized process is compatible with the process of negotiation, discussed in Chapter 7.

consultative selling strategy—A hybrid form combining the best of the transactional selling strategy with the consultative selling strategy, which we previously discussed in their pure forms.

win-win negotiation tactic—A hybrid form combining the best of the negotiation tactic with the relationship tactic, which we previously discussed in their pure forms.

hotel sales force—As noted, we will limit examples in upcoming chapters to a resident sales force of a full-service-property-level hotel selling meetings and convention venues for meeting planners (buyers). We want to stress, however, that the buying/selling exchange process is highly applicable to other selling situations, such as other hospitality firms and their sales forces, sales forces of firms within the supply chain, sales forces at various levels of hospitality firms (corporate level and centralized telemarketing level), and to other industries outside hospitality and tourism.

Each of the phases and steps of the buying/selling exchange process will be explored further in Chapters 7–13. For now, here is a preview of the chapters to follow:

Managing the Buying/Selling Exchange Process

Phase One—Pre-Negotiation Strategy

Negotiation Preparation and Planning (Chapter 7). All exchanges should begin with solid preplanning. The more that a seller knows before meeting with a potential buyer, the more successful the outcome is likely to be.

Phase Two—Negotiation Process Strategy

Step One—Approaching the Buyer (Chapter 8). People often "judge a book by its cover." It's well known that a buyer will make certain assessments about the seller in the first 15 seconds of the meeting. These initial impressions can help or devastate a potential sale. Sellers must get off to a positive start.

Step Two—Investigating Needs (Chapter 9). This is the most important part of selling. How can salespeople recommend the right product or service if they don't really know what a buyer wants or needs, or what problem he/she is trying to solve? We will learn that it is here that competitive advantage can be won. The seller with the most information is in the best position to win the sale.

Step Three—Demonstrating Capability (Chapter 10). Just as English teachers emphasize that compositions must have an *introduction, body,* and *close,* we'll show you why you need a structure when demonstrating capability. This systematic road map to logical presentations will become a natural instinct with experience.

Step Four—Negotiating Concerns (Chapter 11). Successful salespeople invite their potential customers to ask questions, especially in areas where they have concerns. Some people fear this step, sometimes called *handling objections.* Experienced salespeople welcome these buyer questions. They know that when people ask for clarification, they are showing that they are interested. You will want to know buyer concerns so that you can address them! Chapter 11 will show you how.

Step Five—Gaining Commitment (Chapter 12). We like the term *gaining commitment,* as opposed to the traditional terminology, *close.* Often, especially in consultative selling, there are many meetings between buyers and sellers before a close, or signing of a contract. Gaining commitment often refers to a commitment simply to proceed to the next phase. Some selling texts and programs erroneously teach that a salesperson should always attempt to get the contract—to close. In more sophisticated selling, this approach will simply kill the sale.

Phase Three—Post-Negotiation Strategy (Chapter 13)

Most traditional selling prescriptions mention that *follow-up* should come after the *close*. Often, this refers to simply calling up the buyer and finding out if there are any problems. In this text and specifically with consultative selling, the after-sale phase is extremely important. In fact, it is here that long-term relationships deepen, leading to repeat and referral business.

After-Sale Implementation and Relationship Management. Effective implementation sets the stage for a solid and long-term relationship. Consultative sellers understand that their first sale creates a "gate" or portal to a large customer account. It is very important that this first buyer (the gatekeeper) be satisfied and be willing to serve as a referral person within the account. The salesperson wants the gatekeeper to be so happy that he/she will become not only a repeat customer, but also a source of referral business.

After implementation, the consultative seller is interested in developing and penetrating the account. He/she will continue efforts to penetrate or develop the account while simultaneously deepening the relationship bond with the initial buyer and all other referred new buyers within the account.

Conducting Self-Critique and Continual Improvement

To continually improve, consultative sellers measure their performance and analyze where plans fell short. By learning from mistakes or actively critiquing their performance, sales professionals improve their expertise and abilities over time.

In Chapter 13, which discusses this self-critique phase, we will present practical methods to help you implement and manage relationships and develop and penetrate major accounts.

SUMMARY ◇

If we are to believe the majority of sales training programs and sales textbooks, Goldilocks would have been happy with the way all three bowls of porridge were presented. As she clearly loved porridge, she would have been indifferent to whether one was too hot or too cold. The majority of sales literature still teaches a single selling process. Traditionalists would have you believe that one style of selling or one way of preparing the offer will convince buyers to buy based on the fact that they want the product—the porridge.

Goldilocks was presented with an offer that she clearly liked—porridge. Yet, one was presented too hot. Another was presented too cold. Goldilocks unhesitatingly rejected both of these presentations even though she loved porridge. When one bowl of porridge was presented in a way that was just right, she . . . you know the rest.

In this chapter, we have made a case for situational selling. We firmly believe that the appropriate exchange strategies and tactics depend on the way both buyers and sellers perceive the value in the exchange process.

We have presented an exchange process that is a synthesis of both the buyers' and the sellers' views: the buying/selling exchange process. We outlined the process steps and will discuss each in the following seven chapters. Stay tuned to see how we blend transactional and consultative selling strategies and then blend negotiation and relationship tactics.

References

Colletti, J. A., and M. S. Fiss. 1999. *Compensating new sales roles*. New York: American Management Association.

Lewicki, R., D. Saunders, and J. Minton. 2001. *Essentials of negotiations*. 2nd ed. Boston: McGraw-Hill Irwin.

◆ DISCUSSION QUESTIONS

1. What impact has the Internet had on the competitive environment of the hospitality industry? What impact has this influence had on the salesperson?

2. What factors influence a firm to go after all sales during its early life cycle stages? Why do many firms tend to become more selective in terms of their target markets in their later stages?

3. What is meant by a multiple channel selling strategy?

4. Imagine for a moment you are employed by a large hotel company in your community to develop a database of prospects of corporate accounts. How would you go about developing such a database?

Section 3

Managing the Sales Process

CHAPTER 7

Phase One—
Pre-Negotiation
Strategy:

Negotiation Preparation and Planning

After reading this chapter you should be able to

LEARNING OBJECTIVES

- ◆ understand sales as a negotiation process meant to achieve win-win outcomes
- ◆ explain the importance of planning and preparation prior to entering into negotiations
- ◆ identify alternative strategies and tactics useful in negotiating

KEY TERMS & CONCEPTS

negotiations

situational negotiation strategies or tactics

BATNA

interests

proposals

integrative negotiation strategies

distributive negotiation strategies

accommodative negotiation strategies

In Chapter 6, we introduced the buying/selling exchange process composed of three phases: Phase One—*Pre-Negotiation Strategy*, Phase Two—*Negotiation Process Strategy,* and Phase Three—*Post-Negotiation Strategy,* which proves the framework for this text. This chapter is concerned with Phase One. In negotiation preparation and planning, the salesperson: (1) develops and selects the appropriate negotiation strategies and tactics in order to maximize the probability of making a sale and (2) updates and examines his/her prospect/customer database to correctly target the potential buyer that he/she plans to approach with a sales proposition. Phase One of the buying/selling exchange process serves as preparation for the actual sales presentation or face-to-face contact with the buyer that occurs in Phase Two.

This chapter is organized as follows. First, we will integrate the buying/selling exchange process with the negotiation process. This model (Table 7-1) guides the discussion in Chapters 8 through 13. It is important to understand that *selling* is really a form of *negotiation*. Second, we will focus on the primary task of Phase One of the model—understanding **negotiations**. We will accomplish this by discussing the general concept of negotiations and its process (Phase One, Step One). Finally, we will refine the general discussion of negotiations by introducing **situational negotiation strategies/tactics** (Phase One, Step Three). We will defer the essential preselling/negotiations task of building a prospect/customer database (Phase One, Step Two) until Chapter 8.

The Buying/Selling Exchange Process and the Negotiation Process

In Chapter 6, we discussed various situational selling strategies and tactics. Additionally, having discussed the exchange process in Chapter 4 from a buyer-centric perspective and then, in Chapter 5 from a seller-centric perspective, we integrated these two perspectives in Chapter 6. We have labeled the synthesis of the two views the *buying/selling exchange process.* In this chapter we have added a final refinement of the process of exchange. We now link the *buying/selling exchange process* with the *negotiation process* into one model (or overall process) (see Table 7–1). We make this linkage to emphasize and demonstrate that selling is actually a form of negotiations. Although the aforementioned might appear a bit complicated, the model presented in Table 7–1 will remain a constant guide throughout the remainder of this text.

Note the similarities between the buying/selling exchange process and the negotiation process. Our purposes here are illustrative of the need to adopt a negotiation mindset when engaged in selling. As opposed to the popular view of selling as being a take it or leave it proposition, in today's selling, one must see the engagement between buyer and seller as a two-way negotiation where both parties derive benefits. Let's examine the general concept of negotiations.

Table 7–1 Comparison of the Buying/Selling Exchange Process and the Negotiation Process

THE BUYING/SELLING EXCHANGE PROCESS	THE NEGOTIATION PROCESS
Phase One – **Pre-Negotiation Strategy: Negotiation Planning and Preparation (Chapter 7)**	**Phase One** – **Pre-Negotiation Strategy: Negotiation Planning and Preparation (Chapter 7)**
Step One – Understanding Sales Process	**Step One** – Understanding Negotiation Process
Step Two – Research Potential Customer	**Step Two** – Know Your and Your Customers' Interests
Step Three – Sales Tactics	**Step Three** – Negotiation Tactics
Phase Two – **Negotiation Process Strategy**	**Phase Two** – **Negotiation Process Strategy**
Step One – Approaching the Buyer (Chapter 8)	**Step One** – Opening
Step Two – Investigating Needs (Chapter 9)	**Step Two** – Exploring
Step Three – Demonstrating Capability (Chapter 10)	**Step Three** – Proposing Agreement
Step Four – Negotiating Concerns (Chapter 11)	**Step Four** – Clarifying Proposal
Step Five – Gaining Commitment (Chapter 12)	**Step Five** – Gaining Commitment
Phase Three – **Post-Sales Strategy (Chapter 13)**	**Phase Three** – **Post-Negotiation Strategy**
Step One – After-Sale Implementation	**Step One** – Implementing Agreement
Step Two – Maintenance & Development	**Step Two** – Conducting Self-Critique
Step Three – Continuous Improvement	

Understanding the Concept of Negotiations

Negotiations—what is it? Everybody negotiates and they do so either to create something new that neither party could on his/her own, or to resolve a problem or dispute between the parties. We often associate sales *negotiations* with the word *bargaining*. These terms are similar but different. *Bargaining* is often associated with competitive haggling over price. *Negotiation* is more often associated with collaborative agreements and is a formal process that occurs when parties are trying to find a mutually beneficial solution to a buyer's complex problem or need.

A Basic Map of Negotiations

There are five important points along the way to a mutually satisfactory agreement: (1) **interests**, (2) *options* for satisfying those interests, (3) *standards* for resolving differences fairly, (4) *alternatives* to negotiation (BATNA—Best Alternative To a Negotiated Agreement), and (5) **proposals** for agreement (Ury 1991, 17–26).

Interests. Negotiation typically begins when one side's position comes into conflict with the other side's position. In conventional bargaining (distributive/competitive negotiation strategy), your position may be all you need to know in advance of the negotiation session. However, joint problem solving (integrative/collaborative negotiation strategy) revolves around the *interests* that lie behind each side's *positions*. This is a critical distinction: your *position* is the concrete things you say you want—the dollars and cents, the terms and conditions. Your *interests* are the intangible motivations that lead you to take that position—your real and basic needs, desires, concerns, fears, and aspirations. In order to end up with an agreement that satisfies both sides, you need to begin by figuring out each side's interests. This is done in the Phase One—Pre-Negotiation Strategy of the negotiations process model outlined in Table 7–1.

Know *your* interests. It's common to trade off an important interest for a less important one during negotiations, so it's important to rank your interests before you actually enter a negotiation session. As is often said, "Unless you know where you want to go, any road will take you there." Shouldn't you decide in advance where you want to go and choose the path that will take you to satisfaction of your interests?

Know *their* interests. You usually can't satisfy *your* interests unless you also satisfy the other side's. It is therefore just as important to understand their interests as your own. Negotiation is a two-way street. It is a dynamic give-and-take situation whereby both parties attempt to obtain satisfaction of their interests. Put yourself in the other side's shoes. This is the single most important skill in negotiation.

Options. The purpose of identifying each side's interests is to see if you can devise creative options to satisfy them. An option is a possible agreement or part of an agreement. Inventing options for mutual gain is a negotiator's single greatest opportunity. Effective negotiators do not just divvy up a fixed pie. They first explore how to expand the pie.

Although it may not be possible to obtain your *position,* it is often possible to satisfy your *interests*. You may not succeed in obtaining the 30 percent salary increase (a *position* of hope), but you may invent an option that allows you to realize a cost of living gain *(interest)* while keeping your employer satisfied.

A common negotiation mistake is to dwell on a single solution—your original position. By opening yourself up to consideration of a multitude of options, you may generate new possibilities, one of which might meet your interests while also satisfying the other side. The biggest obstacle in the way of generating creative options is a little voice in the back of our heads that is always saying, "That won't work!"

In the preparation phase of the negotiation process, plan to be flexible in searching for options that can satisfy your interests. Don't be fixated on preconceived positions.

Standards. Once you have expanded the pie (created options), you need to think about how to divide it up. How will you jointly select an option (decide among the many created options) with the other side when your interests seem to be opposed? Your employer wants to pay you less for your work; you would like them to pay more. How do you resolve the issue?

Perhaps the most common method is to use a contest of wills (the battle of positions and classic competitive negotiation strategy). Each side insists on its position, trying to get the other to give in, but the problem is that nobody likes to give in. A *contest of wills* usually turns into a *conflict of egos*. This type of contest can destroy trusting relationships and effectively stop future negotiations. People don't forget being bullied. Utilizing a joint-decision-making approach, effective negotiators search for a fair and mutually satisfactory solution. This is an approach that can head off a contest of wills. In this joint selection process (searching and deciding on mutually satisfactory options) they rely heavily on fair standards independent of either side's will (position).

An independent *standard* is a measuring stick that allows you to decide what is a fair solution. Common standards are: (1) market value, (2) equal treatment, (3) the law, (4) common precedents—the way the issue has been resolved before, and so forth. The great virtue of standards is that instead of one side giving in to the other on a particular point, both can defer to what seems fair. It is easier for your client to accept a standard like market rate than it is to pay a certain fee or salary just because *you* say that's what you charge or want.

So think in advance (Phase One—Pre-Negotiation Strategy) about what standards you could appeal to in your negotiation. Do your homework on marketplace, salaries, market rates, scientific criteria, costs, technical measures, and precedents. Think how you and the other party in the negotiation can agree on the standards that you will use during the negotiation. This might be a bit uncomfortable, but having standards will usually guide negotiations to a more satisfactory outcome.

Alternatives. Here we are speaking of alternatives available to us to satisfy our interests. Negotiation is only one way to satisfy interests. All too often people go into a negotiation looking for agreement and examine their alternatives only if things go badly. This is a classic mistake. Knowing what your alternatives are can determine your success in satisfying your interests. We are talking about knowing your BATNA (Best Alternative to a Negotiated Agreement). The purpose of entering into negotiations in the first place is to explore whether you can satisfy your interests better by negotiating an agreement than you could by pursuing your BATNA.

BATNA is your walk-away alternative, your *Plan B,* your best course of action for satisfying your interest *without* the other parties' agreement. BATNA is the key to negotiating power. Your power depends less on whether you are bigger, stronger, more senior, or richer than the other person but more on how good your BATNA is. If you have a viable alternative, then you have leverage in the negotiation.

Identify your BATNA. Your BATNA should be your measuring stick for evaluating any potential agreement. To identify your BATNA, you should consider three kinds of alternatives:

1. What can you do all by yourself to pursue your interests? Depending on your role and circumstances, your *walk-away* alternative may be to find another job or supplier or customer.
2. What can you do directly to the other party in the negotiation to make them respect your interests? Go on strike, go to war, accept a competitor's offer, and so on. But, remember not to threaten! Threatening people usually causes them to resist based solely on principle. Gently, tactfully, but clearly let them know the facts of life. They can draw their own conclusions regarding your BATNA.
3. How can you bring a third party into the situation to further your interests? Your third-party alternative may be to resort to mediation, arbitration, or court.

After generating a set of possible BATNAs, select the one that is most likely to satisfy your interests, and keep it close to your side. If things get tough during the negotiation and you are feeling under pressure, calm yourself and stay rational, remembering that you have an alternative—your BATNA. It is not the end of the world if the negotiation does not end with an agreement.

Strengthen your BATNA. You need to work at developing a good BATNA. Generally, a BATNA doesn't already exist; you need to work at discovering it. This means serious self-examination of your true interests regarding the negotiation situation. If your BATNA is not very strong, you should take steps to improve it. For example, don't just identify your BATNA as your willingness to seek another job if your salary negotiation session doesn't work out. Actually go to the trouble of getting another job offer. Make sure your BATNA is strong and not simply something you hope for.

Decide whether you should enter into negotiations at all. Why negotiate if there is a better way to satisfy your interests? Remember that BATNA stands for *Best Alternative to a Negotiated Agreement.* You might decide that your BATNA provides a better solution than the proposed negotiation could provide. But, keep in mind that it is easy to overestimate how good your BATNA really is. If you know in advance (Phase One—Pre-Negotiation Strategy) that your BATNA is not all that strong, then negotiations might be the best way to attempt to satisfy your interests.

Identify their BATNA.   Knowing the BATNA of the other side (to the negotiation) can be just as important as knowing your own. It gives you an idea of the challenge you face: developing options for a negotiation agreement that will exceed their BATNA. Make sure that you avoid the dual mistakes of: (1) underestimating and (2) overestimating. Don't underestimate or overestimate the strength of their or your BATNA. Your BATNA may be weak or strong and so may theirs. Know the true situation.

Proposals.   Your earlier work on interests and options opens up the challenge of creating a solution (agreement) that will satisfy the interests of both sides of the negotiation. Your list of potential options to satisfy the interests of both parties helps to design a proposal. (Note: Sales proposals are discussed in more depth in Chapters 10 and 12.)

A *proposal* is a description of a final but tentative solution (agreement) that might satisfy the interests of both parties to the negotiation. It is potential and tentative because it is a summary agreement laid before both parties that they are asked to agree to. A proposal is a possible agreement to which both parties are asked to say yes.

If both parties agree to the proposal, then it automatically becomes a contract, either formal or informal. Both parties are expected to abide by its terms. Obviously, some contracts (agreed-on proposals) are more legally binding than others; however, our moral values generally operate on the law of what is fair and honest. Thus, one's word should be his/her bond.

For example, during an interview for a job, if the employer lays out a proposal of salary, starting date, and so forth and you agree, both you and the employer are expected to abide by this agreement. In a selling situation, a tentative proposal is laid out after all parties have discussed it. If both parties say yes, the proposal becomes a contract. If no, the deal does not go through. If maybe, the proposal is discussed further until both parties can firmly commit to a yes or no.

When deciding whether you will say yes or no to a tentative proposal, it is useful to have three comparison (ideal) proposals in mind. This will help you gauge whether the actual proposal laid out before you truly satisfies your interests.

1. *Comparison Proposal #1—What Do You Aspire To?* Those who begin with realistically high aspirations often end up with better agreements. How high is realistic? Realistic means within the bounds set by fairness and by the other side's BATNA.
2. *Comparison Proposal #2—What Would You Be Content With?* You may not be able to get everything you would like; therefore, it is useful to ask yourself a second question: Even though this agreement is not ideal, would it still satisfy my basic interests?

3. *Comparison Proposal #3—What Could You Live With?* This is directly based on your BATNA. If you can't obtain an agreement at least as good as that, you should consider walking away from the negotiation. Then you would exercise your BATNA as an alternative to an unsatisfactory agreement that you sensed coming from the negotiation.

The above comparison proposals are not rigid positions. They are concrete illustrations of the kinds of outcomes that would satisfy your interests. They really are potential scenarios or various imagined situations to achieve your interests and serve as comparisons for any proposals made in the actual negotiation. Use these comparison proposals to judge the acceptability of the actual proposal that is laid out before you. Based on these three comparative proposals, you are in a position to either say yes, no, or maybe.

If maybe, you begin to discuss again the terms and conditions of the actual proposal. You cannot know for certain whether the other side will or will not accept any of the comparison proposal scenarios that you use to improve the chances of achieving your interests.

The Mandatory Characteristics of a True Negotiation

Now that you have a basic map of the negotiation process, let's begin to refine our understanding. First, we will examine the required characteristics that define a negotiation. Second, we will discuss different approaches to negotiation—situational negotiation strategies and tactics.

How do you know if you are in a true negotiation situation? Here are the distinguishing requirements and characteristics for a discussion between parties to be defined as a negotiation.

Relationship of the Negotiating Parties. There must be *interdependence* between the parties. In negotiations, both parties need each other and are mutually dependent. For example, a meeting planner cannot accomplish his/her goals without a supplier of meeting facilities, and vice versa.

The parties must exhibit *mutual adjustment* to one another. Being interdependent, both parties know that they can influence the other's outcomes and that their outcomes can, in turn, be influenced by the other. This knowledge causes progressive change during the negotiation's give-and-take interactions.

Characteristics of the Negotiating Parties. The following characteristics define a true negotiation situation:

1. There are two or more parties: two or more individuals, groups (teams), or organizations.
2. The parties have different interests. What one party wants is offered in return for something of value. The creation and claiming of value is an essential part of the negotiated sales agreement.

3. The parties negotiate because they think they can use some form of influence to get a better deal that way than by simply taking what the other side will voluntarily give them or let them have.
4. The parties, at least for the moment, prefer to search for solutions rather than to: (1) permanently break off contact and leave needs unmet or (2) take the offer to another party (BATNA).
5. When we negotiate, we expect to give and take. We expect that both sides will give in somewhat or modify their opening requests or demands.
6. Successful negotiation involves the management of *intangibles* as well as the resolving of *tangibles*.
   a. *tangibles*—price or terms of agreement, for example.
   b. *intangibles*—psychological motivations such as the need to "look good" or the fear of setting a precedent in the negotiations. Many negotiation observers place basic psychological motivators along a primal fear (of loss) to greed (for gain) continuum.

Understanding Situational Negotiation Strategies and Tactics

Negotiation sessions differ according to the interests of the parties involved. Different negotiations require effective negotiators to choose different approaches or strategies for each negotiation. Thus, various approaches to negotiations can be categorized as *situational negotiation strategies*. We now turn to the topic of which strategies are appropriate for what kinds of negotiation sessions.

There once was a time when all of us were taught this or that magic prescription for negotiation success. "This is the way to stay in control and even to intimidate the customer. You will win every time by claiming more value than you give." "No, the days of win-lose are over; every negotiation must be a win-win. Here is the way to negotiate for gain and long-term relationships." Confusing, isn't it? From our practical experiences in selling, we all know that sometimes you need to control, other times you are the party that is controlled, still other times you need to problem solve, and other times require a blend of the three. Welcome to *situational negotiation strategies*.

Where do we begin in making sense of fuzzy conditions that lead us to *it depends?* We will do this in a two-fold approach. First, we will clarify terminology. We want to make sure that we know what we are talking about and are all on the same page. This requires definitions. In our clarification efforts, we will also present a model that illustrates the wide range and variability of negotiation strategies available to us. Second, we will discuss circumstances when it is appropriate to use or not use various situational negotiation strategies. Here we provide a practical question checklist leading you to select the right negotiation strategy and tactic for your specific negotiation situation.

Modeling Situational Sales Negotiation Strategies

Essentially, sales negotiations are entered into to find solutions to complex needs or problems that derive value for both the buyer and seller. It is the essence of how modern day economies work. Each party is interested in specific outcomes that, at a minimum, will allow them to claim their fair share of the value pie. These outcomes can be balanced so that both parties will win, or they can be unbalanced so that one party wins more than the other. In the following discussion, we will first present four broad classifications of situational negotiation strategies and, second, present a Dual Concerns model that describes multiple variations of negotiation conflict management tactics within these four basic negotiation strategies.

Four Classifications of Situational Negotiation Strategies. Options for sales negotiations can be classified into two sets containing a total of four situational negotiation strategies: (1) engagement strategies—*integrative (collaborative), distributive (competitive),* and accommodative strategies and (2) nonengagement strategies—*avoidance strategy and accommodation strategy.* These strategies are viewed on a two-by-two matrix that relates (1) the importance of maintaining a relationship between parties with (2) the importance of winning substantive gains (see Figure 7–1). All are dependent of each party's BATNA.

Engagement strategies are *active* in the sense that parties to the negotiation attempt to reach resolution; they are actively engaged and work together to seek outcomes. Within this classification of situational negotiation strategies, there are three subsets.

1. **Integrative negotiation strategy** can be generally described as win-win. It uses negotiation tactics that we will describe in Figure 7–2 as *problem-solving* or *collaborating*.
2. **Distributive negotiation strategy** can be generally described as win-lose. It uses negotiation tactics described as *contending, competitive,* or *dominating*.
3. **Accommodative negotiation strategy** has the reverse outcome of a distributive strategy: lose/win. Why would any party strategically plan to lose? It can be the result of a poor BATNA. In other cases, it might be in one's strategic best interest to keep a relationship by giving up more of the value pie than to lose the relationship by winning the substantive outcome or gain in the negotiation. This strategic option can be situationally appropriate depending on each party's objectives. This strategy uses negotiation tactics described as *yielding* or *obliging*. Additionally, as we will later discuss, *compromising tactics* are not really win-win but are a form of accommodative strategy.

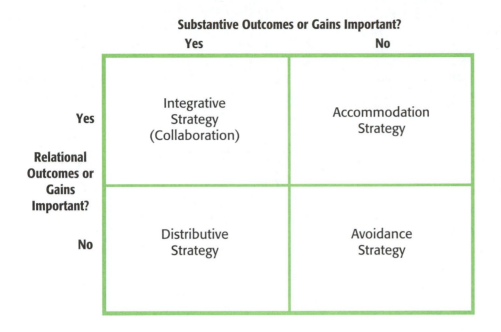

Substantive Outcomes or Gains Important?

	Yes	No
Yes	Integrative Strategy (Collaboration)	Accommodation Strategy
No	Distributive Strategy	Avoidance Strategy

Relational Outcomes or Gains Important?

FIGURE 7–1

Classification of Situational Negotiation Strategies

Source: Adapted from Savage, G. T., J. D. Blair, and R. J. Sorenson. 1989. Consider both relationship and substance when negotiating strategically. *Academy of Management Executive* 3:37–48. Reported in Lewicki, R. J., D. M. Saunders, and J. W. Minton. 2001. *Essentials of Negotiation.* 2nd ed. New York: McGraw-Hill Higher Education, 36.

Nonengagement strategies refer to a negotiation situation in which it is a strategically sound plan to avoid active engagement between parties. When might these be appropriate? Often it is better to walk away from a poor deal than to accept an offer that does not meet your needs. By committing to a poor offer, you remove the possibility of pursuing other alternatives (BATNA). Sometimes it is not worth one of the parties' time and effort to negotiate, especially in the case where one party's alternatives are high. As an illustration, hotel sales staff members seldom attempt to negotiate with tour wholesalers who want to book high transient demand periods—beyond probing if they can move to low demand dates. And sometimes the success in a negotiation engagement is improbable;, thus, active negotiations are avoided and the "chips" allowed to "fall where they may." Within the classification scheme of Figure 7–1, we have illustrated one nonengagement strategy—avoidance strategy. This strategy uses a tactic described as *inaction* (Lewicki, Saunders, and Minton 2001).

The Dual Concerns Model of Situational Negotiation Tactics. *Tactics* are face-to-face actions taking place after *strategies* are planned. In Figure 7–1, we discussed situational negotiation strategies. In Figure 7–2, we turn our attention to the Dual Concerns Model of **situational negotiation tactics**.

This model demonstrates that negotiation tactics are also based on the objectives of the parties and the nature of the need or problem, but deal

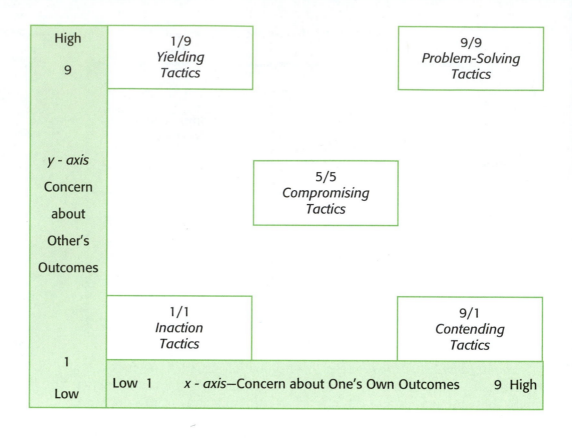

FIGURE 7–2

The Dual Concerns Model of Situational Negotiation Tactics *

* Source: Adapted from Rubin, J., et al. 1994. *Social conflict: Escalation, stalemate and settlement.* 2nd ed. New York: The McGraw-Hill Companies. Reported in Lewicki, R. J., D. M. Saunders, and J. W. Minton. 2001. *Essentials of negotiation.* 2nd ed. New York: McGraw-Hill Higher Education, 17.

specifically with the actions of conflict management during the actual negotiation session. The model is based on two (dual) variable objectives as viewed from the perspective of each of the parties: (1) concern about one's own outcomes and (2) concern about the other's outcomes.

From Figure 7–2 we can describe five situational negotiation tactics, each of which is a subset of the four situational negotiation strategies illustrated in Figure 7–1. The five tactics in Figure 7–2 illustrate extremes and are not inclusive of the many variations that one might find. For example, how would you describe a negotiation tactic located at x = 7 and y = 3? The model illustrates the multiplicity of negotiation tactics possible. Simultaneously, each of the five tactics and their variations fall into one of the four broad strategy classifications illustrated earlier in Figure 7–1. Let's discuss the characteristics of the five situational negotiation tactics:

1. *Problem-Solving Negotiation Tactic*—Fulfills an *integrative strategy* (Figure 7–1). The tactic is also called *collaborating.* Here the two parties actively pursue approaches to maximize their joint outcome from the conflict, so that both sides "win."

2. *Contending Negotiation Tactic*—Fulfills a *distributive strategy* (Figure 7–1). This tactic is also known as *competing* or *dominating.* Parties who use this maintain their own aspirations and try to persuade the other party to yield. Threats, punishment, intimidating, and unilateral action are consistent with a contending approach.

3. *Yielding Negotiation Tactic*—Fulfills an *accommodative strategy* (Figure 7–1). This tactic is also called *obliging.* Yielding involves lowering one's own aspiration in order to let the other win and gain what he/she wants.

4. *Compromising Negotiation Tactic*—Also fulfills an accommodative strategy (Figure 7–1). Additionally, this tactic is known as *half-heartedness.* It represents a moderate effort to pursue one's own outcomes and a moderate effort to help the other party achieve theirs. It can be a "lazy problem-solving approach" involving a half-hearted attempt to satisfy the two parties' interests, or simple *yielding* by both parties.

5. *Inaction Negotiation Tactic*—Fulfills an *avoidance strategy* (Figure 7–1). Inaction is often synonymous with withdrawal or passivity; the party prefers to retreat, be silent, or do nothing. Parties show little interest in whether they attain their outcomes or if the other party attains theirs.

When to Use Situational Negotiation Strategies and Tactics

Now that we have clarified what we mean by negotiations and situational strategies and tactics, we need to apply our knowledge practically. Table 7–2 summarizes the situations in which it is appropriate to use or not use situational negotiation strategies and tactics. Further, Table 7–2 relates situational negotiations to three distinct selling strategies discussed in Chapter 6: transactional, consultative, and alliance selling strategies.

Which situational negotiation strategy is for you? It depends on your BATNA as well as the BATNA of your counterpart. Now we want to present a practical way for you to select the appropriate situational negotiation strategy and tactic to use in your specific circumstances. See Table 7–2.

From Table 7–2, we can observe that there are many situational negotiation strategies and tactics that are appropriate under certain circumstances. If you are a seller using consultative or alliance selling strategies, then an integrative situational negotiation strategy with a problem-solving tactic is most appropriate. On the other hand, if you are a seller using transactional selling strategies, then a distributive situational negotiation strategy with a contending tactic may be more appropriate.

Table 7–2 Appropriate Use of Situational Negotiation Strategies and Tactics Related to Selling Strategies

SITUATIONAL SALES NEGOTIATION STRATEGY/TACTIC	APPROPRIATE SITUATIONS TO USE SELLING STRATEGY	INAPPROPRIATE SITUATIONS TO USE SELLING STRATEGY
Integrative Negotiation Strategy 1. Problem-Solving Negotiation Tactic Distributive Negotiation Strategy	**Win-Win Objectives** **Consultative/Alliance Selling** 1. Value that can be created is great for both buyer and seller. 2. Synthesis of ideas is needed to come up with better solutions. 3. Commitment is needed from the other party. 4. Time is available for problem solving. 5. One party alone cannot solve the problem. 6. Resources possessed by different parties are needed to solve their common problems.	**Win-Lose Objectives** **Transactional Selling** 1. Value is small; task or problem is simple. 2. Immediate decision is required. 3. Other parties are unconcerned about outcome. 4. Other parties do not have problem solving skills. 5. Resources to be committed to decision are not significant.
2. Contending Negotiation Tactic Accommodation Negotiation Strategy	**Win-Lose Objectives** **Transactional Selling** 1. Issue is trivial. 2. Speedy decision is needed. 3. Unpopular course of action is implemented. 4. Necessary to overcome assertive subordinates. 5. Unfavorable decision by the other party may be costly to you. 6. Other party lacks expertise to make technical decisions. 7. Issue is important to you. 8. Resources to be committed to decision are not significant.	**Win-Win Objectives** **Consultative/Alliance Selling** 1. Issue is complex. 2. Issue is not important to you. 3. Both parties are equally powerful. 4. Decision does not have to be made quickly. 5. Other party possesses high degree of competence.

Table 7–2 (Continued)

	Lose-Win Objectives All Three Selling Strategies	Win-Lose Objectives All Three Selling Strategies
3. Yielding Negotiation Strategy	1. You believe that you may be wrong. 2. Issue is more important to the other party. 3. You are willing to give up something in exchange for something from a position of weakness. 4. You are dealing from a position of weakness. 5. Preserving relationship is important.	1. Issue is important to you. 2. You believe that you are right. 3. The other party is wrong or unethical.
4. Compromising Negotiation Tactic Avoidance Negotiation Strategy	1. Goals of parties are mutually exclusive—differ from one another too widely so "splitting the difference" is practical. 2. Parties are equally powerful. 3. Problem solving or contending strategies prove unsuccessful after being tried. 4. Temporary solution to a complex problem is needed.	1. One party is more powerful than the other. 2. Problem is complex enough to need a true problem-solving strategy approach.
	Other Objectives All Three Selling Strategies	**Other Objectives All Three Selling Strategies**
5. Inaction Negotiation Tactic	1. Issue is trivial. 2. Potential downside costs of confronting the other party outweigh benefits of any resolution. 3. Cooling-off period is needed.	1. Issue is important to you. 2. It is your responsibility to make decision. 3. Parties are unwilling to postpone and the issue must be resolved. 4. Prompt attention is needed.

Source: Adapted from Rahim, M. A. 1990. *Organizational conflict inventories: Professional manual.* Consulting Psychologists Press, Inc. Reported in Lewicki, R. J., D. M. Saunders, and J. W. Minton. 2001. *Essentials of negotiation.* 2nd ed. New York: McGraw-Hill Higher Education, 19.

In all three selling strategies, transactional, consultative, and alliance, an accommodative negotiation strategy and/or an *avoidance* negotiation strategy may be appropriate. And, sometimes these negotiation strategies may be used in conjunction with integrative and distributive negotiation tactics.

◈ SUMMARY

Which situational negotiation strategy and tactic should you use? It depends on your specific objectives and circumstances—the situation! The three distinctive selling strategies and four negotiation strategies with their accompanying tactics are situational as well as intertwined. To be an effective salesperson requires you to carry out two important steps. First, you must fully understand and know what type of selling strategy you are using. Second, you must select the appropriate negotiation strategy and tactics for your specific circumstances. At one time salespeople could safely operate using a tried-and-true selling and negotiation strategy and tactic. Our fast-paced world has changed all of that. Successful salespeople must fill their toolbox with a flexible set of tools. A situational approach provides this adaptability.

Selling and negotiation strategies have become situational. This means that the appropriate effective strategy to be used is dependent on circumstances or situations that vary widely. The trick is to know what situation you are facing and be prepared to adapt if needed. Your professional success, if not your very career survival, is dependent on your being prepared to meet a continually changing environment.

In Chapters 8 through 13, we will use the buying/selling exchange process as coordinated with the negotiation process illustrated in Table 7–1. This approach is a consultative selling strategy combined with negotiation tactics (both described in Chapter 6). Although selling and negotiations today are situational, we will use only one strategy in this text for the purposes of clarity and consistency. The consultative selling strategy is the approach to selling that is in ascendancy today.

References

Lewicki, R. J., D. M. Saunders, and J. W. Minton. 2001. *Essentials of negotiation.* 2nd ed. Boston: McGraw-Hill.

Ury, W. 1991. *Getting past no: Negotiating your way from confrontation to cooperation.* New York: Bantam Books.

DISCUSSION QUESTIONS ◈

1. Comment on how the selling process is like and unlike negotiations.
2. It is often said that the party that enters into a negotiation the best prepared will receive the best outcomes. What areas should you consider in preparing for a negotiation?
3. What is meant by the term BATNA? Why is it important for the selling organization?
4. Should you ever accept business whereby from strictly a transactional basis the customer wins but your firm loses? If yes, provide an example.

Phase Two—Approaching The Buyer

In Chapter 7, we discussed Phase One of the buying/selling exchange process: *Pre-Negotiation Strategy*. This strategy is designed for preparing for the actual sales presentation or face-to-face contact with the buyer. Phase One was concerned with two parts: pre-approach planning and planning for the approach. In this preparation phase, the salesperson: (1) updates and examines his/her prospect/customer database to correctly target the potential buyer that he/she plans to approach and (2) develops effective negotiation strategies and tactics in order to maximize the probability of making a sale.

This chapter discusses the process leading up to a salesperson's first appointment with a potential buyer and how to establish the tone or environment of the negotiation session at the very beginning of this appointment. The *approach,* as discussed in this chapter, is the initial face-to-face contact with the buyer during which the seller must make a favorable first impression as well as engage the buyer and stimulate interest. However, anytime a salesperson contacts a potential buyer, an approach or favorable opening introduction is appropriate.

The crucial first face-to-face encounter may or may not create a favorable environment within which negotiations will take place. Obviously, it's best to be prepared for and attempt to favorably control this most important step. The negotiation itself will be challenging enough and filled with often surprising and uncontrollable events; thus, effective sellers attempt to set up conditions for smooth negotiations by first creating an atmosphere of comfort for the buyer. Salespeople build self-confidence by being as knowledgeable and prepared as possible. With a buying/selling exchange process map in hand and a planned negotiation strategy in place, most effective salespeople are well prepared for negotiations. Thorough preparation for the negotiation process yields guidance and a sense of confidence. Before we proceed to discuss Step One of Phase Two, *the approach,* let's remind ourselves of where our discussion from previous chapters has taken us. Let's briefly review the entire buying/selling exchange process that we first introduced in Chapter 7, (Table 8–1).

In addition to knowing where we are on our map of the buying/selling exchange process, we need to remind ourselves that as *consultative salespeople* we should be very selective with the potential buyers that we approach. *Transactional salespeople* rely on the Law of Large Numbers to reach revenue quotas. That is, they make a sales presentation to almost anyone that will let them have an appointment. They see a lot of people, make a lot of sales presentations, and are rejected a lot, but, a small percentage of contacts actually buy. Thus, the larger the numbers presented to, the larger the numbers who buy, even though there is a lot of wasted effort in this approach.

Consultative salespeople, on the other hand, work differently (arguably smarter) by doing a lot of homework in advance of making an appointment. They increase the percentage of the number of people who actually make a

Table 8–1   Comparison of the Buying/Selling Exchange Process and the Negotiation Process

THE BUYING/SELLING EXCHANGE PROCESS	THE NEGOTIATION PROCESS
Phase One – Pre-Negotiation Strategy: Negotiation Planning and Preparation (Chapter 7)	**Phase One – Pre-Negotiation Strategy: Negotiation Planning and Preparation (Chapter 7)**
Step One – Understanding Sales Process	**Step One** – Understanding Negotiation Process
Step Two – Research Potential Customer	**Step Two** – Know Your and Your Customers' Interests
Step Three – Sales Tactics	**Step Three** – Negotiation Tactics
Phase Two – Negotiation Process Strategy	**Phase Two – Negotiation Process Strategy**
Step One – Approaching the Buyer (Chapter 8)	**Step One** – Opening
Step Two – Investigating Needs (Chapter 9)	**Step Two** – Exploring
Step Three – Demonstrating Capability (Chapter 10)	**Step Three** – Proposing Agreement
Step Four – Negotiating Concerns (Chapter 11)	**Step Four** – Clarifying Proposal
Step Five – Gaining Commitment (Chapter 12)	**Step Five** – Gaining Commitment
Phase Three – Post-Sales Strategy (Chapter 13)	**Phase Three – Post-Negotiation Strategy**
Step One – After-Sale Implementation	**Step One** – Implementing Agreement
Step Two – Maintenance & Development	**Step Two** – Conducting Self-Critique
Step Three – Continuous Improvement	

purchase by doing extensive prescreening and pre-qualifying of **suspects** and **prospects** before they spend valuable time in a face-to-face appointment.

In Chapter 7, we stressed the importance of building a prospect/customer database. This computerized database is where all information is collected on prospects and **customers**. From this database, the consultative salesperson is able to mine and access those selective *potential* buyers *(prospects)* that have a high probability of eventually becoming *actual* buyers *(customers)*. In the old days of selling, traditional wisdom talked about the value of *prospecting*, or calling a lot of people to gather information about and determine potential buyers. In the new era of selling, computers have expanded this concept. Although sellers continue to gather information about potential buyers by the telephone, they now gather additional information from many other sources and then store it in computerized databases. The computerized database allows salespeople to massage, manipulate, analyze, and access stored prospect/customer data in ways unimagined in the past (see Chapter 17 for more information on sales and technology). Based on increased amounts of and access to information about their potential buyers, consultative salespeople systematically convert *suspects* to *prospects* to *customers*. Consultative salespeople are selective in the use of their time and resources. They are highly selective in the potential buyers they approach. In this text we present a way to quantify potential buyers using a probability system (see Table 8–2). This probability system can easily be incorporated into the prospect/customer database.

In this probability system, there are two types of suspects who fall into the low- to medium-probability-potential buyers—10 to 49 percent probability. *Prospects* are middle to high-range-probability-potential buyers—50 to 89 percent. *Customers* are high probability and actual buyers—90 to 100 percent. Most customers are not 100 percent because there is always a possibility that they might fail to purchase everything agreed to on a signed contract and sometimes they even cancel contracts or letters of agreement.

Note: The probabilities assigned are based on the salesperson's experienced judgment and on predetermined criteria. For example, a suspect (potential buyer) at a 35 percent probability may be elevated to a higher probability, for instance 60 percent, thus being transformed into a prospect (potential buyer). This can happen based on the salesperson's experienced judgment regarding increased potential buyer interest as well as predetermined criteria such as the potential buyer agreeing to have a face-to-face appointment with the salesperson. We will discuss this in more detail later in this chapter.

Conversion of Suspects to Prospects to Customers

If the salesperson has little to no information on a potential buyer's true needs and has had little contact with this potential buyer, this is a situation that should be considered as a low probability of eventual purchase (see Table 8–2). Only when more information is gathered and more contact with the potential buyer is made can the salesperson estimate whether the probability of an eventual purchase is increased or lessened. The basic idea here is that a salesperson should continually develop suspects into eventual customers or stop working with suspects that do not have the potential of ever becoming customers. This is the way smart consultative salespeople operate.

The potential buyer increases in **qualifications** (factors that indicate potentiality or probability of eventually becoming a customer) as the salesperson learns of his/her ability to purchase the product or service, **authority** to do so, interest in purchasing, and willingness. As a potential buyer's qualification increases, a salesperson generally assigns a higher probability that they will eventually make a purchase. Increased qualification information can also lead to a lower probability of eventual purchase: for instance, in the case in which the salesperson discovers that the potential buyer's company has just

Table 8–2 Evolving Buyer Status Related to Buying/Selling Exchange Process and Accompanying Sales Communication Documents

THE BUYING/SELLING EXCHANGE PROCESS	EVOLVING BUYER STATUS	PROBABILITY OF BECOMING A CUSTOMER	SALES ON GENERATED COMMUNI-CATIONS	EXPLANATIONS
Phase One – **Pre-Negotiation Strategy: Negotiation Planning and Preparation (Chapter 7)**	Suspects	10% to 29%	Basic Direct Mail	*Stock* letter with #10 Brochure
Step One – Understanding Negotiations **Step Two** – Essential Skills **Step Three** – Negotiation	Suspects	30% to 49%	Customized Direct Mail (Proposal Letter)	*Detailed* letter noting basic prospective buyer needs such as dates, basic rates, and meeting name sent with extensive materials: large brochures, videos, etc. These are usually sent out with requests for proposals (RFP) and at this level of suspect probability. This is sometimes called a proposal letter.
Phase Two – **Negotiation Process Strategy** 1st Appointment – Purpose to Discover Buyer Needs **Step One** – Approaching the Buyer (Chapter 8) **Step Two** – Investigating Needs (Chapter 9) **Step Five** – Gaining Commitment (Chapter 12)	Prospects	50% to 69%	Proposal Checklist	This is essentially a blank proposal form used to aid the salesperson as a checklist during questioning appointment with potential buyer.
2nd Appointment – Purpose to Make the Sale **Step One** – Approaching the Buyer (Chapter 8) **Step Three** – Demonstrating Capability (Chapter 10) **Step Four** – Negotiating Concerns (Chapter 11) **Step Five** – Gaining Commitment (Chapter 12)	Prospects Customer	70% to 89% 90% to 100%	Proposal Contract or Letter of Agreement	A written document estimating pricing and giving working numbers for known potential buyer needs. It also provides basic seller policies and other important information on which a potential buyer is able to make a decision. A signed proposal plus any appendices added as they develop.

filed for bankruptcy. Thus, a salesperson's estimate of raising or lowering a potential buyer's probability of purchase is a guide informing him/her to expend more effort and expense in attempting a sale or to stop wasting effort and resources.

From Suspects to Customers

Suspects. A salesperson wants to approach only those potential buyers with a certain probability of actually purchasing his/her product or service. Potential buyers with an estimated probability of conversion are called suspects. The probabilities are estimated and assigned by experienced salespeople using certain criteria. When these suspects are converted to prospects and then actually make a first purchase, they are transformed and known as *customers* (see Table 8–2). The job of a salesperson is to identify suspects and work with them to develop them through a process that leads to them eventually becoming *customers*.

Usually a salesperson needs to find and work with many suspects in order to eventually end up with a few customers. The selling process is like sifting a mixture of sand, gravel, and twigs through a screen. Only the desired finely grained sand passes through the narrow openings of the screen's mesh. Similarly, not all suspects can pass through the buying/selling exchange process screen. Some can't afford the product that the salesperson is selling, some don't need the product or service, some are loyal to other sellers, and so on.

At the time that someone is classified as a suspect, the estimated probability range that he/she will make a purchase is approximately 10 to 49 percent. If a salesperson identifies a suspect, he/she will work with them until the suspect converts to the next level and a higher probability or the salesperson determines that it is impossible to convert or refine the suspect to a higher level (see Table 8–2). You will see in the table that the salesperson attempts to refine him/her to a higher level by providing the suspect with increasing levels of communication such as direct mail brochures. The salesperson uses these communication pieces as a reason to talk with the suspect to learn more about his/her **interests** in the salesperson's product or service. This communication is also used as a way to obtain a face-to-face appointment and make an approach, especially for a first appointment in a multi-call negotiation session.

As the salesperson makes more contact with these suspects, learns more about their needs, and receives increased indications of growing interest from them, *suspects* convert into *prospects*. Once a suspect is converted into a prospect, the salesperson attempts to obtain a first face-to-face appointment.

Prospects. A prospect is a qualified suspect who has not yet made a commitment to purchase. *Qualified* means that the potential buyer has been determined by the salesperson to have: (1) authority to purchase or influence the purchase, (2) **means** (money), (3) basic **need**, and (4) interest in purchasing the product or service. Due to increased qualifications and characteristics, a prospect has a higher probability (50 to 79 percent) than a suspect of eventually becoming a customer.

As a general operating rule, the consultative salesperson should only conduct a face-to-face appointment with mid- to high-range-probability prospects—those falling in the 50 to 69 percent range. This means that the salesperson will use his/her valuable and expensive time targeting suspects (potential buyers) about whom they have already gained significant information and systematically transforming them into prospects.

As mentioned, a multi-call negotiation session ideally consists of a minimum of two face-to-face meetings between the salesperson and the potential buyer: a first appointment for the sole purpose of **investigating needs** (see Chapter 9) and a second appointment for the purpose of **demonstrating capability** (see Chapter 10). In each of these appointments, the salesperson must *approach* the prospect.

In the first appointment, the salesperson and the potential buyer engage in a conversation of questions and answers about the buyer's needs. The salesperson takes extensive notes using a *proposal checklist* (discussed in Chapter 9) as a type of questioning guideline. This proposal checklist, along with information regarding the potential buyer's needs, is the foundation for the actual *proposal* (discussed in Chapter 10) that the salesperson later prepares and uses in his/her second appointment of a multi-call negotiation session.

In the second appointment, the salesperson attempts to have the prospect make a purchase. If a purchase is actually made, the prospect is converted into a customer.

Customers. A *prospect* who has agreed to the terms of the proposal presented by the salesperson is defined as a *customer*. The probability assigned to customers ranges from 90 to 100 percent. Usually a 90 percent probability is assigned to allow for uncertainty due to convention/conference group business not fully living up to letter-of-agreement terms or due to cancellations. The purchase is official when the buyer and seller are in agreement as evidenced by a signed contract or letter of agreement.

Two conversions take place with the signing of this agreement. First, with a buyer's signature on the *proposal,* this document converts into a *contract* or *letter of agreement*. Second, by signing the proposal, the prospect is converted into a *customer.* We will discuss letters of agreement in detail in Chapter 12.

How does all of this relate to the subject of this chapter, the *approach?* As we will see, the probabilities of a potential buyer (suspect or prospect) becoming an actual buyer (customer) are increased or decreased during the process leading to the first face-to-face appointment between the salesperson and the potential buyer. At this first appointment the salesperson makes his or first crucial approach.

The Approach

In Chapter 7 we discussed *Phase One—Pre-Negotiation Strategy* of the buying/selling exchange process. In that phase, the seller prepared to make an appointment to meet with a buyer face-to-face or by telephone. We have stated that the consultative seller should have face-to-face appointments only with *qualified prospects* (those with probabilities in the 50 to 69 percent range). The initial contact with these targeted prospects any time the salesperson has an appointment is called the *approach*. It is the first step of *Phase Two—Negotiation Process Strategy.* All the planning, thought, and effort put into pre-negotiation preparation and planning can now be applied to Phase Two, or the process flowing from approach through commitment or close.

When we speak of the approach, we are talking about the time when the salesperson first walks up to greet the potential buyer. This occurs any time a salesperson walks in the door and shakes hands, but the importance of the approach should also be considered any time a telephone call or other contact is made. The approach, in any of these settings, establishes the tone and environment for the rest of the dialogue between the salesperson and the potential buyer. In this chapter, we will specifically discuss the approach as it relates to a salesperson's meeting with the potential buyer in his/her first appointment for the purposes of investigating needs.

How Salespeople Get to the Approach

Stages Leading to the Approach. Briefly, the following are the stages leading to the first face-to-face approach (see Table 8–2):

Direct Mail and Telephone Contacts—There are series of direct mailings followed by a salesperson telephoning the potential buyer. The mailings are for the purpose of providing the salesperson a reason to speak directly with the potential buyer. During these follow-up telephone conversations, the salesperson asks questions to further qualify the potential buyer (*suspect* at this point). With increased qualification information, the potential buyer's probability level usually is raised but sometimes is lowered.

First Face-to-Face Appointment—The first approach occurs here. This appointment is for the purpose of thoroughly *investigating needs*. Once the suspect is qualified to probability levels in the range of 50 to 69 percent, he/she is now known as a *prospect*. A salesperson conducts this first appointment for the purposes of investigating needs. After the needs are discovered, the salesperson sets up a second appointment with the prospect.

Second Face-to-Face Appointment—A second approach occurs here. This appointment is for the purpose of *demonstrating capability*. Since it always establishes the tone of the discussion to follow, the approach is just as important here as it was in the first appointment. Demonstrating capability in this appointment is accomplished by explaining and discussing the proposal that was prepared in between the first and second appointments. The proposal is the salesperson's best attempt to solve the prospect's needs using the features and benefits of his/her product or service. The prospect's needs, of course, were discovered at an earlier time: during the first appointment.

Additional Face-to-Face Appointments—Although we assume a two-appointment multi-call negotiation session in this text, it is not uncommon for the negotiation to take more face-to-face appointments; thus, in all contacts with the potential buyer, on the telephone, by mail, or face-to-face, the importance of thorough preparation for the approach is imperative.

The Approach in a Two-Appointment Multi-Call. The purpose of the first appointment of the multi-call negotiation session is to gain more information: to thoroughly investigate needs. This increased information will most likely raise the prospect's estimated probability level. In Table 8–2 we indicate that a prospect in the Investigating Needs step should be at an estimated 50 to 69 percent probability range. Conversely, this first appointment may provide the salesperson with information that will cause him/her to lower the probability estimate or eliminate it altogether. In this latter case, the salesperson would cease to work with the prospect having determined that further efforts would be a waste of valuable time and resources.

With a successful first appointment, the probability estimate is raised again as the salesperson plans for a second appointment for the purpose of demonstrating capability. When the salesperson has progressed this far into the buying/selling exchange process, the probability should be in the 70 to 89 percent range. The consultative salesperson who has systematically qualified and selected potential buyers should feel fairly confident that he/she will make a sale at this point.

Should the prospect agree to the salesperson's proposal presented during the second appointment (demonstrating capability) and then sign it, the proposal becomes a binding letter of agreement or contract. Simultaneously, the prospect converts to a customer with a probability raised to a 90 percent level. When the customer actually takes delivery of the product or holds his/her group meeting, the probability is raised to 100 percent.

Consultative salespeople ideally will, at a minimum, make two appointments with a qualified prospect; thus, they will have two pre-negotiation phases and two approaches to make. First, they will have an appointment for the sole purpose of investigating needs. Second, they will prepare a proposal based on discovered needs and then have a second appointment to demonstrate capability. Successful salespeople go through a pre-negotiation phase for each appointment where they need to approach the prospect. Each time the salesperson needs to have an appointment and make an approach, he/she must obtain a scheduled appointment, or *gain entry*. We now turn our discussion to the following:

> How to Gain Entry or Make an Appointment—First, we will present the tools used and a proven strategy. Second, we will provide tips on how to use the telephone more effectively for making appointments as well as for transactional selling by telemarketers and telesales.

> How to Make an Effective Face-to-Face Approach—Here we will discuss the do's and don'ts of an effective approach as well as provide an outline of steps to be taken.

Gaining Entry for a Face-to-Face Appointment

It is clearly easier to obtain an appointment with an existing customer, with a referred potential buyer, or where a previously established social or business relationship exists. To obtain a second appointment in a multi-call negotiation session is also usually not a problem. Salespeople find it more challenging to obtain a first appointment with someone they have never met or talked with. When contacting a potential buyer (either suspect or prospect) for the first time, salespeople should have patience, persistence, and a strategy. Often it takes several contacts by mail and phone to lead up to an actual face-to-face appointment. There are three basic tools to establish contact with a first time prospective buyer: letter, telephone, and cold call.

Letter Combined with Phone Call. Letters can be sent via snail mail, fax, or e-mail. A letter of any type by itself, not followed by a personal telephone call or personal visit, is next to worthless. Too often, salespeople believe that the potential buyer will call them. This is possible but not probable. So, at the onset, let's clearly understand that it is the salesperson's responsibility to be proactive. Also, e-mail is not recommended at this stage of the process since it is too easily ignored or deleted. We recommend hard copy to be on the prospective buyer's desk for a specific reason that will be explained.

The following is a proactive letter/telephone appointment acquisition strategy designed specifically for a consultative selling strategy (McNeill 2001).

Step One: Preselect Only Qualified Suspects—Remember that you are a consultative salesperson who is selling complex products; thus, you need to adequately preselect the prospective buyers that you will approach. Use of a computerized, well-maintained, and well-developed prospect/customer database is essential in selecting qualified suspects. As presented in Table 8–2, these initially selected prospective buyers (now called *suspects*) should be in an estimated probability range of 10 to 29 percent of eventually becoming a customer. You should be prepared to devote focused and disciplined efforts to learn more about these suspects and move them upward on the probability scale, transforming them into prospects. Prospects are the potential buyers with whom you want to make appointments.

Potential buyers who are not at a suspect probability level are simply unqualified people: people about whom the salesperson has no information to make an informed guesstimate about their potential to become an actual buyer. Mailing to an unqualified list is usually unproductive, expensive, and a waste of time. To obtain qualified suspects means that in Phase One of the buying/selling exchange process and on an ongoing basis, you should have developed a solid database of qualified potential buyers.

The database used by salespeople contains both potential and actual buyers at all probability levels (see Table 8–2). In seeking new suspects, it pays to research your existing database and look at characteristics of actual customers who have purchased from you in the past. You then seek out suspects with similar characteristics. For example, you might notice that you have done a large number of national sales meetings with major corporations. Thus, you would go to directories such as *Dun and Bradstreet Directory* or *Directory of Corporate Affiliations* (both available in public libraries) to find other large corporations and enter basic information into your database. From this database, you would begin your multiphase process of obtaining a face-to-face appointment. Refer to Table 8–2 to follow the flow from suspect to customer.

Step Two: Send Basic Direct Mail to Suspects (probability 10–29 percent)—Here we are still dealing with suspects in a probability range of 10 to 29 percent. The basic direct mail piece should be a standardized letter accompanied by a letter-sized (#10) brochure and be mailed only to the number of suspects who you can logistically telephone personally. This means that if your schedule only permits time to make 15 prospecting calls per day, then you should only mail at the rate of 15 direct mail pieces per day.

To schedule your telephone calls, you should keep in mind the time it will take for the direct mail piece to move through the mail system: approximately five business days (three days through the U.S. Postal Service and two days through the intracompany mail system of a large corporation). You want to call the prospective buyer at approximately the same time the mail is moving across his/her desk. If you miss this window, your direct mail will usually go into the *round file* (garbage can) and be forgotten. The only reason to mail is to give you an excuse to call and speak directly with the suspect: "I recently sent you some information. Did you receive it?" This icebreaker permits you to introduce yourself and provide more information regarding your hotel property.

Step Three: Send Customized Direct Mail to Suspects (probability 30–49 percent)—If the previous telephone call stimulated the suspect to a higher level of interest, you automatically raise his/her probability rating and record this change in your database. With increased interest, the suspect now has a higher probability of eventually becoming a customer. At this point, you might suggest sending *customized direct mail* (see Table 8–2). This customized mailing piece is known in the industry as a *proposal letter*. In this text we generally avoid using this term in order to minimize confusion with the proposal, which is a different and more extensive document and will be discussed in Chapter 10.

Note: This customized direct mail piece or proposal letter is usually sent when a suspect directly requests an RFP (request for proposal) by mail, phone, fax, Internet, or other means.

The customized direct mail piece is sent after the suspect has indicated increased interest in the salesperson's product or service. The salesperson has also discovered additional needs such as his/her meeting name, dates, number of attendees, and basic sleeping and meeting room specifications. The salesperson sends a stock or template letter that acknowledges this new information and also provides rate information and general attractive selling features and benefits of the lodging or hospitality organization or property. This *customized* letter will be accompanied by collateral material such as a full conference kit (big brochure and more information), a videotape of your property, and/or the URL to your Internet site. The effective salesperson, of course, follows this mailing or fax with a timely phone call.

Should you fax this information? Do it only if the buyer needs it immediately. Your color brochure and other material will be more attractive if it is received in a nonfaxed condition. Also, people tend to notice incoming packages larger than standard letters.

Note that a relationship is beginning to develop between the seller and potential buyer. Yes, this takes time, but a 250-attendee corporate meeting for three days at a full-service hotel or resort might be revenue of approximately $200,000 to $300,000. It's worth your time.

Step Four: The First Appointment with the Prospect (probability 50–69 percent)—After the customized direct mail has been sent to the suspect in Step Three, the salesperson follows up with a phone call. If the suspect shows an even higher level of interest in the product or service, the salesperson raises the probability range and transforms the suspect into a prospect (see Table 8–2). At this stage, your relationship with the prospective buyer has intensified. You have given him/her as much information as can be given over the telephone or by mail. During the telephone follow-up of the customized direct mail piece, the salesperson's objective is to make a face-to-face appointment.

In the hospitality business, appointments are of two types: *off-property*—the seller goes to the prospect's office—and *on-property*—the prospect visits the hospitality venue or place of business. On-property appointments are the best unless the prospect will be negatively impacted by his/her visit. Just like a consumer receiving a sample of soap in the mail, there is no replacement for an actual demonstration of the hotel's service. Additionally, the hospitality industry is in the service industry and services are intangible. Thus, prospective buyers want to see, feel, touch, taste, and hear the level of service that they might consider purchasing. For the service industry, the buying/selling exchange process can more effectively be conducted on-property than off-property.

Here are two suggestions for making a face-to-face appointment to conduct a buying/selling exchange process negotiation. These suggestions depend on the geographic location of the prospective buyer.

> Buyer Located in the Local Area—First, try to have the buyer visit your hotel for lunch and a tour. Second, if this is inconvenient, the salesperson should make an appointment to visit the buyer at his/her office.
>
> Buyer Located in a Distant City—First, invite the buyer for a complimentary *(comp)* visit to your property over a weekend or anytime that they might be traveling in the area. Remember that decision makers for complex meetings usually travel regularly around the country. Additionally, a formal meeting planner has a budget to conduct "site visits" to prospective properties. Second, hotel salespeople often make trips to trade shows where the prospective buyer may be in attendance. Hotel salespeople also make trips to geographic areas where their other customers are based. Is the prospective buyer also based in one of these areas? If so, attempt to coordinate a visit with the prospective buyer while traveling for other reasons. Third, if the potential account is clearly worth it and has given indications of high interest, make an appointment and book a flight specifically to visit that prospective buyer.

Note: Sometimes a prospect cannot meet face-to-face with the salesperson. In this situation, the salesperson simply does the best that he/she can by conducting the investigating needs appointment over the telephone or by other means such as teleconferencing or other electronic means. Needless to say, a face-to-face appointment is the best situation to have but is not always possible.

Telephone Tips for Telemarketers/Telesales Making Appointments

Many people starting their career in sales will begin in telemarketing or tele-sales. For example, Hilton Direct, Marriott's Event Booking Centers, and Wyndam Express all hire new salespeople to begin a career in selling through their centralized inbound and outbound telesales operations. With increasing experience, these beginning salespeople will move toward consultative selling. Thus, it's important to be familiar with the basics of using the telephone either to make appointments for other salespeople or to sell simple products or services such as small meetings over the telephone (transactional selling). Ron Marks (1997, 212) offers some key tips for telephone effectiveness.

Identification. The attention-getting effort begins when the prospect answers the telephone and the salesperson introduces himself/herself. The introduction contains three clearly enunciated elements: the prospect's name (use the appropriate title—Mr. or Ms.), the salesperson's name, and the salesperson's company. At this early point in the conversation, the salesperson should speed up the rate of conversation, because it is likely that the prospect begins to prepare himself/herself to say "not interested." A faster paced rate of conversation allows the salesperson to move quickly to the *lead-in*.

The Lead-In. A lead-in is a statement that attracts the prospect's attention and is meant to cause him/her to allow the salesperson to continue the conversation. The lead-in statement might include

- a third-party reference—this is an especially effective lead-in
- mention of literature sent to the prospect by the salesperson or the company
- reference to the prospect's or the salesperson's recent company advertising
- a statement of a known problem in the prospect's industry
- pertinent points made by a recognized figure in the prospect's industry at a recent conference or in an article
- the inactive account approach: "We haven't heard from you in a while."

Interest-Capturing Statement. Once the salesperson has attracted the prospect's attention with a lead-in, the objective is to give the prospect a reason to continue the conversation. Ideally, the statement would be a benefit statement that would be matched with a known and pressing need that the prospect has. This pressing need might have been learned through research during the pre-negotiation phase. For example, "Ms. Meeting Planner, I understand that you are looking for a quality hotel that offers a training facility at a price that will meet your significantly constrained budget. As a new conference center, we are offering introductory rates to build up our business."

Of course, you may not have such detailed information on the prospective buyer. You may have to approximate pressing needs, gaining this information from general trade reading or other experienced sources.

Stating Purpose and Asking for an Appointment. Following an interest-capturing statement, the salesperson continues logically. For example, "Ms. Meeting Planner, our low introductory rates will provide you a high-quality conference facility that should be within your constrained budget. Can we set up an appointment to meet next Wednesday at 3 PM or Thursday at 10 AM to discuss this and other needs in more detail?"

Your goal is to get the appointment so that you or the salesperson for whom you are setting up an appointment can enter into a full buying/selling exchange process. Only a full process can actually sell. An abbreviated telephone call will not sell, so don't be tempted. Giving away too much information on the phone runs the risk that you will be turned down for your real objective: getting the appointment.

Handling Objections or Resistance on the Telephone. The prospective buyer may object to setting an appointment. What do you do? Recognize that objections indicate a need for clarification, not a personal slight. First, if the objection is real, such as suggested appointment times don't work, ask for other times that are convenient. Or, if you have caught the prospect at an inconvenient time, recognize this and offer to call back at another time. If the objection is not real—for instance if the prospective buyer stalls—he/she is not interested; try to get an appointment based on the fact that he/she really doesn't know enough about the product unless you can hold the appointment. "How about an appointment limited to 15 minutes to provide you additional information? If you still are not interested, I promise I will stop persisting." It is especially tough to deal with objections over the phone. It's an impersonal situation and one that allows a prospective buyer to simply disengage. This is why most complex products need to be sold person-to-person and face-to-face.

Voice Mail. The reality is that it is getting more and more difficult to contact prospective buyers in the age of voice mail and phone machines that are used to screen phone calls. Thus, when leaving a recorded message:

1. Have a pleasant phone voice and follow the above rules to have impact.
2. Use a referral name if possible in the lead-in.
3. Give a sound reason for them to call back: usually a benefit.

4. Consider setting a firm appointment when you will call back, and thus maintain control of the situation.

How to Make an Effective Face-to-Face Approach

After obtaining an appointment to meet with the prospective buyer, the seller has an opportunity to enter the negotiation process face-to-face. As mentioned earlier, consultative salespeople have different purposes in mind during multi-call negotiating sessions: in the first session (appointment) they seek to discover needs and in the second session seek to gain commitment or make a sale. Also, in the hospitality and hotel business, it is an ideal situation if you can conduct the second appointment during a prospective buyer's on-property site visit.

The first thing that happens is initial contact with the potential buyer: the buyer and seller approach one another. If the approach is effective, the seller will be given the opportunity to complete the full negotiation process. If it is not effective, his/her opportunity to proceed toward commitment or close may be lost. Without an effective approach there may be little chance for a sale.

The approach in both the first and second appointments of a multi-call negotiating session has two objectives: (1) to establish or reestablish *rapport* with the prospective buyer and (2) to capture the potential buyer's full *attention*. In a first appointment to investigate needs, a third objective is to have the prospective buyer reveal his/her complete list of needs, desires, wants, and problems needing a solution. In the second appointment, to demonstrate capability, a third objective is to generate *interest* in the salesperson's proposed solution to the prospective buyer's need, desire, or problem to be solved using a product or service. The approach is analogous to the aesthetics, headline, and subline of an advertisement, which generally follow the AIDA formula: *attention, interest, desire,* and *action*. The salesperson must be aesthetically pleasant, unthreatening, and perceived as helpful rather than adversarial. The salesperson must obtain the prospective buyer's attention by connecting with the buyer's need to solve his/her problem or satisfy his/her need. And, the salesperson must translate this initial attention into enough interest so that the buyer will commit time to continue the conversation. Successfully achieving these three objectives sets the stage for a detailed give-and-take negotiation process. Let's look at each of these objectives in more detail.

Establishing Rapport.   It's a commonplace phrase: "First impressions are lasting impressions." And, it's also well known that people generally form first impressions within the first several seconds to minutes of meeting you. What does a positive or negative first impression mean for conducting a negotiating session? It can be the difference between success and failure. Within this short period of time a relationship can be established or denied. The meaning and ramifications of the approach are crucial. According to Mark McCormack, author of *What They Don't Teach You at the Harvard Business School:*

> *In any new business situation there is a kind of mutual sizing up that goes on between the players. Each is trying subtly to exert his/her influence over the other. Whoever is better equipped to control the impressions being formed will walk away accomplishing the most, certainly in the short term and most likely in the long term as well (Manning and Reese 1997, 204).*

Manning and Reese (1997) report some of the findings of a Wilson Learning Corporation study that help to better understand the first short period of building rapport. The study tested the idea that "a certain degree of social penetration (interpersonal comfort) is necessary for a buyer/seller relationship to develop to the degree that the two parties can engage in a decision-making process [negotiation process]." As seen from the buyer's viewpoint, three factors emerged as essential to establish the initial rapport that would provide the foundation to effectively proceed with the negotiation process.

competence—The salesperson is technically qualified to help solve a buying problem.

propriety—The salesperson is the "right" kind of person to be working with. "This person is enough like me to understand and deal with my problem." Propriety is an intangible that is connected with communication styles (see Chapter 7). Propriety can be positively or negatively affected by a mannerism, gesture, style of dress, breach of etiquette, or conversational topic that is offensive to the customer.

trustworthiness—The salesperson can be trusted. "This person really wants to help me solve my problem." Like propriety, trustworthiness is an intangible that is positively or negatively affected by the same factors (Manning and Reese 1997, 205).

According to Ron Marks (1997, 237–244), establishing rapport is concerned with the following issues:

appearance—Appearance extends beyond just the appropriateness of the salesperson's dress. For example, a salesperson may make a poor impression by handing the receptionist a grimy business card instead of a crisp new one or by pulling an obviously worn sample or a crumpled flyer out of his/her briefcase. Something as small as an appointment book may detract from a positive image. One bulging with papers sticking out is distracting and sends a negative image. Another example of a negative appearance would be taking the prospect to lunch in a cluttered car.

shaking hands—Not too much and not too little. Shake hands firmly but don't overdo or underdo it. Don't pump, give limp digits, give a wet rag, or present a nonrelease clamp. Not everyone shakes hands. If the prospect holds back, don't force it. Be aware of how much of the hand is involved in the shake. Offering only the front half of the fingers says, "I don't want to become too involved with you." Palm to palm, web to web is a safe choice.

posture—Some people make assumptions about another person's self-esteem and the product that he/she is selling based on his/her posture. "How shallow," you say, but it's true—just think about your own experiences with people. The body projects confidence, competence, dignity, and enthusiasm when held upright, with the head straight and shoulders pulled back. On the other hand, the body projects insecurity, disinterest, and lack of conviction when it is slumped with rounded back, a bowed head, and slack shoulders. Distribute your weight in a balanced way: feet should be shoulder-width apart, knees should be slightly bent and relaxed, and do not rock or sway.

eye contact—Another important element of first impressions is eye contact. In our society, the salesperson should make immediate eye contact. This projects honesty, sincerity, and attentiveness. Failure to make eye contact, on the other hand, may convey dishonesty, insincerity, and lack of attention. Just as a handshake should be balanced between limp and bone crushing, eye contact must also be balanced in the duration of the gaze. A prolonged gaze could be interpreted as a threatening stare, whereas rapid darting of the eyes from place to place is often interpreted as somewhat sneaky and perhaps much less than sincere. The right amount of time is no longer than a gaze eye-to-eye followed by a brief break.

etiquette—As you learned in Chapter 7, different people respond to different communication styles. Although etiquette may vary somewhat depending on the prospective buyer's communication style, there are some general rules that need to be observed, especially if you are unaware of the prospective buyer's style.

◆ Driving a nice car is a good idea, but a flashy car might awaken a buyer's mind to those negative stereotypes of salespeople. And, it might make the buyer question whether or not buyers are overcharged.

◆ Don't make pushy demands to see the buyer. This usually will be perceived as discourteous and result in the buyer finding reasons not to see you.

◆ If you smoke, don't do it around the buyer. Simply assume he/she doesn't smoke.

◆ Absolutely, remember the buyer's name and use it frequently. However, this must be kept in balance to avoid the impression that the salesperson is practicing techniques.

◆ When in the buyer/seller exchange process, take notes, but ask for permission first. This shows courtesy as well as attention to detail.

◆ Use common pleasantries often: please, thank you, and you're welcome.

◆ Avoid unconscious mannerisms and habits of speech. For example, some people pull at their chins, rub their noses, flick their hair, tap a pen, drum fingers, hitch up a skirt or slacks, and many other such mannerisms. When speaking, many people use filler words such as *well, now, frankly, bottom-line, you know*, and so on. All these things distract the buyer and get in the way of an effective buying/selling exchange process. How do you know about *unconscious* mannerisms and habitual speech? Ask a trusted friend or coworker. After all, you want to maximize your potential for success.

◆ Don't waste a busy buyer's time. Often a buyer will already know about many of the points the salesperson is prepared to talk about. Be sensitive and adjust accordingly.

◆ Be friendly but do not take this to the extreme. Again remember that people have different communication styles. A salesperson may like being touched on the arm and shoulder and being called by his/her first name; the buyer, on the other hand, may be offended by such behavior.

◆ Most important, be honest. Especially in consultative selling, credibility and integrity are the glue of building relationships. If you don't know something, say so, but also suggest that you will find the answer and report back. Then make sure you deliver on your promise. Not delivering will send negative signals and sabotage a sale and the ability to build relationships.

social conversation or small talk—This is part of establishing the social rapport that breaks tensions that often characterize the first meeting of a buyer and seller. Small talk is expected in our society and culture. In some cultures more is expected, whereas in others less is expected. Doing your homework during the pre-negotiation phase of the buying/selling exchange process can help in understanding your prospective customer's interests. If you don't know them, you can obtain many clues simply by looking around the buyer's office for plaques, pictures, and so forth, which can provide some clues. The last fallback position is to talk about general news and the old favorite, the weather. Some topics for icebreaker conversations can be helpful.

◆ a personal interest of buyers or their families, if the salesperson has such information from the pre-negotiation phase

◆ a sincere and deserved compliment (not an obvious attempt to please) about the prospect's plant, products, office, or community activities—an obviously insincere flattering remark will backfire and cause a negative impression

◆ some pleasant news about the industry: favorable legislation, economic upturns, or new technology

Remember that most people like to hear positive remarks about themselves. As the old saying goes, "If you want to be perceived as a gifted conversationalist at a cocktail party, simply ask good questions about the person you are speaking with."

When does the salesperson know when to shift the conversation from social talk to business talk? It varies by individual situation, but this comes with experience. Don't engage so long that the prospective buyer must say, "Let's get down to business." If this happens, the social conversation has gone on too long and might cause a negative impression about the salesperson.

It's best to attempt a smooth transition from the social conversation to the business conversation. This transition statement leads to the final two objectives of the approach: obtaining buyer attention and activating interest.

How-To's—**Capturing the Prospective Buyer's Attention and Activating Interest.** As stated earlier, the approach step of the buying/selling exchange process has three objectives: (1) to establish rapport with the prospective buyer, (2) to capture the prospective buyer's full attention, and (3) to generate interest in the potential solution (your product or service) to his/her need, desire, or problem to be solved. We have just completed a discussion of how to obtain an appointment and establish rapport once the salesperson has gained entry to meet with the prospective buyer. After the rapport-building stage, the salesperson must capture the prospective buyer's attention and activate his/her interest in the business at hand. This is done by making a transition statement to the business at hand.

As we discussed earlier, you may find yourself in a multi-call negotiation session. For example, the purpose of your appointment with the prospective buyer might be only to learn about his/her needs (see Chapter 9). Or, you may have already completed a sales call so that you know your prospective buyer's needs, and the purpose of your sales appointment might be to present a proposal that you have worked up that you believe will satisfy the customer's needs. The transition statement to the business at hand should reflect the purpose of your appointment.

Approach: First Appointment—Investigating Needs. If you are on the first sales appointment to learn about your prospective customer's needs, then a transition statement after establishing initial rapport and leading from the social conversation to the business conversation might go something like this:

First, pause after the social conversation. Next, introduce an attention and interest statement about your company or your product or service. If you have a unique product, service, or company, state why it's unique. This is like a headline in an advertisement: for example, you could say, "Ms. Meeting Planner, we have talked about the importance of successful meetings. Do you know anything about the Scottsdale Conference Center? Were you aware that we only host corporate meetings? Our extensive audiovisual equipment inventory, large number of meeting rooms, and custom-made conference furniture were specifically designed for meetings such as yours. We are focused specialists on corporate meetings."

This statement linked the social conversation to the business conversation while simultaneously differentiating this property from other competitive properties. It gained the meeting planner's attention and will activate the meeting planner's interest. Of course, there are other ways to make statements that grab attention and activate interest. Next, we must transition to the purpose of the appointment.

State the purpose of your first appointment. "Ms. Meeting Planner, I'm not here today to try to sell you anything. Your national sales meeting is too important, and I'm sure too complex, to make any decisions without fully exploring what you need. So, let's just talk about your meeting needs and the goals that you want to achieve with this national sales meeting. How does this sound?" Notice that the salesperson clearly informed the meeting planner of the purpose of the appointment and also asked him/her to confirm whether the agenda of the conversation was acceptable.

Approach: Second Appointment–Demonstrating Capability. The multi-call negotiation session is almost always used when the salesperson is using the consultative selling strategy and a win-win negotiation tactic. Why? Because he/she is selling complex and high-priced products and services. At a minimum, the salesperson meets with the prospective buyer and discovers his/her needs, wants, desires, and problems that need to be solved. After discovering the potential buyer's needs in the first appointment and making a second appointment for the near future, the salesperson goes back to his/her office or a location away from the prospective buyer and designs a proposal. A proposal is nothing more than a document that outlines the salesperson's creative solution to the prospective buyer's needs or problems. It packages, lists, and prices specific products and services that are matched to the known prospective buyer needs. A sales presentation *demonstrating capability* is nothing more than a salesperson showing the proposal to the prospective buyer and discussing whether it will satisfy their needs.

If you are a salesperson in a multi-call negotiation session and the purpose of your appointment is to present the proposal, you makes a transition from social conversation in the following manner:

Similar to the above discussion, first, pause after the social conversation. Next, as we illustrated above, introduce an attention and interest statement about your company or product or service.

State the purpose of your second appointment. "Ms. Meeting Planner, I'm sure that you want your national sales meeting to successfully motivate and energize your sales force. I would like to go over the proposal that I worked up for you. How does that sound?" Again, after creating attention and interest, you stated the purpose of your appointment and asked the meeting planner if this agenda was agreeable to him/her. With this preface, we are now about to proceed to the *demonstrating capability* step of the buying/selling exchange process that will be fully discussed in Chapter 10.

SUMMARY ◆

The buying/selling exchange process is composed of three phases: Phase One—Pre-Negotiation Strategy, Phase Two—Negotiation Process Strategy, and Phase Three—Post-Negotiation Strategy. This chapter has been concerned with the first step in Phase Two. Step One, approaching the buyer, is the initial opening introduction and contact between the buyer and the seller. This initial period establishes the overall environment within which the entire negotiation process (buying/selling exchange process) will take place. Starting off on the right foot is essential for final success in any endeavor, especially in selling.

Specifically, we have discussed how to select and qualify potential buyers. We introduced a probability system that advances potential buyers (suspects) with a low probability of eventually becoming an actual buyer to potential buyers (prospects) who actually make a purchase and transform into customers. Probability advancement of suspects to prospects to customers is based on increased qualifications or likelihood of eventually becoming an actual buyer, and assessments of these probabilities are made by experienced salespeople.

We discussed methods to obtain a first face-to-face appointment with a prospective buyer and the effective actions to be practiced by salespeople in the approach. We also stressed the importance of the approach step in setting the tone of the entire negotiation process and as the first of several steps that are systematically designed to lead to a salesperson's gaining commitment in Step Five, which is fully discussed in Chapter 12.

References

Manning, G. L., and B. L. Reece. 1997. *Selling today.* 7th ed. Upper Saddle River, NJ: Prentice Hall.

Marks, R. B. 1997. *Personal selling: A relationship approach.* Upper Saddle River, NJ: Prentice Hall.

McNeill, R. G. 2001. The successful salesperson of the future: A master of complex consultative selling. *Marketing Review* 18(1):24–31.

◈ DISCUSSION QUESTIONS

1. What three types of information does a salesperson need to qualify a potential buyer?
2. Consider for a moment that you would like to gain a management-level position with a hotel company in Las Vegas, Nevada. Describe the strategies and tactics you believe would be effective in developing suspects into prospects and prospects into potential employers.
3. Imagining the same scenario described in question #2, describe the tactics you would use to gain an appointment with a potential employer. How would you prepare yourself for that first meeting?
4. Contrary to the old adage "Don't judge a book by its cover," what social skills and aspects of appearance are important for the salesperson to develop?

CHAPTER 9

Phase Two—Investigating Needs

After reading this chapter, you should be able to

- explain the importance of questioning skills and active listening skills for discovering and understanding customer needs
- identify types of questions by purpose and function

- describe the range of potentially complex customer motives and needs

active listening techniques

buying motives

situation questions

problem questions

implication questions

need-payoff questions

probing questions

confirmation questions

Intimate knowledge and deep understanding of a prospective buyer's needs, wants, desires, value perceptions, and problems are the mandatory keys to achieving competitive advantage. The salesperson who has first established a trusting relationship, sincerely projects a genuine problem-solving attitude, and is highly skilled in questioning and creating an atmosphere of open discussion will usually have the advantage over his/her competitors and win the sale.

A doctor does not prescribe medication until the patient's symptoms have been identified. A lawyer does not give a client advice until the legal problem has been carefully studied and confirmed. A financial consultant does not recommend a stock or bond without knowing about a customer's investment objectives or ability to handle risk. Like a doctor who uses various instruments to conduct an examination of patients, a consultative salesperson uses questions as his/her instruments to conduct an examination of the prospective buyer (Marks 1997; and Manning and Reese 1997).

When a consultative selling strategy is being used, thorough questioning is even more important. Why? Because the products and services being sold are usually complex and have a high price tag. Complex products and services are usually associated with complex customer needs and related complex customer problems that require a solution. Only after many in-depth and **probing questions** can the salesperson learn enough about these customer requirements in order to customize a solution.

Obviously, having a developed relationship between seller and buyer creates an atmosphere of trust wherein customers feel free to openly discuss their business needs and desires. This is the reason that consultative sellers use relationship tactics in order to practice win-win negotiations.

In Chapters 3 and 4, we discussed customer needs as related to their perception of *value*. Customers will pay only for value and value can be found in the product or service itself or in the way the salesperson handles the buying/selling exchange process. So, if the salesperson wants to make a sale, he/she must give the customer the value that he/she seeks. And, the only way to discover the value sought by a prospective buyer is by asking questions and actively listening in order to thoroughly investigate customer needs.

Before we proceed to discuss Step Two of Phase Two, investigating needs, let's remind ourselves of where our discussion from previous chapters has taken us. Let's briefly review the entire buying/selling exchange process that we first introduced in Chapter 7 (see Table 9–1).

In Phase One of the buying/selling exchange process, we thoroughly prepared and preplanned our negotiation strategy before we approached the prospect in Phase Two, Step One (Chapter 8). During our actual approach in our first appointment, we accomplished two objectives. First, we established rapport with the buyer, which helped to create an effective environment for

Table 9–1 Table Comparison of the Buying/Selling Exchange Process and the Negotiation Process	
THE BUYING/SELLING EXCHANGE PROCESS	**THE NEGOTIATION PROCESS**
Phase One – Pre-Negotiation Strategy: Negotiation Planning and Preparation (Chapter 7)	**Phase One – Pre-Negotiation Strategy: Negotiation Planning and Preparation (Chapter 7)**
Step One – Understanding Sales Process	**Step One** – Understanding Negotiation Process
Step Two – Research Potential Customer	**Step Two** – Know Your and Your Customers' Interests
Step Three – Sales Tactics	**Step Three** – Negotiation Tactics
Phase Two – Negotiation Process Strategy	**Phase Two – Negotiation Process Strategy**
Step One – Approaching the Buyer (Chapter 8)	**Step One** – Opening
Step Two – Investigating Needs (Chapter 9)	**Step Two** – Exploring
Step Three – Demonstrating Capability (Chapter 10)	**Step Three** – Proposing Agreement
Step Four – Negotiating Concerns (Chapter 11)	**Step Four** – Clarifying Proposal
Step Five – Gaining Commitment (Chapter 12)	**Step Five** – Gaining Commitment
Phase Three – Post-Sales Strategy (Chapter 13)	**Phase Three – Post-Negotiation Strategy**
Step One – After-Sale Implementation	**Step One** – Implementing Agreement
Step Two – Maintenance & Development	**Step Two** – Conducting Self-Critique
Step Three – Continuous Improvement	

an open and honest dialogue. Second, we made a transition from our rapport-building social conversation to a business conversation. Here we stated the reason and purpose for our appointment. Our reason and purpose for this first appointment is investigating needs. We will not attempt to sell anything at this time. We are in this first appointment to do one thing only: to thoroughly discover and understand all of the prospect's needs.

As a consultative salesperson your task is to discover all the needs and problems that the prospective buyer has so you can help him/her solve them using the benefits of your product or service. At the end of this appointment in a multi-call negotiation session, you will thank the prospective buyer for his/her time and set up a future appointment to meet again at a second appointment. At the second appointment you will present your proposal, which is the written and priced plan of how your product or service can solve the prospective buyer's problems or satisfy his/her needs (discussed in Chapter 10). Then, you will excuse yourself and return to your office to write up this proposal.

So, how do you accomplish the purpose of your appointment? How do you investigate the prospective buyer's needs and problems to be solved? By asking good questions and actively listening to the answers. These two skills result in an active and, ideally, honest dialogue between the buyer and the seller. The successful results of this dialogue process are threefold: (1) *joint decision making* through which the buyer and seller, consultatively and in partnership, arrive at a sound buying decision, (2) *a high-quality customized solution* to the buyer's need or problem, and (3) the creation of *foundations for a strong and ongoing relationship*.

In this chapter, we will first discuss *questioning skills*. Second, we will discuss *active listening skills*. Third, we will illustrate these skills with a role-play script between a seller and buyer.

Questioning Skills

Questioning skills are dependent first on having knowledge about the various types of questions and second on the ability to apply these questions in the appropriate situations. There are two types of question categories: (1) questions classified by the type of information they hope to gain and (2) questions categorized by their functional purpose. The first category of questions is designed to obtain a specific type of information. The second category is concerned with the way the first category of questions is asked. This will become clearer as we proceed in our discussion.

The First Category of Questions, Classified by Type of Information Sought

Investigating needs is probably the most important opportunity within the buying/selling exchange process for a consultative salesperson to add value. By uncovering complex buyer needs, the salesperson immediately puts himself/herself in a position to help the prospective customer find a successful solution to his/her buying problems. Generally, when selling complex products and services, the more needs that the salesperson can uncover, the greater competitive advantage this salesperson will have over other salespeople. Salespeople uncover needs through extensive questioning.

There are four general classifications of questions categorized by their purpose or information that they attempt to obtain. These four classifications are prioritized in a specific order. The order proceeds from the simplest to the most sophisticated. The first two—the simplest classifications—are adequate when using a transactional selling strategy. All four types are necessary when using a consultative or alliance selling strategy. Neil Rackham has popularized this classification list well in his 1988 book, *SPIN Selling* (Rackham 1988, 17).

Questions Sufficient for Noncomplex Selling or Transactional Selling Strategies.
Situation Questions—These are data-gathering questions sometimes referred
to as *fact-finding* questions. Since consultative salespeople do a lot of preplanning and investigation, these should not be overused.

For example, "How many attendees?" "What is your budget?" "What hotels are you also considering?"

Problem Questions—After the fact-finding questions, successful salespeople tend to move to *feel-finding* questions. These are called *problem questions*
because they explore problems, difficulties, and dissatisfactions in areas where
the seller's product or service can help. Inexperienced people generally don't
ask enough of these.

For example, "Are you worried that your meeting will not be successful?"
"Have you encountered problems and disappointments with past meetings
and the meeting hotel?"

Additional Questions Necessary for Complex Consultative/Alliance Selling.
Implication Questions—These questions start with the customer's problems
and explore the problems' effects or consequences. This helps the salesperson
to understand the seriousness or urgency of the problem. Also, these help to
amplify the seriousness to the customer (bring urgency to the forefront of
his/her mind). These questions are particularly important in complex (con-
sultative/alliance) selling situations. Even very experienced salespeople rarely
ask them well, but these are the key to success.

For example, "What effect does the lack of seamless and flawless coordination have on your meeting's success?" "Is the success of this meeting important to your career advancement?"

Need-Payoff Questions—The goal of these questions is to get the customer deeply involved—to get the customer to recognize and tell the salesperson (verbalize) the benefits that the seller's product or service can provide.
It's clear that the buyer is very interested and involved when he/she actually
verbalizes or suggests the benefits himself/herself.

For example, "If we could provide you certainty of a successful meeting,
how would that help you?" "Would it be useful for us to assign a conference
service manager (CSM) on a full-time basis to coordinate your meeting?"

In summary, within the first category of questions, we find four classifications designed to obtain specific types of information regarding the prospective buyer's needs and problems to be solved. The information sought in each
of these four classifications is obtained by using a second category of questions.
This second category of questions is classified into *purpose* questions and *type
of information sought* questions. For example, a *situation question* (classification #1) might be asked using a *probing question* (#2 in Table 9–2). The purpose of a probing question is to extract additional information.

The Second Category of Questions, Classified by Purpose

Whereas the first category of questions informs the salesperson of the type of information that he/she is attempting to obtain, the second category of questions can be viewed as *tools* used for a specific purpose. For example, as previously discussed, a *probing question* (#2, Table 9–2) is a *tool* to pry or extract more information out of a reticent prospective buyer. The buyer may not be giving enough information in his/her answers, so the salesperson probes further. Another example is the use of a **confirmation question** (#3, Table 9–2).

Table 9–2 Purpose Questions: Definitions, Uses, and Examples

QUESTION	DEFINITION	WHEN USED	EXAMPLES
1. Information Gathering	General questions designed to get the prospect to disclose certain types of basic information. Classified: 1. Fact-finding (factual motives/needs) and 2. Feel-finding (emotional motives/needs).	Usually at the beginning of the sale and during the need discovery stage.	How many attendees do you have for this meeting? *(fact-finding)* What is your measure of success for this meeting? *(feel-finding)*
2. Probing	More specific questions designed to uncover and clarify the prospect's perceptions and opinions. Probing questions are of two types: Open-ended: invites an expansive answer. Closed-ended: short answers, yes or no.	When you feel the need to obtain more specific information to fully understand the problem. Usually used when the prospect has not fully answered a previous question.	What do you mean by your statement that, "you want this meeting to create a feeling of camaraderie?" (*open-ended* question) So you are saying that you don't want an open bar for the reception (*closed-ended* question—yes or no answer)
3. Confirmation	Designed to find out whether or not your message is understood by the prospect.	After each important item of information is presented. Especially during their presentation of matching product benefits with needs.	Is that what you had in mind? Do you see the merits of having your VIPs housed in suites?
4. Summary Confirmation	Designed to clarify your understanding of the prospect's needs. Also used at end of presentation.	Usually used at the beginning of the sales presentation (to confirm that you have all of the needs correctly identified). Also used periodically to summarize if a lot of information is being discussed.	I would like to summarize what you have told me so far: You need one meeting room. You need lunch for 50. You need . . . etc., until all needs are summarized.

The salesperson uses this *tool* to find out if the prospective buyer agrees or disagrees with a statement that the salesperson has just made.

Listening and Acknowledging Customer Response

The listening rate for most people is about 25 percent, meaning they miss about 75 percent of the messages spoken by other people. This ratio can be improved by developing *active listening skills*—the process of sending back to the speaker what you as a listener think he/she meant, in terms of both content and feelings. It involves taking into consideration both verbal and nonverbal signals.

Four Active-Listening Techniques. When the listener uses **active listening techniques,** the feedback allows a check on accuracy and gives the speaker the opportunity to confirm or amend the listener's perceptions (object to inter-pretation/feedback). Active listening involves five techniques (Manning and Reese 1997).

1. **Encourage Talking.** "I see," "good point," and "go on." These short prompts or cues indicate that you are listening and that you understand the person's message and want him/her to keep talking.

2. **Take Notes.** Although not necessary at every sales presentation, taking notes is critical during complex selling (consultative selling) where accurate and detailed information is essential to create a good written proposal. To be polite, be sure to ask for permission to take notes. And remember that the customer is often taken off the defensive (thinking, "here comes a sales pitch") to a feeling of "my needs are important."

3. **Paraphrase the Customer's Meaning with a Confirmation Question.** This is also called "reflective" listening. It clarifies meaning and also shows the customer that you are interested in gaining accurate information. For example, "Ms. Client, what I here you saying is . . . Is that right?" Also, echo your perceptions of what the customer is feeling or perceiving: "You seem to be a little concerned with what I just presented. How are you feeling?"

4. **Obtain Feedback.** Make sure that you get the customer to respond to your questions above. This will actively involve the customer and demonstrate your interest in him/her.

5. **Establish Buying Motives.** The primary goal of questioning, listening, and acknowledging is to uncover prospect needs and establish **buying motives.** Our efforts to discover prospect needs will be more effective when the buyer's primary reasons for buying are uncovered. As mentioned in earlier discussions, buyers usually have both *rational* and *emotional* reasons for buying.

Some observers of the art of selling have made this poignant statement: "Buyers buy on emotion and justify their purchase on rationale." Think about a time when you personally bought something that might have been too expensive. If asked why you bought it, did you give the real reason or justify your purchase with creative rational reasons? Think hard! Emotional motivation is usually an underlying factor in most purchases and is often prevalent in business-to-business (B2B) markets where one might think rationale is *always* the guiding motivation.

Although a prospective buyer may state many needs, there usually is a primary motive for buying. This primary motive or buying need is often referred to as a *hot button* in selling terminology. Be sure you don't miss this primary motive. It is essential to know this motive when making a selling presentation.

While speaking of motivators, some observers of the art of selling have distilled emotional motivators down to two primary sources: gain/desire or loss/fear. You should think about this *stark statement* in more depth. Does one want to *gain* status? Does one *fear loss* of love? Does one want to *gain* wealth? Does one *fear loss* of managerial power? More subtly, does one *desire* to be thought of as giving? Does one *fear loss* of credibility? We could continue, but you get the idea and probably can think of examples on your own to verify the statement above.

So, how do you uncover prospective buyers' needs that also are related to underlying motivations? You ask thorough questions and actively listen to their answers. At a minimum, sellers should always ask *fact-finding questions* (to discover rational needs) and *feel-finding questions* (to discover the underlying emotional motivators). As more sophisticated selling strategies are used, the seller should begin to ask all four types of questions suggested by Neil Rackham in his book *SPIN Selling,* as discussed earlier (Rackham 1988).

The Investigating Needs Appointment

Remember, we have already prepared and preplanned for our multi-call negotiation session (Phase One—Pre-Negotiation Strategy: Negotiation Preparation and Planning—Chapter 7). And, in Chapter 8, we learned how to approach prospects effectively in face-to-face appointments.

Phase Two, Step Two of the buying/selling exchange process (see Table 9–1) is our first appointment in a multi-call negotiation session. Our purpose is to investigate the prospective buyer's needs. After we have discovered these needs, we will prepare a *proposal* and return for a second appointment to present this proposal (see Chapter 10). Our second appointment is meant to accomplish different purposes. These will be examined three times in increasing complexity: in Chapter 10—demonstrating capability, Chapter 11—negotiating concerns, and Chapter 12—gaining commitment. In our second appointment, we will ideally make a sale or have the prospective buyer agree to continue considering working with us in other future sales appointments after which we hope the sale will be made.

Let's look at the logical steps of systematically investigating needs by magnifying Step Two of Phase Two in the buying/selling exchange process presented above in Table 9–1. In Table 9–3 we will look at the details of the *investigating needs* step.

Table 9–3 Objectives in the Investigating Needs Negotiation Session

PHASE TWO – NEGOTIATION PROCESS STRATEGY

Step One – Approaching the Buyer (Chapter 8)

Objective #1 – Approach and Establish the Relationship

1. Establish rapport and a relationship. This is the first appointment of a multi-call negotiation session. The salesperson knows some things about the prospective buyer either from research, from information in his/her prospect/customer database, or from prior contact from other social or business settings. This is the social conversation. The salesperson makes enthusiastic comments about information he/she may have and about commonalities that are now known.
2. Communicate positive *body* language (good entrance, carriage, handshake, and seating posture).
3. Communicate positive *verbal* language (use positive words, show enthusiasm with a well-modulated voice).
4. Use the prospect's name effectively (at least three times).

Objective #2 – Transition from Social to Business Conversation

1. Make a transition statement from social conversation to business conversation and purpose. Communicate the sales appointment objectives (share with the prospect why the salesperson is on this appointment).
2. Ask permission to take effective nondistracting notes (salesperson was organized and prepared to take notes). Use a proposal checklist form as described in Chapter 8, Table 8–2.

Step Two – Investigating Needs (Chapter 9)

Objective #3 – Question to Investigate Customer Needs

1. Ask quality information-gathering questions (salesperson is prepared and questions were both *information* [SPIN] and *purpose* questions).
2. Ask quality probing questions (follow-up questions to clarify and secure all details of the customer's meaning).
3. Verify special customer needs by asking good confirmation questions (salesperson needs to be accurate and correct in interpreting all of the prospect's needs).

Step Five – Gaining Commitment (Chapter 12)

1. Set up the next appointment (salesperson requests another meeting to be able to *demonstrate capability* of his/her product or service features and benefits that will "solve" customer's meeting needs). Suggest and write down the date, time, and place in day planner or record in Palm Pilot or laptop.
2. Thank the prospect (salesperson communicates appreciation and indicates enthusiasm for second and/or next meeting appointment).

◆ SUMMARY

For a consultative salesperson, *investigating needs* is the most important step in the buying/selling exchange process. A doctor does not prescribe medication until the patient's symptoms have been identified. A lawyer does not give a client advice until the legal problem has been carefully studied and confirmed. A financial consultant does not recommend a stock or bond without knowing about a customer's investment objectives or ability to handle risk. Like a doctor who uses various instruments to conduct an examination of patients, a consultative salesperson uses questions as his/her instruments to conduct an examination of the prospective buyer. In this chapter, we discussed the tools that a consultative salesperson uses to thoroughly examine his/her prospective buyer: first, we discussed *questioning skills;* second, we discussed *active listening skills;* and finally, we will conclude by illustrating these skills with a role-play script between a seller and buyer.

Intimate knowledge and understanding of a prospective buyer's needs, wants, desires, value perceptions, and problems that need to be solved are the mandatory key to achieving competitive advantage. A salesperson who has first established a trusting relationship, sincerely projects a genuine problem-solving attitude, and is highly skilled in questioning and creating an atmosphere of open discussion will usually have an advantage over his/her competitors and win the sale.

Only a thorough knowledge of a prospective buyer's needs, wants, desires, and problems to be solved can prepare a salesperson to seamlessly move to the next step of the process: Phase Two, Step Three—demonstrating capability. Now that the salesperson thoroughly understands the needs of his/her prospective buyer, he/she will prepare a written *proposal* and present it at the next appointment, the *demonstrating capability* step. How to prepare a proposal and effectively present it is the topic of the next chapter.

References

Manning, G. L., and B. L. Reece. 1997. *Selling today.* 7th ed. Upper Saddle River, NJ: Prentice Hall.

Marks, R. B. 1997. *Personal selling: A relationship approach.* Upper Saddle River, NJ: Prentice Hall.

Rackham, N. 1988. *SPIN selling.* New York: McGraw-Hill.

◆ DISCUSSION QUESTIONS

1. Someone once commented that it is important to "first understand and then be understood." Why is this advice important to the salesperson?
2. Probing questions are useful in acquiring what types of information?

3. Describe the five active listening techniques explained in this chapter. What does their use communicate to the buyer?

4. Do organizational buyers ever have emotional reasons that motivate their purchase decisions? Describe such a potential hot button.

ROLE-PLAY: A Seller and Buyer Engaged in Investigating Needs

Role-Play Members

1. Hotel Park Plaza salesperson—Jim Parker
2. YWCA meeting planner, prospective buyer—Erin Massey

Role-Play Specifications

1.   The purpose of this first appointment is to discover the prospect's needs or buying conditions. *Investigating needs* is the most important thing a consultative salesperson can do. (Thoroughly understanding needs allows the salesperson to later address these needs with product or service solutions.)

2.   Jim will not attempt to sell anything at this meeting. He has made this first appointment and meeting for the sole purpose of discovering Erin's YWCA meeting needs.

3.   Jim will end the conversation by telling Erin that he will go back to his office to write a *proposal*. (The proposal will contain Jim's priced product or service solutions, explicitly addressing Erin's stated needs.)

4.   Jim will make a second appointment to come back the next week to meet with Erin. At the second appointment, Jim will present or demonstrate capabilities of his proposed solutions for her needs. Jim will refer to his written proposal. (Note: A formal *sales presentation* or *demonstrating capability* is nothing more than a salesperson's presenting a written proposal that spells out solutions to the customer's needs.)

5.   The role-play model script follows the buying/selling exchange process model beginning at Phase Two, Step One and ending with Phase Two, Step Two.

6.   This is the first formal appointment on a multi-call negotiation session. Jim knows certain things about Erin. He has met her before and knows her cousin, Joan Winters. He has information about Erin stored in his prospect/customer database. Before setting up this appointment with Erin and based on information he has gathered, Jim has determined that Erin is a 60 percent probability prospect.

Role-Play Investigating Needs—Model Script

Phase Two—Negotiation Process Strategy (First Appointment)

Step One—The Approach

Objective #1—Approach and Establish the Relationship

JIM: Good morning, Ms. Massey. It's great to put a face with the voice. We've been talking for some time by phone and mail, so I'm happy to meet you at last. Thanks for inviting me over. By the way, did you catch the Wizards vs. the Celtics the other night? I can't believe Jordan. He's incredible for someone who has retired a couple of times . . . 46 points in one game . . . a true legend in his own time. *(Jim makes a good entrance, smiles, shakes hands, hands Erin his business card, and takes a seat when invited.)*

Note: Jim had learned from Erin's cousin, Joan Winters, that Erin was a Michael Jordan fan. Jim had recalled this information from his prospect/customer database while preparing for this appointment.

ERIN: I was there! In fact, I was seated right behind the players . . . fantastic experience. I didn't know you were a fan, too. And please, just call me Erin.

JIM: Yes, I'm a longtime fan.

Objective #1 (Continued)—Comment on Known Items about Erin Massey

JIM: Well, Erin, I also saw Joan Winters at the mall the other day. She told me to tell you, "Hi."

ERIN: We have a family reunion coming up in two weeks and I'm sure that I'll see her then, but thanks.

JIM: Six months ago, my family got together at their annual reunion. You know, in the end, there's no replacement for family.

ERIN: I'm happy you feel that way; I do.

Jim pauses.

Objective #2—The Transition from Social to Business Conversation

JIM: (transition statement away from social conversation to business conversation) I certainly appreciate your call to consider the Hotel Park Plaza for your upcoming meeting. I'm especially appreciative that you specifically asked for me.

I have always found that thoroughly understanding a customer's needs is the most important thing that I can do. I know that only if I have this information can I suggest how my hotel can help my client to have a successful meeting. Do you mind if I take notes while I ask you some questions?

ERIN: Sure, fire away.

Jim accomplishes several things here:

1. He states his purpose for the appointment.
2. He establishes an agenda for the appointment and has Erin agree.
3. He asks to take a few notes, thus showing interest as well as capturing information that might be difficult to remember.

Objective #3—Questioning to Investigate Customer Needs

Jim is using a *proposal checklist form* (see Chapter 8) to guide his questioning. He should learn enough about Erin's needs to allow him to prepare a proposal that he will present in a second appointment. Watch for two basic types of need questions: (1) fact-finding and (2) feel-finding. Remember, feel-finding questions are very important to uncovering the customer's true motivation for buying.

Fact-Finding Questions

Note: Jim writes down Erin's needs, as she talks.

JIM: First, what type of meeting are you planning?

ERIN: It's called the YWCA Physical Fitness Seminar.

JIM: Okay. When do you want to hold your meeting?

ERIN: The last Thursday of next month for one day.

JIM: Great. And how many people will be attending?

ERIN: There will be 150 people at the meeting, but 40 nonsmoking singles will stay overnight the night before.

JIM: Good. So what are your meeting accommodation needs?

ERIN: One meeting room theater style for 150 from 1:00 to 3:00 and a 3,000 square foot display (trade show) room from 3 PM to 7:30 PM.

JIM: Okay. And food and beverage needs?

ERIN: We will have a chicken banquet lunch at noon for 150 on the day of the meeting.

JIM: Will all of your attendees be flying in?

ERIN: The 40 seminar leaders, but no others. I'm glad you brought that up. We have to be sure to have a convenient downtown location with convenient parking.

JIM: (while writing) Downtown parking. Okay. *(looks up from notes at Erin)* Erin, everyone is seeking maximum value for cost, yet sometimes there are budgetary constraints. Do you have a budget for this meeting?

ERIN: We need to be in the neighborhood of $10,000.

Feel-Finding Questions

JIM: Erin, what is the objective of this meeting? What would be a mark of a successful meeting for you?

ERIN: I'm happy you asked this. While it's a physical fitness meeting and sounds ordinary, actually this is the kickoff meeting for a major series. This meeting has to "wow" the attendees. I want them to tell their friends. The success of this meeting is an important part of the YWCA's marketing plan. Its success is extremely important to me.

Probing—Open-Ended Question

This solicits anything else that the salesperson did not remember to ask.

JIM: We've covered a lot of things that are important to you in making this meeting standout. What other concerns do you have?

ERIN: Nothing else really. I think we have just about covered everything.

Probing—Closed-Ended Question

JIM: Are you sure?

ERIN: Yes.

At this time, Erin should have revealed enough meeting needs to Jim so that he can later prepare a proposal.

Step Five—Gaining Commitment

Gaining commitment does not always mean "closing a sale." Here, Jim simply wants Erin to commit to two things: (1) that she agrees to have Jim prepare a proposal and (2) that she will set a firm second appointment (in the multi-call negotiation session) so that Jim can present that proposal to her.

In the *investigating needs* step during a multi-call negotiation session, Jim *gains commitment* from Erin by having her agree to set up a *demonstrating capability* appointment at a future time.

JIM: (transition to wrap up interview) Erin, thanks for sharing your meeting needs with me. I appreciate your spending time with me today. I feel confident that Hotel Park Plaza can satisfy your meeting needs.

What I would like to do is to go back to my office and write up a proposal of how our hotel can satisfy your needs. I need a day to thoroughly consider how we can help you.

Can we set an appointment for the day after tomorrow to meet again so that I can go over the proposal with you?

ERIN: Sure. Between 1 PM and 4 PM would be best; how about 3 PM?

JIM: *(writing in his day planner)* I'll be here at 3 PM the day after tomorrow. I appreciate your time and look forward to discussing how we can help you have a successful meeting next month.

CHAPTER 10

Phase Two— Negotiation Process Strategy:

Step Three— Demonstrating Capability

Everybody sells. Everybody influences. Everybody persuades. Whether or not you go into sales, you deal with people in all areas of your life. Influence and persuasion are an ongoing and integral part of our society and economic life. As a leader, you need to influence or persuade others to follow you. There can be no leaders without followers. As a manager, you need to influence or persuade employees to implement your direction. The days of autocratic managers are ending and people must be persuaded.

As an aspiring employee, you need to influence or persuade others that you should be rewarded with increased responsibility and promotion. As a small business entrepreneur, you need to influence and persuade bankers, competitors, customers, and others regarding your business concepts. As a parent, son, or daughter, you need to influence or persuade your family to harmonize and synchronize with your individual wishes. Everybody sells, influences, and persuades all of their lives.

In this chapter, we will discuss how to demonstrate product or service capability to satisfy a potential buyer's needs. We will do this in an *informative* presentation (see Chapter 7). The term **demonstrating capability** refers to what most salespeople call a **sales presentation**. Demonstrating capability, Phase Two, Step Three of the buying/selling exchange process, involves following a guideline, but it is not a canned presentation. It is a model that presents categories or steps that most successful salespeople follow. With experience, salespeople develop their own style to implement these steps and unique words to describe them. Over time, salespeople naturally flow through this model. The content of this model is always *customized* and *modified* for each prospective buyer, whereas the general steps remain constant.

Most new salespeople find this process a bit artificial at first. But don't be concerned with a little discomfort. Only know that each step should be covered and that, with experience, artificiality and discomfort disappear. This is similar to learning a new skill. Skiing, skating, riding a bike, and many other newly learned abilities feel clumsy and artificial until you have experience.

Before we discuss demonstrating capability, let's remind ourselves of where our discussion from previous chapters has taken us. Let's briefly review the entire buying/selling exchange process introduced in Chapter 7 (see Table 7–1). In the preceding chapter, Chapter 9, we discussed the first appointment of a multi-call negotiation session. The purpose of that first appointment was to investigate needs. In that appointment, we followed the buying/selling exchange process model by making an appropriate approach: establishing rapport, transitioning from social conversation to business conversation, and stating why we were meeting with the potential buyer ("to investigate your meeting needs so that we can determine if our hotel can meet those needs"). We investigated needs by asking many types of questions to discover the buyer's needs.

To end our first appointment, we moved to Phase Two, Step Five of our process model, *gaining commitment*. Normally, Step Five is gaining commitment to purchase. However, it was not our purpose to make a sale in the first appointment. The first appointment was primarily for the purpose of thoroughly understanding the prospective buyer's needs.

In the first appointment, we were successful in gaining commitment (a commitment to continue the buying/selling exchange process). The prospective buyer agreed to set another appointment to discuss the **proposal** that the salesperson would write.

Having a *second appointment* to discuss the proposal or for demonstrating capability is the subject of this chapter. We will demonstrate capability by explaining how our written proposal will satisfy the buyer's needs. In simple terms, a sales presentation, or demonstrating capability, is a systematic way of discussing a proposal. Preparing a proposal will also be discussed in this section, as well as the different types of proposal documents.

We will discuss the demonstrating capability step of the buying/selling exchange process over the next three chapters, as follows:

1. Chapter 10, the present chapter, introduces all steps of the demonstrating capability process. Here we do not complicate the process by introducing buyer concerns during the process itself or at the gaining commitment step.
2. Chapter 11 adds the first level of complexity to the demonstrating capability process. During the process, the prospective buyer will voice concerns about what the salesperson is presenting. This is the negotiating concerns step. Here we will discuss how to deal with these concerns.
3. Chapter 12 further complicates the demonstrating capability process. In addition to voicing concerns during the presentation, the buyer again expresses concerns when the salesperson asks the buyer to make the purchase. This is the gaining commitment step. Here we will discuss how to deal with these concerns.

The Proposal—Basis for Demonstrating Capability

The word *proposal* was first introduced in Chapter 8 in Table 8–2. We used the word *proposal* several times: (1) *proposal letter,* (2) *proposal checklist,* and (3) *proposal.* We even said that once a potential buyer signed the proposal, it was transformed into a contract or letter of agreement. At this point, let's clarify any confusion that may exist by defining the word *proposal.* According to one dictionary, the word *proposal* means

"The act of offering or suggesting something for acceptance, adoption or performance. A plan or scheme proposed. An offer or suggestion. Syn-

onyms are: recommendation, suggestion, design, and plan" (Webster's Encyclopedic Unabridged Dictionary *1996, 1551).*

Proposal

In this chapter, we are discussing the salesperson's *second appointment* with the potential buyer, in which the salesperson is demonstrating capability. In the first appointment, the salesperson met with the potential buyer for investigating needs. Having discovered the potential buyer's needs, the salesperson went back to the office and prepared a proposal. Table 10–1 shows the proposal form that the salesperson completes.

As we have learned, the proposal is a plan or suggestion—in this case, of how the salesperson's product or service can satisfy the potential buyer's needs. At the second appointment, and with the written proposal in hand, the salesperson explains how the proposal was written. The salesperson, using a formatted discussion for demonstrating capability, suggests the proposal for acceptance and adoption by the potential buyer. If the potential buyer accepts the proposal and signs it, the proposal becomes a legally binding contract or letter of agreement. But what about the other confusing uses of the word proposal letter and proposal checklist?

Proposal Letter

The *proposal* must be reasonably detailed, since it has the potential to be transformed into a legal contract. On the other hand, a *proposal letter* is very general. We said that another term we prefer is *customized direct mail.* The proposal letter or customized direct mail is used when a suspect is first elevated to a probability level indicating a greater likelihood that the suspect will become a customer. This form of direct mail is also sent out to suspects requesting **RFPs** (requests for proposal) by letter, e-mail, fax, Internet, or other means. These suspects are also still at a low probability since the salesperson knows very little about their complete meeting needs. So, a proposal letter is a form of more sophisticated direct mail—customized direct mail.

Proposal Checklist

What is a *proposal checklist?* This is simply the blank proposal form (see Table 10–1). A salesperson takes this form to the first appointment when *investigating needs.* It is a good checklist to remind the salesperson of important questions and to record responses from the potential buyer. Since this proposal has the potential to be transformed into a letter of agreement, doesn't it make sense that all of the information needed is captured in the same format? A proposal checklist is simply that: a blank form used as a checklist to systematically capture a potential buyer's needs.

Matching Statements—The Heart of Demonstrating Capability

As we will see in the illustrative role-play script following, the core of a sales presentation (traditional term) or demonstrating capability presentation is the salesperson's ability to match the product or service features and benefits with the stated needs of the prospect. Let's look at what we mean by **matching statements**.

When Are Matching Statements Used?

After the salesperson has established rapport and summarized the prospect's needs, matching statements become the core of the presentation.

What Do Matching Statements Look and Sound Like?

Matching statements match potential buyer's needs with **proof devices** and the features and benefits of the salesperson's product and service. Too often salespeople simply state a feature of their product or service. In effect, they assume that the potential buyer will see the obvious benefit.

Let's clearly restate what we spent considerable time discussing in Chapters 3, 4, and 5: *Buyers don't buy things. They buy value and benefits.* So a salesperson can't leave it up to chance that the buyer will always see the benefits. This is the reason that salespeople must use fully developed matching statements (see Table 10–2).

A fully developed matching statement contains the following components, each represented by a column in Table 10–2:

1. Restatement of the Prospect's Need
2. Display or Demonstration of a Proof Device
   This reinforces the product or service feature. (This could be a brochure or, better yet, an opportunity for the customer to view or experience the real thing. For example, it's powerful to demonstrate your food service by having the customer eat a meal at the property. Also, you could offer the customer a complimentary night at your hotel, complete with a site tour. Or, if you are presenting in the prospect's office, show brochures or use your laptop computer to either access your property's Web site or show pictures from a CD.)
3. Statement of the Product or Service Feature
   A salesperson presents the statement of features while demonstrating or displaying the proof device that will address the customer's need. A feature is usually something tangible.

MEETING PROPOSAL
HOTEL PARK PLAZA

1.0 CUSTOMER INFORMATION

Customer Name: _____ Title: _____

Organization Name: _____ Telephone: ___/___-_____ Fax:__/____-____

Address: _____ E-mail: _____ Official Dates of

Meeting: Arrival (4 PM):___/___/_____ Departure (12 N):____/___/_____

Name of Meeting: _____

Peak Number of Attendees: _____ Full Value of Meeting (# 6.0) $_____ Meeting Deposit $_____

Cancellation Policy: No Charge for Cancellation 120 days prior to meeting. Thereafter, on a sliding scale: 119 to 90 Days Prior = 25% of Meeting Full Value (FV), 89 to 60 Days Prior = 50% of FV, 59 to 30 = 75% of FV and under 30 Days = 100% of FV.

2.0 GUEST/SLEEPING ROOM INFORMATION & CHARGES

Day	Date
Sunday	__/__/__
Monday	__/__/__
Tuesday	__/__/__
Wednesday	__/__/__
Thursday	__/__/__
Friday	__/__/__
Saturday	__/__/__
Total	

Guests Room/Nights
Room   Rate

Total Room
Cost

Guests
Single   Double   Suites

Room Nights

Guest Rooms $_____ + Room Tax (1%) $_____ + Sales Tax (8.2%) $_____= Total Guest Room Charges $_____ (# 2.0)

3.0 MEETING FACILITY INFORMATION & CHARGES

Day	Date
Sunday	__/__/__
Monday	__/__/__
Tuesday	__/__/__
Wednesday	__/__/__
Thursday	__/__/__
Friday	__/__/__
Saturday	__/__/__
Total Room	
Costs	

Attendees

Times

Style

Total Costs

Meeting Rooms $_____ + Sales Tax (8.2%) $_____ = _____ Total Meeting Room Charges $_____ (# 3.0)

4.0 FOOD & BEVERAGE INFORMATION & CHARGES

Day	Date
Sunday	__/__/__
Monday	__/__/__
Tuesday	__/__/__
Wednesday	__/__/__
Thursday	__/__/__
Friday	__/__/__
Saturday	__/__/__

Total

Costs

Guests

Breakfast #1	Lunch	Dinner	Refresh
Break #1	Refresh	Break #2	Cocktail

Party

Total Costs

F&B $___ + Sales Tax (8.2%) $____ + Gratuity $____ + Service $____ = Total Food & Beverage Charges $_____ (# 4.0)

5.0 OTHER CHARGES
1. There will be a $2.00 per person per bag Bellperson added to the Master Folio = Attendees Xs 4 bags Xs $2 = $_____
2. There will be a $3.00 per room per day Housekeeping Charge added to the Master Folio = Room Nights Xs $3 = $____
3. Miscellaneous Charges: _____

Bellperson $_____+ Housekeeping $_____ +Miscellaneous $_____   = Total Other Charges $_____ (# 5.0)

6.0 TOTAL CHARGES (From Subtotals Above)
2.0 $_____ plus # 3.0 $_____ plus # 4.0 $_____ plus # 5.0 _____= Total Meeting Charges $ _____ (# 6.0)

7.0 BILLING INSTRUCTIONS
1. Accounts/Folios: a. __All Charges on Master Folio b. __All Charges on Individual Folio c. Specific Folio Split
2. Payment Method: a. $_____Deposit on Signing b. $_____Before Departure c. $_____Due 30 Days of Departure

8.0 AUTHORIZATION

_____   _____
Hotel Authorized Signature   Date   Customer Signature   Date

_____   _____
Title   Title

Table 10-2 Matching Statements					
1. NEED	**2. PROOF DEVICE**	**3. FEATURE**	**4. TRANSLATION WORDS**	**5. BENEFIT**	**6. CONFIRMATION QUESTION**
#1 Need: "You indicated that . . you wanted 40 sleeping rooms."	"Here is . . . a picture of one of our guest rooms."	"which has . . . just been remodeled."	"which means to you"	"that . . . your people will enjoy clean, comfortable, spacious, and attractive sur-roundings."	"Is that what you had in mind?" or "What do you think?" Or, any other way of asking a "confirmation" question and obtaining the customer's agree-ment or disagreement.
#2 Need:					
#3 Need:					
#4 Need:					
#5 Need:					
#6 Need: (Price/Budget— always done last)					

4. "Translation" Words

   These words convert the feature into a benefit. A benefit is the value of the feature to the prospect, or what the feature can accomplish for the prospect. Salespeople must ensure that the prospect clearly under-stands the benefit offered by the feature. **Translation words**, such as "what this means to you" and "thus" and "so," as well as other words, act as translations of features into benefits (see Table 10–2).

5. "Confirmation Question"

   Confirmation questions help the salesperson learn whether the cus-tomer agrees that this benefit satisfies the stated need. Here the sales-person is inviting the prospect to agree or disagree with the matching statement. If the prospect agrees, the salesperson begins to select the next prospect need and starts a new matching statement.

   a. If the customer does not agree (with a confirmation question), "resis-tance" must be negotiated. (This will be covered in Chapter 11.)

b. If the customer agrees (with a confirmation question), then the salesperson moves to the next need/benefit matching statement.
c. The matching statement process continues until all needs have been addressed.

The Demonstrating Capability Appointment

Let's look at the logical steps of systematically discussing the proposal in the second appointment by magnifying Phase Two of the buying/selling exchange process presented in Table 7–1. In Table 10–3 we will look at the details of the

Table 10–3 Objectives in the Demonstrating Capability Negotiation Session

PHASE TWO—NEGOTIATION PROCESS STRATEGY

Step One—Approaching the Buyer (Chapter 8)

Objective #1—Approach and Establish the Relationship

1. Establish rapport and a relationship. This is the first appointment of a multi-call negotiation session. By now you should know some things about the prospective buyer either from research, from information in your prospect/customer database, or from prior contact from other social or business settings. This is the social conversation. Make enthusiastic comments about information you may have and about commonalities that are now known.

2. Communicate positive *body* language (good entrance, carriage, handshake, and seating posture).

3. Communicate positive *verbal* language (use positive words, show enthusiasm with a well-modulated voice).

4. Use the prospect's name effectively (at least three times).

Objective #2—Transition from Social to Business Conversation

1. Make a transition statement from social conversation to business conversation and purpose. Communicate the sales appointment objectives (share with the prospect why the salesperson is on this appointment).

2. Ask permission to take effective nondistracting notes (you should be organized and prepared to take notes). Use a proposal checklist form as described in Chapter 8, Table 8–2.

Step Two—Investigating Needs (Chapter 9)

Objective #3—Question to Investigate Customer Needs

This step was completed in the first appointment of this multi-call negotiation session (Chapter 9).

Step Three—Demonstrating Capability (Chapter 10)

Objective #4—Summarize and Confirm Needs

1. Show a clear understanding of each of the customer's needs (from the first appointment in Chapter 9—investigating needs role-play).

2. End this summary of needs with, "Is there anything else I have not covered?"

Objective #5—Give a Brief Differentiation Statement

1. Communicate something unique about your facility (this is a type of "headline" that puts the customer on alert to look for

(continued)

something special). You can state this differentiation statement in the first appointment, but it is usually done in the second appointment. Simply reword it if you have already used it before.

Example: "Did you know that our facility specializes in corporate meetings? We rarely host functions for transient guests, preferring instead to focus on businesses. In fact, our entire property is geared to handle meetings—we're corporate specialists, unlike most hotel properties."

Objective #6—Match Each Need with a Product or Service Feature/Benefit

1. Make effective need/product matching statements. The components of a matching statement are

   a. Restate need (do one need at a time with a full matching statement for each).

   b. Match each need with a feature.

   c. Support each feature with a proof device. This could be a picture or other visual proof such as a report document, map, property schematic, and so on. You should have a brochure (paper or electronic on your laptop computer) with you if you are presenting at the customer's office. The best way to offer proofs is to present as you are giving the customer a site visit of your hotel: real experience is better than pictures.

   d. Use translation words to convert features to benefits.

   e. End each matching statement with a confirmation question or statement. (*Note:* The confirmation question will either receive an affirmative or a negative answer that would indicate a *buyer's concern* or *objection.*)

Step Four—Negotiating Concerns (Chapter 11)

Objective #7—Recognize and Negotiate Concerns As They Arise

Note: You will not encounter any resistance or need to *negotiate concerns* in this chapter's discussion. However, in the next chapter we will fully discuss them. Normally, the resistance or customer concerns would have come during your matching statements, specifically, when you asked the confirmation question.

Step Five—Gaining Commitment (Chapter 12)

Objective #8—Select an Appropriate Closing Method

This objective is discussed in Chapter 12.

Objective #9—Ask for the Buyer's Commitment

1. Summarize the benefits as discussed in the matching statements in Step Three. Although *summary of benefits* is a type of closing method (see Chapter 12), it is *always* a good idea to summarize here even if you used a different closing method in Objective #8.

2. Ask for the order or purchase in a clear and direct way. (Be sure that there is no mistake that you are asking for the order.) Some salespeople become wishy-washy here. Since so much time and effort have been invested up until this point, avoid a common salesperson's weakness of getting cold feet at this step.

Objective #10—Negotiate Any Customer Concerns about Making a Commitment

In the concluding role-play for this chapter, the salesperson will not meet any buyer resistance or concerns at the closing or gaining commitment step. In Chapter 12 we will fully discuss resistance or concerns from the prospect at the gaining commitment step.

Objective #11—After-Sale Service Statements

1. Thank the customer (the *prospect* has been transformed into a *customer* since he/she is making a purchase) for the business.

2. Give the customer an idea of what actions will take place after the order is placed. (This keeps the customer from feeling that the salesperson is only interested in making this sale, and assures him/her that implementation will be taken care of.)

demonstrating capability step. Remember, we have already investigated needs during the first appointment of this multi-call negotiation session; therefore, we have a different purpose for this second appointment: *gaining commitment,* by ideally making a sale or having the prospective buyer agree to continue considering working with the salesperson in other sales appointments to complete the sale.

SUMMARY ◆

Demonstrating capability is what is traditionally referred to as the *sales presentation.* This text philosophically believes that an exchange between buyers and sellers requires their equal involvement and must be viewed from both the buyer's and seller's perspectives. Thus, we have combined the buyer-centric view of exchange, the *buying process,* with the seller-centric view of the exchange, the *selling process,* and created a hybrid, the *buying/selling exchange process,* which reflects both perspectives. Similarly, the step called *demonstrating capability* reflects the open discussion dialogue between buyer and seller when using a consultative selling strategy.

Demonstrating capability can logically take place only when the buyer's full needs and desires are clearly understood by the salesperson. In our presentation of the buying/selling exchange process, these needs were ascertained in a separate appointment. The salesperson then returned to the office and digested all of the potential buyer's needs and then matched these needs with the product or service features and benefits. This matching process was recorded in a written document called a proposal (see Table 10–1).

In the second appointment that has already been set up, the salesperson demonstrates capability by discussing the proposal. The core of this discussion is in constructing and delivering effective matching statements (see Table 10–2). The salesperson knows that buyers only buy benefits, so the salesperson will match each of the buyer's needs with a product or service feature and translate the feature into a benefit. The effective salesperson will then ask the prospect, using a confirmation question, if the prospect agrees with the matching statement. If so, the salesperson moves on to the next need. If the prospect disagrees or has questions or concerns, the salesperson addresses or negotiates these concerns (discussed in Chapter 11).

Finally, after discussing the concepts involved in demonstrating capability, we will finish by illustrating these through a model role-play script.

In the next chapter, we will add to the complexity of demonstrating capability by introducing concerns raised during this presentation by the prospect. Negotiating concerns is the topic of Chapter 11.

References

Webster's Encyclopedic Unabridged Dictionary. 1996. New York: Random House Publishing.

◈ DISCUSSION QUESTIONS

1. A sales proposal contains what three key elements?
2. What is meant by presenting features as benefits? What does the technique attempt to achieve?
3. Describe two proof devices a hotel salesperson can use to demonstrate to a prospect a firm's unique qualities and capabilities.
4. What are confirmation questions? When are they used? Why are they used?

ROLE-PLAY: A Seller and Buyer Engaged in Demonstrating Capability

Role-Play Members

1. Hotel Park Plaza salesperson—Jim Parker
2. YWCA meeting planner, prospective buyer—Erin Massey

Recap of the Evolving Role-Play Scripts

1. *Investigating Needs* Role-Play (Chapter 9). This was the first appointment of a multi-call negotiation session. Here Jim's sole purpose was to discover Erin's needs. He did not try to sell her at this appointment. In-depth discovery of needs is for a future appointment. Jim told Erin that he would go back to his office to write up a written proposal that would detail and price how the Hotel Park Plaza could satisfy her meeting needs. The purpose of the second appointment was to present the contents of the written proposal or demonstrate capability.

2. *Demonstrating Capability* Role-Play (Chapter 10). Jim returned to visit with Erin at the second appointment, which was scheduled at the first appointment. Jim presented his proposal in a formatted way. He systematically demonstrated capability—how the Hotel Park Plaza could satisfy Erin's meeting needs. For illustration purposes, Erin agreed with everything that Jim presented. In a real situation, the customer would probably not say yes to

everything. We will see more of the real world of prospective buyer concerns and objections in the next two role-plays.

3. *Negotiating Concerns* **Role-Play (Chapter 11).** Jim goes through the same demonstrating capability role-play as in #2, but this time Erin has concerns. She will object or have questions that Jim must answer before he can expect to gain commitment or have Erin agree to purchase.

4. *Gaining Commitment* **Role-Play (Chapter 12).** In Chapter 12, Jim will attempt the same demonstrating capability role-play with Erin as in #2. She will again have concerns and object during this step as in #3. Additionally, she will have more concerns at Jim's *gaining commitment* or *close* attempt. Jim will have to satisfactorily answer all questions or concerns if he expects Erin to buy.

Demonstrating Capability Role-Play Specifications

1.   In his first appointment, Jim discovered Erin's needs or buying conditions. Knowing these needs, Jim set a future appointment with Erin to return to her office to present a proposal. Jim is now at this future appointment. The purpose of this appointment is to demonstrate capability—how the Hotel Park Plaza can satisfy Erin's needs that Jim discovered in his first appointment.

2.   Jim will demonstrate capability by discussing the proposal (see Table 10–1) he has prepared. Jim will do this by naming each of Erin's needs and then matching each need with a feature/benefit of the Hotel Park Plaza by using matching statements.

3.   By satisfying needs with hotel features/benefits, Jim will be influencing Erin in order to get her to decide to use his hotel. Jim will attempt to have Erin sign the prepared written *proposal* (that he is discussing). This will transform into a *contract* (*letter of agreement*). For purposes of illustration, Erin will sign the contract in the following script.

4.   Jim will end the conversation by thanking Erin and then telling her what will happen after the contract is signed. This helps her to anticipate the steps that will follow regarding her meeting at the Hotel Park Plaza.

5.   The role-play model script follows the buying/selling exchange process model beginning at Phase Two, Step One and ending with Phase Two, Step Five. For illustrative purposes, we will not meet customer resistance in either Step Four or Step Five.

6.   This is the second formal appointment of a multi-call negotiation session. Jim knows about Erin's needs and has prepared a written proposal that he will discuss in detail. He has brought his laptop computer on which he has an electronic brochure of all the features of the Hotel Park Plaza. He also has

information on competitors, along with maps of the area, stored on his laptop's hard drive. Jim is well prepared.

Role-Play Demonstrating Capability—Model Script

Model scripts in all subsequent chapters build on Jim and Erin's negotiation session to provide consistency in our illustrations.

PHASE TWO—Negotiation Process Strategy

STEP ONE—The Approach

Objective #1—Approach and Reestablish the Relationship
> **JIM:** Good morning, Ms. Massey. It's great to see you. Thanks for inviting me again. By the way, I saw your new YWCA advertisement on TV. Looks great. You seem to be gearing up for a major fund-raising campaign. *(Jim makes a good entrance, smiles, shakes hands, and takes a seat when invited.)*
> **ERIN:** Thanks. We're really excited about the new campaign. And like I said last time, just call me Erin. "Ms. Massey" sounds so formal.

Jim pauses.

Objective #2—Transition from Social to Business Conversation
> **JIM:** *(transition statement away from social conversation to business conversation)* I certainly appreciate the opportunity to let you know about how the Hotel Park Plaza can help you have a successful meeting. I believe that you will like what I have put together for you. *(Jim states the purpose of this appointment: to demonstrate how his hotel can satisfy Erin's meeting needs.)*

STEP TWO—Investigating Needs

Objective #3—Question to Investigate Customer Needs
Jim has preplanned and prepared his strategic sales plan around the six needs or buying conditions as revealed to him by Erin at the investigating needs meeting at his first face-to-face appointment with Erin. Jim will use these needs as the main portion of his demonstrating capability presentation.

Erin's Six Needs

1. "I need a meeting facility for a one-day YWCA physical fitness seminar."
2. "I need a meeting room for the first Thursday of next month that will accommodate 150 people from 1:00 PM to 3:00 PM with theater-style seating along with a 3,000 square foot room for vendors to display their products from 3:00 PM to 7:30 PM."
3. "I want nonsmoking single guest rooms for 40 seminar leaders the night before the seminar."
4. "I want a chicken banquet lunch served at noon for 150 people."

5. "I want a convenient downtown location with a lot of convenient parking."
6. "I need all of this on my budget of $10,000."

Jim will use these needs to develop his proposal and will discuss each of them in the main portion of his demonstrating capability presentation.

STEP THREE—Demonstrating Capability

Objective #4—Summarize and Confirm Needs

JIM: *(continuing a transition to business)* Erin, the last time we spoke, you indicated you had some needs that were very important to you. Let me see if I have them all. *(Jim begins to summarize the needs.)*

JIM: *(need #1)* Let me see. You said that you wanted to hold your one-day YWCA physical fitness seminar the first Thursday of next month for 150 attendees. Is that right? *(The last part is a confirming question to find out if Jim is on the right track.)*

ERIN: That's right.

JIM: *(need #2)* You also indicated you needed a theater-style meeting facility for 150 attendees and that you needed 3,000 square feet for a trade show.

ERIN: You bet! It's important that we have plenty of space. *(Jim didn't have to ask a confirmation question here as Erin automatically confirmed.)*

JIM: *(need #3)* Erin, your sleeping accommodation needs are for 40 nonsmoking singles for seminar leaders the night before. Do you want VIP treatment packages for these?

ERIN: No VIPs, just 40 single rooms.

JIM: *(need #4)* You also said that you wanted to have the 150 attendees enjoy a chicken luncheon on the seminar day. Is that right? *(Again, Jim adds a confirmation question.)*

ERIN: That's right.

JIM: *(need #5)* You said that a convenient location was very important, along with convenient parking.

ERIN: That is extremely important. Even though this is a physical fitness seminar, I don't want my attendees to get lost or have to do too much exercise *before* they get to the meeting by having to walk for miles.

JIM: *(need #6)* Erin, I hear what you're saying. You also indicated you have a budget for this meeting of about $10,000. Is this right?

ERIN: I think you have it about right.

JIM: Excellent. Are there any other meeting needs you have thought about since I was last here? *(Jim makes sure that Erin has all of her needs "on the table.")*

ERIN: No, we have covered the most important things.

Objective #5—Give a Brief Differentiation Statement

Jim pauses.

JIM: How familiar are you with the Park Plaza?

ERIN: Not very, but I do drive by it every day on my way to work.

JIM: *(gives a differentiation statement to get Erin's attention and interest)* Our hotel specializes in meetings. We were specifically designed to host groups ranging in size from 15 to 700 attendees. We have recently renovated and have an extensive on-property inventory of audiovisual equipment. We also have a large number of meeting rooms that can be flexibly adjusted to comfortably accommodate meeting needs. In other words, we are meeting and convention specialists and, as such, we do everything possible to make a meeting successful.

ERIN: I didn't know all that, Jim. It already sounds like your property is a place I might seriously consider.

The attention-getting differentiation statement has caused Erin first to pay attention and then to listen for these different qualities of the Hotel Park Plaza.

Objective #6—Match Each Need with a Product or Service Feature/Benefit

Jim uses his preplanned strategic sales plan to discuss one customer need at a time. He saves the *budget* need for last!

JIM: What I'd like to do is to go over each of your needs and let you know how the Hotel Park Plaza proposes to handle your meeting. How does this sound? *(Note: Jim presents an agenda and then uses a confirmation question to see if Erin agrees and will allow him to proceed.)*

ERIN: That's fine with me.

JIM: *(matching statement for need #1)* About your meeting dates, you indicated that you need to hold the meeting the first Thursday of next month *(restate buying condition/need)*. I have checked our rooms control book *(proof device)* and we have availability *(feature)*. This means *(translation phrase)* that you can have your meeting at the times that you planned *(benefit)*. How does this sound *(confirmation question)*?

ERIN: Great.

JIM: *(matching statement for need #2)* You indicated that you needed a theater-style room for 150 attendees and a trade-show room of 3,000 square feet *(buying condition/need)*. Here is a layout of our meeting and display rooms *(proof device)*. We have reserved the Curtis A/B room for your theater seating and the 3,344 square foot Sundance room for your trade show *(feature),* which means *(translation phrase)* that your attendees and vendors displaying at the trade show will have a spacious and comfortable environment *(benefit)*. Is that what you had in mind *(confirmation question)*?

ERIN: Jim, this is exactly the type of thing I was thinking of.

Conversation continues through matching statements for needs #3, #4, and #5, then ends with #6.

JIM: *(matching statement for need #6—price, the tough one!)* Erin, you indicated that you have a budget of around $10,000 *(buying condition/need)*. As you can see by the calculations on the proposal *(proof device)*, I have been able to get the total price within the range of your budget: $10,800 *(feature)*. This means *(translation phrase)* that all of your meeting needs can be met by a total price that approximates your budget *(benefit)*. Is that what you had in mind *(confirmation question)*?

ERIN: Well, Jim, I told you that my budget was in the range of $10,000. $10,800 is a little over, but close. And from what you've told me, I think the Hotel Park Plaza can solve my meeting needs. I believe this budget will work. *(A verbal "buying signal" is given, which invites Jim to ask for commitment.)*

STEP FOUR—Negotiating Concerns

Objective #7—Recognize and Negotiate Concerns As They Arise
Jim does not encounter any buyer concerns in this role-play, but will in Chapter 11.

STEP FIVE—Gaining Commitment

Objective #8—Select an Appropriate Closing Method
Jim chooses the common *summary of benefits* closing/commitment method. (The six closing methods are discussed in Chapter 12.) The reason this method of summarizing benefits is chosen is because Jim wants benefits in the front of Erin's mind just before closing the sale. Jim makes this summary loose and free flowing. Jim summarized *needs* at the beginning of the presentation. Now *benefits* are summarized.

Objective #9—Ask for the Buyer's Commitment
Preface with Summarized Benefits

JIM: I'm happy to hear that. Let's review where we've been: We have your dates available *(benefit #1)* and we have provided spacious accommodations for both the meeting and trade show *(benefit #2)*. Our oversized and newly renovated sleeping rooms provide comfortable accommodations for your seminar presenters *(benefit #3)*. The chicken luncheon prepared by our award-winning chef will be artistically presented and delicious *(benefit #4)*. Easy access to our downtown location and our free adjacent parking garage will provide your guests convenience *(benefit #5)*. And, most important, all of this is within your budget range *(benefit #6)*. How does all this sound *(confirmation question)*?

ERIN: I like it. From everything that you have told me, it sounds like my meeting will be a success.

JIM: *(after hearing a buying signal or reading body language for the signal)* Can we formalize our agreement with your signature? *(Jim places the written proposal in front of Erin along with a pen.)*

Objective #10—Negotiate Any Customer Concerns about Making a Commitment
In this role-play, Erin has agreed to every one of Jim's suggestions as written on the proposal. Of course, it is rare that 100 percent agreement is achieved. In Chapters 11

and 12, Erin will have concerns with the statements on the proposal and, after discussing modifications with Jim, the proposal (now a "contract") will need to be rewritten.

Objective #11—After-Sale Service Statements

ERIN: (while signing the letter of agreement) Jim, what happens next?

JIM: Thanks, Erin. We at the Hotel Park Plaza want to make your meeting a very successful one. As soon as you sign the letter of agreement, this becomes the marching orders of the house (the *house* is language for the hotel). We will immediately assign you a conference service manager (CSM) who will call and let you know about various time lines and meeting details.

Of course, I am always in the background and watching over your meeting to make sure that everything runs smoothly.

ERIN: This sounds great. Having a person to help me with my meeting sure takes a load off my mind. Jim, it's been great working with you.

JIM: Erin, I am enjoying working with you and helping you to have a successful meeting. I appreciate your time and look forward to working with you. We'll stay in frequent contact. Thanks again for your business.

CHAPTER 11

Phase Two—Negotiation Process Strategy:

Step Four—Negotiating Concerns

LEARNING OBJECTIVES

After reading this chapter you should be able to

- describe the types of concerns customers may have that keep them from committing
- explain how to advance a sale by overcoming a customer's concerns or resistance
- identify the importance of finding win-win solutions to problems

KEY TERMS & CONCEPTS

distributive strategies
integrative strategies
customer objections

indirect denial
direct denial

People don't always agree with statements that they hear; they have questions or concerns and seek clarification.

A sales presentation, or the demonstrating capability step of the buying/selling exchange process, is a conversation between a prospective buyer and a seller. The topic of the conversation is how the seller's product or service can meet the needs of the buyer. Based on a pre-prepared proposal (see Chapter 10), the seller makes statements and suggestions as to how the product can solve or satisfy the prospective buyer's problem or need. The buyer may not agree with the seller's suggestions. The buyer has *concerns* and the seller must answer or *negotiate* these concerns.

It's important to recognize that if the buyer asks questions, voices concerns, or has objections, the buyer is showing interest. If the buyer did not have interest, he/she would simply end the conversation. Thus, sellers should welcome concerns or objections and not fear them as do most salespeople. By asking questions, the buyer permits the seller to engage in an open conversation to answer them.

This chapter builds on Chapter 10, where we introduced the demonstrating capability process. In Chapter 10, we did not complicate the process. We did not introduce buyer concerns or have the buyer resist the seller's suggestions.

This situation, of course, is unrealistic. Buyers almost always express concerns. In this chapter, we introduce the first level of complication to the demonstrating capability process: *negotiating concerns*. These concerns will arise during the selling conversation.

Before we discuss Step Four of Phase Two, negotiating concerns, let's remind ourselves of where our discussion from previous chapters has taken us. Let's briefly review the entire buying/selling exchange process that we first introduced in Chapter 7 (see Table 7–1).

In Chapter 9, we discussed the first appointment of a multi-call negotiation session. The purpose of that first appointment was investigating needs. Having discovered the prospective buyer's needs, at the end of this first appointment we set up a second appointment for a future date. Before the second appointment, we prepared a proposal (see Chapter 10). The purpose of the second appointment was to present this proposal or demonstrate capability showing how our product or service could satisfy the buyer's needs.

In Chapter 10, we presented the format of steps showing how to demonstrate capability in the second appointment. In this chapter, we will again go through the steps of demonstrating capability but will complicate the process by adding buyer concerns. This chapter focuses on methods of negotiating concerns.

Negotiating Concerns

Win-Win Negotiation Is Crucial to Relationship Maintenance

Most salespeople have somehow been led to believe that any time the potential customer raises a problem, issue, objection, question, or concern about the salesperson's matching statement (see Chapter 10), something has gone wrong. Often they believe that this concern needs to be handled with some technique that makes the concern go away. Old sales training taught salespeople that, in such circumstances, they needed to: (1) *overcome the objection,* (2) *apply the correct manipulative technique,* and (3) *outtalk, outsmart,* and *outmaneuver* the customer. In actuality, when the potential customer asks questions, he/she is showing interest. If the customer were not interested, he/she would simply say no or say nothing.

As we learned in Chapter 7, there are several possible strategies to approach negotiations. The two most common strategies are win-lose (distributive) and win-win (integrative).

With a *win-lose* (also called *competitive* or *distributive*) strategy, the salesperson (negotiator) is taught to do everything possible to overcome and to outmaneuver the other party so that the salesperson will emerge victorious. In the win-lose strategy, substantive outcomes, not relationship outcomes, are the most important measure of success. Although this strategy may be necessary in appropriate situations, it is more related to the transactional selling strategy and is clearly not appropriate for the consultative selling strategy.

As we learned in previous discussions, the consultative selling strategy depends on building strong relationships with the customer. To accomplish both substantive outcomes and relationship outcomes, a win-win negotiation strategy is more effective. The *win-win* strategy goes by other names such as *integrative, cooperative, collaborative,* or *problem-solving* strategy. The idea is to have both buyer and seller satisfied with the outcome of the negotiation. It assumes that both the potential buyer and the seller can achieve their goals while preserving, as well as enhancing, the relationship. This approach is more than a simple compromise. Compromise does not always ensure that both parties will be happy or satisfied with the outcome.

Two definitions of a win-win negotiation are:

1. Working to reach an agreement that is mutually satisfactory to both buyer and seller
2. The way to reach a common understanding of the essential elements of the [exchange] (Manning and Reese 1997, 270)

Using a consultative selling strategy, the salesperson initially enters the buying/selling exchange process step, negotiating concerns, with a joint problem-solving philosophy. It is hoped that the potential buyer also wishes to engage using a win-win strategy. With this philosophy in mind, both the salesperson and the potential customer have the opportunity to work together to achieve the best possible solution for both parties. Both must gain benefits or, otherwise, someone will lose. And anyone who loses usually will not engage with the other party again; thus, the relationship is severed.

Consultative sellers utilize a win-win strategy throughout the entire buying/selling exchange process and especially in the negotiating concerns step. Their objective is to maintain long-term relationships while also achieving substantive outcomes.

As was noted in Chapter 7, sometimes the consultative seller attempts to engage with the potential buyer using a win-win strategy, but the potential buyer begins to engage in a win-lose strategy. What is the appropriate response? The consultative seller should be trained in win-lose strategies so he/she will be prepared to effectively recognize and counter the buyer employing win-lose tactics. However, the consultative seller should only use his/her countering win-lose methods to realign the potential buyer back to a win-win approach. Why? Because if this negotiation session clearly calls for relationship building, then a win-lose strategy, whereby a winner emerges and a loser is vanquished, will destroy relationships as well as potential repeat and referral business.

Five Common Types of Concerns

Whether in a win-lose or win-win situation, there are many types of questions or concerns that a potential customer can raise. Here are five common categories of questions that a salesperson can expect:

1. need—Concerns related to the need for the product or service. For example, "I don't need your product or service."
2. product or service—Concerns related to the product or service itself. For example, "I'm not familiar with your brand."
3. source—Concerns related to the source of supply. For example, "I have been buying from Marriott for years."
4. time—Concerns that delay the decision. For example, "I want time to think it over."
5. price—Concerns related to price are the most common form of concern. For example, "This is too far above my budget."

Knowing the most common customer concerns is an advantage to salespeople. With this knowledge, in the pre-negotiation phase of the buying/selling exchange process, the salesperson can anticipate customer concerns and prepare potential responses to them. Of course, a salesperson can only prepare and anticipate possible concerns the customer might have. However, if the potential customer's personal characteristics and past negotiation practices are researched, an approximate guess will get the salesperson into the ballpark.

One practical way to get a better understanding of the potential customer's characteristics is to ask him/her (in earlier telephone conversations) where he/she has held previous meetings or conferences. A phone call to a salesperson at the lodging facility where the last meeting was held will generate valuable information. Salespeople will usually share their experiences freely. With this advance information, the salesperson is better prepared to respond to potential customer concerns.

Seven Types of Responses to the Customer's Concerns

After recognizing that the customer is expressing concerns (or objections or resistance), the salesperson should first determine which of the following methods of response or combination of responses would be the most appropriate. When a *combination* approach is used, the **indirect denial** is usually the first method, followed by one or several of the following methods.

1. **Indirect Denial**—Sometimes the customer's concern is valid. Here the salesperson will acknowledge that the prospect is partially right. This is a "soft" and "conditional" denial, as in the following example.

    > **Prospective Buyer:** "I understand that you have hired a lot of new people at the hotel recently; to me, this indicates that there may be internal problems."
    >
    > **Salesperson:** "You're right; we have hired many new people, but this is due to our new expansion."

2. **Direct Denial**—This involves directly refuting or denying what the prospect has stated. It's considered a high-risk method, but in some cases what the prospect has stated or believes may be very wrong or misperceived. In any case, if this misperception is left unaddressed, the prospect will probably not buy.

    > **Prospective Buyer:** "I understand that your company has filed for bankruptcy."
    >
    > **Salesperson:** "That's not true."

3. **Superior Benefit**—A superior benefit is something that will usually outweigh a prospect's specific concern. It is most commonly used in combination with an indirect denial.

    > **Prospective Buyer:** "You don't have enough audiovisual (AV) equipment at the hotel property to fully accommodate our needs."
    >
    > **Salesperson:** "You're right; we only stock the basic AV on property *(indirect denial),* but one of our subsidiaries here in town is an AV supplier and, of course, they carry a full assortment of equipment to which we have first rights. And because we don't have to store and maintain this equipment, we can give you a better price than most people who do maintain the equipment" *(superior benefit).*

4.   **Demonstration**—This is used when you know both your product and your competitor's product or service very well. The idea here is that seeing (and experiencing) is believing. Demonstration is very powerful and can effectively overcome concerns. It is often used in combination-method approaches.

> **Prospective Buyer:** "I really don't know anything about the level of service that your property can provide. I don't know anything about you."
>
> **Salesperson:** "Why don't you and your family come and stay, as my guests, over a weekend? We would love to host a minivacation for you. You could relax and check us out."

5.   **Trial Offer**—This involves giving the prospect an opportunity to try the product without making a major purchase commitment. This has often been used in the case of large association meetings where a smaller board of directors meeting is given a very inexpensive rate so that the decision makers can try out the property.

> **Prospective Buyer:** "We really can't make a commitment for our annual association meeting at this time."
>
> **Salesperson:** "I know that you have a board meeting coming up soon. What if we could host it at a very small cost to you? You can look at this as our marketing cost to acquaint you with our property."

6.   **Third-Party Testimony**—In consultative selling, this is powerful. Third parties are people who refer business to you or are neutral parties who agree to act as a referral source.

> **Prospective Buyer:** "I really don't know anything about your company. It sounds good, but I'm not sure."
>
> **Salesperson:** "Were you aware that Bob Shoemaker, the VP of marketing in your company's medical division, held a successful meeting here two months ago? If you would like, I will ask him to call you. How does that sound?"

7.   **Questions**—Questions are not only an effective way to gather information and clarification, they also can be used to convert a concern into a question that may cause the prospect to rethink his/her position.

> **Prospective Buyer:** "You don't have evening room service?"
>
> **Salesperson:** "How many hosted functions will you be holding?"
>
> **Prospective Buyer:** "One running late every night through the entire meeting."
>
> **Salesperson:** "When do you think your attendees would want room service? I had initially been under the impression it was unneeded due to the late meetings, but perhaps we can work something out if this is not the case."

How to Respond to Customers' Concerns

The following are practical illustrations showing you how a salesperson might respond to customer concerns. The successful salesperson will always *prepare* for any sales presentation by anticipating areas where the customer may resist or have concerns. With this information, the salesperson will prepare some possible responses.

Here is a suggested format (series of steps) guiding the negotiating of **customer objections/resistance/concerns**:

Step #1: Recognize Objections As They Arise (during the presentation)

    a. Verbal and nonverbal signals

    b. Type of objection (of the five common types)

Step #2: Validate the Objection (use "reflective listening")

Example: "I think I understand your concern. You feel that the meeting room is not large enough to accommodate your people. Is that correct?"

Step #3: Answer the Objection (Use one or a combination of seven ways to respond.)

    a. Decide which of the seven techniques or combinations will answer the objection. Example: For a *source* type of objection, use a combination technique of indirect denial and demonstration.

    b. Use a *feel/felt/found* statement.

Prospective Buyer: "I'm going to check with the Marriott."

Salesperson: (validates and indirectly denies) "I understand your need to compare. You *feel* that obtaining the best price/value is important. Is this correct? My customers have always *felt* the same way. When they decided to use the Park Inn, they *found* us to be a superior value for the price."

    c. The salesperson could also use a second technique in combination, *demonstrates* "I know our competition very well. The Marriott is a fine property. Let me show you some price/value comparisons." The salesperson could then show a matrix of all competitive properties from a course pack as proof.

Step #4: Trial Close or Confirmation Question (Attempt to get the customer to see your point or agree that you have answered his/her concerns.)

Example: "Can we formalize our agreement?" or "What do you think?"

Note: After the customer's concern has been resolved, then the salesperson is free to move on to the next need to be matched with a product or service benefit statement.

The Demonstrating Capability Appointment with Negotiating Concerns

Let's look at the logical steps of discussing the proposal by magnifying Phase Two of the buying/selling exchange process presented in Table 7–1. In Table 11–1 we will look at the details of the demonstrating capability step

Table 11–1 Objectives in the Demonstrating Capability Negotiation Session With Negotiating Concerns

PHASE TWO – NEGOTIATION PROCESS STRATEGY

Step One – Approaching the Buyer (Chapter 8)

Objective #1–Approach and Reestablish the Relationship

1. Effectively reestablished relationship that was strengthened in the first appointment of this multi-call negotiation session (made enthusiastic comments about information from the last meeting and what commonalities are now known). This is the social conversation.

2. Communicated positive *body* language (good entrance, carriage, handshake, and seating posture).

3. Communicated positive *verbal* language (used positive words, showed enthusiasm with well-modulated voice).

4. Used customer's name effectively (at least three times).

Objective #2–Transition from Social to Business Conversation

Made transition statement from social conversation to business purpose. Communicated sales appointment objectives (shared why salesperson was calling).

Step Two – Investigating Needs (Chapter 9)

Objective #3–Questioning to Investigate Customer Needs

This step was completed in the first appointment of this multi-call negotiation session (Chapter 9).

Step Three – Demonstrating Capability (Chapter 10)

Objective #4–Summarize and Confirm Needs

1. Show a clear understanding of each of the customer's needs (from investigating needs role-play).

2. End this summary of needs with, "Is there anything else that I have not covered?"

Objective #5–Give a Brief Differentiation Statement

1. Communicate something unique about your facility. (This is a type of "headline" that puts the customer on alert to look for something special.) The salesperson can state this differentiation statement a second time if it was also used in the first appointment. Simply reword it.

Objective #6–Match Each Need with a Product or Service Feature/Benefit

1. Make effective need/product matching statements. The components of a matching statement are

   a. Restate need (do one need at a time with a full matching statement for each).   *(continued)*

b. Match needs with a feature.

c. Support each feature with a proof device. This could be a picture or other visual proof such as a report document, map, property schematic, and so on. You should have a brochure (paper or electronic on your laptop computer) with you if you are presenting at the customer's office. The best way to offer proofs is to present as you were giving the customer a site visit of your hotel: real experience is better than pictures.

d. Use translation words to convert features to benefits.

e. End each matching statement with a confirmation question or statement. (*Note:* The confirmation question will either receive an affirmative or a negative answer that would indicate a buyer's concern or objection.)

Step Four—Negotiating Concerns (Chapter 11)

Note: The salesperson will normally encounter buyer concerns when presenting matching statements in the demonstrating capability step. Specifically, the prospective buyer will show this concern when the salesperson asks the confirmation question.

Objective #7—Recognize and Negotiate Concerns As They Arise

1. Recognize the concern.

    a. Verbal and nonverbal signals

    b. What type of concern is it (of the five common types)?

2. Validate the concern—Use "reflective listening."

3. Answer the concern—Use one or a combination of seven methods to respond.

    a. Decide which of the seven techniques or combinations will answer the concern.

    b. Use a feel/felt/found statement.

Step Five—Gaining Commitment (Chapter 12)

Objective #8—Select an Appropriate Closing Method

The six Closing Methods are discussed in Chapter 12.

Objective #9—Ask for the Buyer's Commitment

1. Summarized the benefits that were discussed in the matching statements in Step Three. Although *summary of benefits* is a type of closing method (see Chapter 12), it is *always* a good idea to summarize here even if the salesperson also used a different closing method in Objective #8.

2. Ask for the order or purchase in a clear and direct way. (Be sure that there is no mistake that you are asking for the order.) Some salespeople become wishy-washy here. Since so much time and effort have been invested up until this point, avoid a common salesperson's weakness of getting cold feet at this step.

Objective #10—Negotiate Any Customer Concerns about Making a Commitment

The salesperson will not meet any buyer resistance or concerns at the closing or gaining commitment step in this chapter. In Chapter 12 we will fully discuss resistance or concerns from the prospect at the gaining commitment step.

Objective #11—After-Sale Service Statements

1. Thank the customer (the *prospect* has been transformed into a *customer* since he/she is making a purchase) for the business.

2. Give the customer an idea of what actions will take place after the order is placed. (This keeps the customer from feeling that the salesperson is only interested in making this sale, and assures him/her that implementation will be taken care of.)

when the prospective buyer has questions, objects, or resists some of the matching statements in the salesperson's proposal presentation. Remember, we have already investigated needs during the first appointment of this multi-call negotiation session. Therefore, we have a different purpose for this second appointment: *gaining commitment* by making a sale or having the prospective buyer agree to work with the salesperson in other sales appointments to complete the sale.

◆ SUMMARY

In this chapter we repeated the demonstrating capability step of the buying/selling exchange process. We first introduced this step in Chapter 10, but we added complications. In Chapter 10, the potential buyer agreed with all the salesperson's statements and the entire written proposal. In this chapter, the potential buyer raised concerns or questions. These questions occurred when the salesperson made a matching statement followed by, "Is this what you had in mind?" The potential buyer said, "No, that's not what I had in mind." The salesperson responded by negotiating concerns.

Consultative salespeople should use a win-win rather than a win-lose negotiation strategy. Why? Because they need to maintain a long-term relationship with the potential buyer. Sometimes a win-win strategy is not initially possible because the potential buyer uses a win-lose strategy. In this case, the consultative seller should have knowledge of win-lose strategy skills and counter the potential buyer in order to return the negotiation back to a win-win.

In this chapter, we introduced five common types of concerns and seven possible responses to these concerns. We demonstrated how to respond to potential buyer concerns in two illustrations: (1) a specific technique using feel/felt/found approach; and (2) a role-play script between a salesperson and meeting planner.

In the next chapter, we will introduce methods to make an effective transition from *demonstrating capability* and *negotiating concerns* to *gaining commitment* or asking for the purchase/order. As we will see, the potential buyer may *again* have concerns at this stage. We will demonstrate the entire process through a role-play script.

References

Manning, G. L., and B. L. Reece. 1997. *Selling today.* 7th ed. Upper Saddle River, NJ: Prentice Hall.

DISCUSSION QUESTIONS ◆

1. What are a buyer's concerns or objections barring him/her from committing to a sale agreement an indication of?
2. Imagine that you are the catering sales manager of a downtown resort. Demonstrate a feel/felt/found approach to responding to a customer concern that your product or service costs more than the alternatives.
3. In sales negotiations the authors of your text argue the importance of finding win-win solutions to customer needs and problems in which both buyers and sellers get what they need to sustain themselves. Should one expect that all buyers will be so inclined? Should a seller react to a buyer who is trying to get the most concessions in a negotiated deal by responding in kind? Why or why not?

ROLE-PLAY: A Seller and Buyer Engaged in Demonstrating Capability with Negotiating Concerns

Role-Play Members

1. Hotel Park Plaza salesperson—Jim Parker
2. YWCA meeting planner, prospective buyer—Erin Massey

Recap of the Evolving Role-Play Scripts

1. *Investigating Needs* Role-Play (Chapter 9). This was the first appointment of a multi-call negotiation session. Here Jim's sole purpose was to discover Erin's needs. He did not try to sell her at this appointment. In-depth discovery of needs is for a future appointment. Jim told Erin that he would go back to his office to write up a written proposal that would detail and price how the Hotel Park Plaza could satisfy her meeting needs. The purpose of the second appointment was to present the contents of the written proposal or demonstrate capability.

2. *Demonstrating Capability* Role-Play (Chapter 10). Jim returned to visit with Erin at the second appointment, which was scheduled at the first appointment. Jim presented his proposal in a formatted way. He systematically demonstrated capability—how the Hotel Park Plaza could satisfy Erin's meeting needs. For illustration purposes, Erin agreed with everything that Jim presented. In a real situation, the customer would probably not say yes to everything. We will see more of the real world of prospective buyer concerns and objections in the next two role-plays.

3. *Negotiating Concerns* Role-Play (Chapter 11). Jim goes through the same demonstrating capability role-play as in #2, but this time Erin has concerns. She will object or have questions that Jim must answer before he can expect to gain commitment or have Erin agree to purchase.

4. *Gaining Commitment* Role-Play (Chapter 12). In Chapter 12, Jim will attempt the same demonstrating capability role-play with Erin as in #2 above. She will again have concerns and object during this step as in #3 above. Additionally, she will have more concerns at Jim's *gaining commitment* or *close* attempt. Jim will have to satisfactorily answer all questions or concerns if he expects Erin to buy.

Negotiating Concerns Role-Play Specifications

1. In his first appointment, Jim discovered Erin's needs or buying conditions. Knowing these needs, Jim set a future appointment with Erin to return to her office to present a proposal. Jim is now at this future appointment. The purpose of this appointment is to demonstrate capability—how the Hotel Park Plaza can satisfy Erin's needs that Jim discovered in his first appointment.

2. Jim will demonstrate capability by discussing the proposal that he has prepared. Jim will do this by naming each of Erin's needs and then matching each need with a feature/benefit of the Hotel Park Plaza by using matching statements.

3. By satisfying needs with hotel features/benefits, Jim will be influencing Erin in order to get her to decide to use his hotel. Jim will attempt to have Erin sign the prepared written *proposal* (that he is discussing). This will transform into a *contract (letter of agreement)*. For purposes of illustration, Erin will sign the contract in the following script. However, in Chapter 12, Erin will have concerns at this commitment step and will resist.

4. Jim will end the conversation by thanking Erin and then telling her what will happen after the contract is signed. This helps her to anticipate the steps that will follow regarding her meeting at the Hotel Park Plaza.

5. The role-play model script follows the buying/selling exchange process model beginning at Phase Two, Step One and ending with Phase Two, Step Five. Erin will have concerns during the presentation. Jim will negotiate these concerns. For illustrative purposes, we will not meet customer concerns or resistance in Step Five, gaining commitment. We will meet resistance in this step in Chapter 12.

6. This is the second formal appointment of a multi-call negotiation session. Jim knows about Erin's needs and has prepared a written proposal that he will discuss in detail. He has brought his laptop computer on which he has

an electronic brochure of all the features of the Hotel Park Plaza. He also has information on competitors, along with maps of the area, stored on his laptop's hard drive. Jim is well prepared.

Role-Play Demonstrating Capability with Negotiating Concerns—Model Script

Model scripts in previous and subsequent chapters build on the Jim and Erin's negotiation session to provide consistency in our illustrations.

PHASE TWO—Negotiation Process Strategy

STEP ONE—The Approach

Objective #1—Approach and Reestablish the Relationship

JIM: Good morning, Ms. Massey. It's great to see you. Thanks for inviting me again. By the way, I saw your new YWCA advertisement on TV. Looks great. You seem to be gearing up for a major fund-raising campaign. *(Jim makes a good entrance, smiles, shakes hands, and takes a seat when invited.)*

ERIN: Thanks. We're really excited about the new campaign. And like I said last time, just call me Erin. "Ms. Massey" sounds so formal.

Jim pauses.

Objective #2—Transition from Social to Business Conversation

JIM: *(transition statement away from social conversation to business conversation)* I certainly appreciate the opportunity to let you know about how the Hotel Park Plaza can help you have a successful meeting. I believe that you will like what I have put together for you. *(Jim states the purpose of this appointment: to demonstrate how his hotel can satisfy Erin's meeting needs.)*

STEP TWO—Investigating Needs

Objective #3—Question to Investigate Customer Needs

Jim has preplanned and prepared his strategic sales plan around the six needs or buying conditions as revealed to him by Erin at the investigating needs meeting at his first face-to-face appointment with Erin. Jim will use these needs as the main portion of his demonstrating capability presentation.

STEP THREE—Demonstrating Capability

Objective #4—Summarize and Confirm Needs

JIM: *(continuing a transition to business)* Erin, the last time we spoke, you indicated that you had some needs that were very important to you. Let me see if I have them all. *(Jim begins to summarize the needs.)*

JIM: *(need #1)* Let me see. You said that you wanted to hold your one-day YWCA physical fitness seminar the first Thursday of next month for 150 attendees. Is that right? *(The last part is a confirming question to find out if Jim is on the right track.)*

ERIN: That's right.

JIM: *(need #2)* You also indicated you needed a theater-style meeting facility for 150 attendees and that you needed 3,000 square feet for a trade show.

ERIN: You bet! It's important that we have plenty of space. *(Jim didn't have to ask a confirmation question here as Erin automatically confirmed.)*

JIM: *(need #3)* Erin, your sleeping accommodation needs are for 40 nonsmoking singles for seminar leaders the night before. Do you want VIP treatment packages for these?

ERIN: No VIPs, just 40 single rooms.

JIM: *(need #4)* You also said that you wanted to have the 150 attendees enjoy a chicken luncheon on the seminar day. Is that right? *(Again, Jim adds a confirmation question.)*

ERIN: That's right.

JIM: *(need #5)* You said that a convenient location was very important, along with convenient parking.

ERIN: That is extremely important. Even though this is a physical fitness seminar, I don't want my attendees to get lost or have to do too much exercise *before* they get to the meeting by having to walk for miles.

JIM: *(need #6)* I hear what you're saying. And you indicated that you have a budget for this meeting of about $10,000. Is this right?

ERIN: I think you have it about right.

JIM: Excellent. Are there any other meeting needs that you have thought about since I was last here? *(Jim makes sure that Erin has all of her needs "on the table.")*

ERIN: No, we have covered the most important things.

Objective #5—Give a Brief Differentiation Statement

Jim pauses.

JIM: How familiar are you with the Park Plaza?

ERIN: Not very, but I do drive by it every day on my way to work.

JIM: *(gives a differentiation statement to get Erin's attention and interest)* Our hotel specializes in meetings. We were specifically designed to host groups ranging in size from 15 to 700 attendees. We have recently renovated and have an extensive on-property inventory of audiovisual equipment. We also have a large number of meeting rooms that can be flexibly adjusted to comfortably accommodate our customers' meeting needs. In other words, we are meeting and convention specialists and, as such, we do everything possible to make a meeting successful.

ERIN: I didn't know all that, Jim. It already sounds like your property is a place I might seriously consider.

The attention-getting differentiation statement has caused Erin first to pay attention and then to listen for these different qualities of the Hotel Park Plaza.

Objective #6—Match Each Need with a Product or Service Feature/Benefit

Jim uses his preplanned strategic sales plan to discuss one customer need at a time. He saves the budget need for last!

JIM: What I'd like to do is go over each of your needs and let you know how the Hotel Park Plaza proposes to handle your meeting. How does this sound? *(Note: Jim presents an agenda and then uses a confirmation question to see if Erin agrees and will allow him to proceed.)*

ERIN: That's fine with me.

JIM: *(matching statement for need #1)* About your meeting dates, you indicated that you need to hold the meeting the first Thursday of next month *(restate buying condition/need)*. I have checked our rooms control book *(proof device)* and we have availability *(feature)*. This means *(translation phrase)* that you can have your meeting at the times that you planned *(benefit)*. How does this sound *(confirmation question)*?

ERIN: Great.

JIM: *(matching statement for need #2)* You indicated that you needed a theater-style room for 150 attendees and a trade show room of 3,000 square feet *(buying condition/need)*. Here is a layout of our meeting and display rooms *(proof device)*. We have reserved the Curtis A/B room for your theater seating and the 3,344 square foot Sundance room for your trade show *(feature),* which means to you *(translation phrase)* that your attendees and vendors displaying at the trade show will have a spacious and comfortable environment *(benefit)*. Is that what you had in mind *(confirmation question)*?

STEP FOUR—Negotiating Concerns

Objective #7—Recognize and Negotiate Concerns As They Arise

Objective #7 appears sporadically throughout the demonstrating capability step of the negotiation process.

Buyer Concern #1: Source Concern/Objection

ERIN: Jim, I need to check with the Marriott.

Recognize the Concern (source type of concern/objection)

Note: Jim will use the *feel/felt/found* approach. Pay attention to the language and structure of the way the concern or objection is phrased and answered by Jim.

Validate the Concern

Jim answers Erin's concern by reflective listening and paraphrasing.

JIM: I understand your need to compare and your sense of loyalty to a familiar supplier. You *feel* that obtaining the best price/value is important and that you have been satisfied in the past. Is this correct *(confirmation question)*?

ERIN: Yes.

Answer the Concern

Methods: *indirect denial* plus *superior benefit* (a combination of two of the seven methods used to negotiate concerns)

JIM: My customers have often *felt* the same way *(indirect denial)*. When they decided to try the Hotel Park Plaza, they *found* us to offer a superior value for the price and were happy that they tried us *and* now they had two choices of suppliers *(superior benefit)*.

Method: *demonstration* (another one of the seven methods used to negotiate concerns)

JIM: I know our competition very well and the Marriott is a fine property. Let me show you some price/value comparisons *(demonstration)*. *(Jim demonstrates what he is saying by showing a competitive pricing matrix of his competitor hotels; this is stored in his laptop computer.)*

Trial Close

This is similar to a confirmation question. Jim wants, first, to ascertain whether Erin agrees with his answer and, second, to establish a pattern of her saying yes to his suggested proposal solutions.

JIM: How does this sound?

ERIN: Well, I think you have a good point.

Note: Erin has accepted Jim's answer to her concern. This acceptance is a signal that allows Jim to continue with matching statements. Jim proceeds to the next matching statement since Erin's concern/objection has been answered.

JIM: *(matching statement for need #3)* You indicated that you needed 40 nonsmoking sleeping rooms *(buying condition/need)*. Here's a picture *(proof device, on laptop computer screen or brochure)* of our newly renovated and oversized sleeping rooms *(feature)*. This means to you *(translation phrase)* that your seminar leaders will enjoy state-of-the art and comfortable accommodations *(benefits)*. Is this what you have in mind *(confirmation question)*?

ERIN: Yeah, this looks great. I'm sure that my speakers will be pleased. *(Erin agrees and has no concerns with this matching statement.)*

JIM: *(matching statement for need #4)* You also said that you wanted to have the 150 attendees enjoy a chicken luncheon on the seminar day *(buying condition/need)*. Our award-winning chef *(proof device, his/her picture with awards)* will personally prepare this meal *(feature)*, which means to you *(translation phrase)* that your meeting attendees will enjoy the superb preparation and flavors as well as be treated to an artistic presentation on their plates *(benefits)*. How does this sound *(confirmation question)*?

ERIN: Great! I'm impressed that the chef will personally prepare our luncheon.

JIM: *(matching statement for need #5)* Now, you said that a convenient location was very important, along with convenient parking *(buying condition/need)*. Here is a map of the freeways converging on our downtown property and the blueprint showing our oversized parking garage attached to the hotel *(proof device)*. This means to you *(translation phrase)* that your attendees can easily find the hotel and have a short walk to your meeting room *(benefits)*. Is this the type of thing you're looking for *(confirmation question)*?

Objective #7—Recognize and Negotiate Concerns As They Arise

Objective #7 appears sporadically throughout the demonstrating capability step of the negotiation process.

Buyer Concern #2: Time Objection

ERIN: Jim, all of this sounds great, but I'd like to take a day to think it over. I'm just feeling that I can't make a decision right now.

Recognize the Concern (time type of concern/objection)

Validate the Concern

Jim answers Erin's concern by reflective listening and paraphrasing. Jim will use the *feel/felt/found* approach. Pay attention to the language and structure of the way the concern or objection is phrased and answered by Jim.

JIM: I understand your need to give adequate consideration to important decisions. You feel that it is important to take additional time to weigh this decision. Is this correct *(confirmation question)*?

ERIN: Yes.

Answer the Concern

Methods: indirect denial plus *third-party testimony* (a combination of two of the seven methods used to negotiate concerns)

JIM: My satisfied customers have often *felt* the same way *(indirect denial)*. But sometimes circumstances required that they act quickly *(third-party testimony)* and they found their action to be a good decision.

Jim's use of a third-party testimony here is not a true use because he only alleged satisfied customers felt and found acting quickly to be satisfactory. Obviously, if Jim could have named a specific third party or had proof, this would be stronger.

Method: demonstration (another one of the seven methods used to negotiate concerns)

JIM: We have a situation that requires decisive action. Our space availability is becoming very tight. Let me share with you the current situation *(demonstration)*.

Jim demonstrates what he is saying by showing the current Hotel Park Plaza "Rooms and Function Book" as tentatively and definitely sold to-date. Jim now has his laptop computer connected by phone lines to the Park Plaza's central computer.

Method: question (another one of the seven methods used to negotiate concerns)

JIM: Do you feel that waiting a few extra days to make this decision outweighs the benefits that you would receive by meeting at the Park Plaza?

Jim uses a fairly complex combination of methods to negotiate Erin's time concern/objection. This illustrates how many ways the seven methods can be effectively and creatively combined.

ERIN: You make a pretty good case for acting more quickly.

Trial Close

Jim uses a confirmation question. He wants, first, to ascertain whether Erin agrees with his answer to her concern and, second, to continue her pattern of saying yes to Jim's suggested proposal solutions.

JIM: Erin, what do you think?

ERIN: As I said throughout our meeting today, what I've seen so far looks very good. I am leaning heavily toward holding my meeting at the Park Plaza. . . . I really don't want to lose the space.

Erin has accepted Jim's complex combination answer to her concern. This acceptance is a signal that allows Jim to continue with matching statements. Jim proceeds to the next matching statement now that Erin's concern/objection has been answered.

JIM: (*matching statement for need #6—price*) Erin, you indicated that you have a budget of around $10,000 (*buying condition/need*). As you can see by the calculations on the proposal (*proof device*), I have been able to get the total price within the range of your budget: $10,800 (*feature*). This means (*translation phrase*) that all of your meeting needs can be met by a total price that approximates your budget (*benefit*). Is that what you had in mind (*confirmation question*)?

Objective #7—Recognize and Negotiate Concerns As They Arise

Objective #7 appears sporadically throughout the demonstrating capability step of the negotiation process.

Buying Concern #3: Price Objection

ERIN: Well, Jim, as you know, I told you that my budget was in the range of $10,000. $10,800 is too much. I can't afford it!

Recognizing and Validating the Concern

Jim answers Erin's concern by reflective listening and paraphrasing. Jim will use the *feel/felt/found* approach. Pay attention to the language and structure of the way the concern or objection is phrased and answered by Jim.

JIM: I understand your need to meet your budget. You *feel* that obtaining the best price for the value is important and you *feel* that our proposed budget is a bit higher than yours. Is this correct *(confirmation question)*?

ERIN: Yes, we are a nonprofit organization and dollars are very hard to come by. I need to make sure that we get maximum bang for our buck.

Answering the Concern

Methods: *indirect denial* plus *third-party testimony* (combination of two of the seven methods used to negotiate concerns)

JIM: My customers have often *felt* the same way *(indirect denial).* However, their budgets were a starting point and a ballpark figure. When they saw the excellent price/value offered and decided to use the Park Plaza, they *found* us to be a superior value for the price *(third-party testimony).*

Methods: *superior benefit* and *question* (combination of two of the seven methods used to negotiate concerns)

JIM: Let me show you some additional benefits that will increase the value you receive for the proposed budget. Were you aware that we offer free airport pickup? I know that you planned to pay for 20 of the 40 seminar leaders' airport transportation. Let's see, 20 attendees times $20 round trip to the airport is $400. (Use any additional benefits not mentioned earlier—always save an *ace* for this.)

ERIN: Jim, I didn't know about your airport pickup. Yes, this $400 will help to reduce my costs almost to my $10,000 budget.

Erin mentally calculates: proposal ($10,800) less $400 equals Erin's cost ($10,400). Since she likes the many benefits Jim has already discussed with her, she is willing to compromise and pay slightly above her budget. Saving a discussion of price until *after* all other benefits have been discussed is very important. Only when a buyer knows the benefits or value to be received can he/she possibly make a decision about the purchase price.

Trial Close (similar to a confirmation question)

JIM: How does this sound?

ERIN: Well, it's slightly above my budget, but from everything you have told me about Park Plaza, I guess I can find another $400. Sounds good.

This is a clear verbal buying signal that should cause Jim to move toward the gaining commitment step.

Objective #8—Select an Appropriate Closing Method

Jim chooses the *summary of benefits* closing/commitment method. (The six closing methods are discussed in Chapter 12.) This method is chosen because: (1) Erin has agreed to all of Jim's matching statements even though Jim had to negotiate concerns three times; and (2) Jim wants all the agreed-on benefits clearly in the front of Erin's mind just before he directly asks for the order (*objective #9*).

Objective #9—Ask for the Buyer's Commitment

Preface with Summarized Benefits

Briefly summarize benefits that were discussed in the matching statements in Step Three above. Even though summary of benefits is a type of closing method (see Chapter 12), it is always a good idea to summarize here even if the salesperson used a different closing method in objective #8.

Jim makes this summary loose and free flowing. Jim summarized *needs* at the beginning of the presentation. Now *benefits* are summarized. These benefits are associated with each of the six matching statements above.

> **JIM:** I'm happy to hear that. Let's review where we've been: We have your dates available *(benefit #1)* and we have provided spacious accommodations for both the meeting and trade show *(benefit #2)*. Our oversized and newly renovated sleeping rooms provide comfortable accommodations for your seminar presenters *(benefit #3)*. The chicken luncheon prepared by our award-winning chef will be artistically presented and delicious *(benefit #4)*. Easy access to our downtown location and our free adjacent parking garage will provide your guests convenience *(benefit #5)*. And, most important, all of this is within your budget range *(benefit #6)*. How does all this sound *(confirmation question)*?
>
> **ERIN:** I like it. From everything you have told me, it sounds like my meeting will be a success.

Jim receives a clear buying signal that indicates he can move to the next objective.

Directly Ask for the Order (Gain Commitment)

Ask for the order in a clear and direct way. Be sure that there is no mistake that you are asking for the order. Some salespeople become wishy-washy here. Since so much time and effort have been invested up until this point, avoid a common salesperson's weakness of getting cold feet at this step.

> **JIM:** Can we formalize our agreement with your signature?

Jim places the written proposal along with handwritten changes that were negotiated in the negotiating concerns step in front of Erin with a pen.

The signed proposal, even with handwritten changes, is now a formal and legal contract or letter of agreement. Of course, a clean copy will be retyped and re-signed. The salesperson should always get a signature.

If massive changes are negotiated, it is best to make another appointment to go over a clean revised contract with the buyer and have him/her sign it.

Objective #10—Negotiate Any Customer Concerns about Making a Commitment

You will not meet any resistance in this chapter. We will fully discuss gaining commitment in Chapter 12.

Step Five—Gaining Commitment

ERIN: (*while signing the letter of agreement*) Jim, what happens next?

Objective #11—After-Sale Service Statements

Give the customer an idea of what actions will take place after the order is placed. This keeps the customer from feeling that all the salesperson is interested in is making this sale.

Also be sure to thank the customer.

JIM: Thanks, Erin. We at the Hotel Park Plaza want to make your meeting a very successful one. As soon as you sign the letter of agreement, this becomes the marching orders of the house (the *house* is language for the hotel). We will immediately assign you a conference service manager (CSM) who will call and let you know about various time lines and meeting details.

Of course, I am always in the background and watching over your meeting to make sure that everything runs smoothly.

ERIN: This sounds great. Having a person to help me with my meeting sure takes a load off my mind. Jim, it's been great working with you.

JIM: I am enjoying working with you and helping you to have a successful meeting. I appreciate your time and look forward to working with you. We'll stay in frequent contact. Thanks again for your business.

CHAPTER 12

Phase Two— Negotiation Process Strategy:

Step Five—Gaining Commitment

After reading this chapter you should be able to

- ◆ explain why gaining a customer's commitment can at times be difficult
- ◆ describe the guidelines and methods that will increase the chances that a salesperson can overcome such resistance
- ◆ list the elements of a letter of agreement and sales contract

gaining commitment

minor closing

assumption close

direct-appeal close

letter of agreement

nonperformance clauses

insurance and indemnification clauses

legal jurisdiction and arbitration clauses

special-concession close

single-problem close

limited-choice close

Gaining commitment or *closing* is the point in the buying/selling exchange process at which the salesperson asks the potential buyer to make a purchase. In other negotiation situations, at this step the other party is asked to take an action of some sort. While this culminating step seems to be a logical outcome of all the work and effort from both buyer and seller, it is surprising to learn that sellers often are afraid to ask for the purchase and buyers often have additional concerns when the gaining commitment step is reached. Ideally, a salesperson who is well prepared and capable should not fear, but welcome this step. And, ideally, all potential buyer questions or concerns should have been asked and addressed before this step.

In this chapter we will discuss five issues related to gaining commitment:

1. why gaining commitment is difficult
2. guidelines for gaining commitment
3. the methods used to gain commitment
4. how to negotiate additional buyer concerns
5. the **letter of agreement** or contract

We will end our discussion with a model role-play script that illustrates the topics we have covered.

Before we proceed to discuss Step Five of Phase Two, gaining commitment, let's remind ourselves of where our discussion from previous chapters has taken us. Let's briefly review the entire buying/selling exchange process that we first introduced in Chapter 7 (see Table 7–1).

In Chapter 9, we discussed the first appointment of a multi-call negotiation session. The purpose of that first appointment was investigating needs. Having discovered the prospective buyer's needs, at the end of this first appointment we set-up a second appointment for a future date. Before the second appointment, we prepared a proposal (see Chapter 10). The purpose of the second appointment was to present this proposal or demonstrate capability by showing how our product or service could satisfy the buyer's needs.

In Chapter 10, we presented the format of steps for demonstrating capability in the second appointment. In Chapter 11, we proceeded through the steps of the demonstrating capability process for a second time, but we complicated the process by introducing buyer concerns and resistance to show how a salesperson is able to negotiate concerns or questions raised by the potential buyer.

In this chapter, we will again go through the steps of the demonstrating capability (Step Three) process along with negotiating concerns (Step Four), but this time we will even further complicate the process by adding buyer resistance and concerns at the very end of the process. This is the step at which the seller attempts to close or obtain commitment from the buyer. This chapter focuses on methods of *gaining commitment (Step Five)*.

Why Gaining Commitment Is Difficult

This step in the buying/selling exchange process is stressful and difficult for both the potential buyer and the salesperson. Brian Tracy, the author of *Advanced Selling Strategies* (1995, 355–356), gives several reasons.

Potential Buyer

The first and foremost reason that a prospect has difficulty at this step is the *fear of failure*. The prospect may have had negative buying experiences in the past, over which the salesperson now has no control. Buyers are conditioned to be suspicious, skeptical, and wary of salespeople and sales approaches. They are afraid of making a mistake. They are afraid of paying too much. They are afraid of being criticized by others for making the wrong buying decision. Fear of failure or making a mistake is the major reason why people object, hesitate, and procrastinate on the buying decision.

The second reason potential buyers have difficulty at the gaining commitment step is that they may be very *busy and preoccupied*. It's not that they are not interested or wouldn't enjoy the benefits of the product or service. They are sometimes simply overwhelmed with their work and don't have the time to thoroughly consider the salesperson's product or service. So, salespeople must be patient and persevere and deliver convincing and persuasive presentations.

Third, sometimes it's a matter of inertia. Prospects are usually comfortable doing what they have done in the past. Thus, a salesperson has to be able to find a way to break the resistance to making change. This is particularly true if a prospect is currently loyal to a competitor.

Salesperson

Fear of rejection or fear of criticism and disapproval is the most common reason salespeople have a difficult time at the gaining commitment step. The salesperson has worked long and hard to convert suspects to prospects, so when they are at the step when they are about to convert the prospect into a customer, they freeze. They fear that they might be rejected by the prospect saying no to their request to make a purchase.

Guidelines for Gaining Commitment

There are a number of factors that will increase the chances that the salesperson will gain commitment (Manning and Reese 1997, 297–301).

Focus On the Prospect's Dominant Buying Motive

In sales language, this has been called the prospect's *hot button*. During the demonstrating capability step, many features and benefits have been discussed, but there is usually one that generates the most excitement in the prospect. Be alert to this hot button, and give it the greatest emphasis at the gaining commitment step.

Before the Gaining Commitment Step, Negotiate the Toughest Points

Gaining commitment should be a positive step and not the place to deal with controversial issues or problems. If your product or service has a weak point, make sure that it surfaces *before* attempting to gain commitment. Even if you must bring tough issues to the surface, it's better to do so and openly discuss them.

Avoid Surprises at the Gaining Commitment Step

Similar to negotiating tough points before gaining commitment, salespeople should ensure that potentially surprising information is not revealed to the prospect at the last step. Bring these items up during the matching statements part of demonstrating capability, and deal with them openly and honestly. Don't let a last-minute surprise damage the relationship and threaten the completion of a sale.

Display Self-Confidence at the Gaining Commitment Step

If you truly believe that you have honestly done the best job possible to consultatively help the prospect solve problems or satisfy needs, there is no reason for lack of confidence. Be confident in yourself, your product or service, your organization, and your proposed solution to the prospect's problem. Never be apologetic in this step of the buying/selling exchange process. A display of self-confidence is particularly important.

Ask the Prospect to Purchase More Than Once

Statistics have shown: (1) 50 percent of all salespeople asked for the purchase once; (2) 20 percent asked twice; and (3) the most productive salespeople asked three times or more. Furthermore, a large number of purchases were made on the fourth or fifth attempt. Does a salesperson obnoxiously ask a prospect five times in a row to purchase? No. After a first no, the salesperson questions further and engages the prospect in more discussion and asks for the purchase at an appropriate moment. In many cases, the salesperson finds a reason to break off the negotiation session and return at a later time when the situation has cooled and/or the salesperson has more information. So, don't give up after one no!

Recognize Clues That Invite Moving to Gaining Commitment

These clues are often referred to as *buying signals*. These clues are of two types: verbal clues and nonverbal clues.

Verbal Clues. *Verbal clues* come in several forms: (1) questions (for example, "How soon can we get delivery?"); (2) recognitions, positive statements toward the seller's product, organization, or factor related to the sale (for example, "I've always wanted to hold a meeting in a five-star property like this."); and (3) requirements, a statement about a condition that must be met before a purchase can be made (for example, "We will need to have all of our audiovisual equipment shipped in two weeks before our meeting dates. Is that a problem?").

Nonverbal Clues. *Nonverbal clues* are more difficult to recognize than verbal clues. And they are not easy to interpret. Sometimes the popular interpretation may not apply in the specific case where it is being observed. For example, arms folded over the chest do not always signal distancing oneself. Here are a few nonverbal clues that might be sending a buying signal: (1) prospect's facial expression changes (for example, eyes widen and genuine interest is shown on the face); (2) prospect begins to nod head in agreement; (3) prospect leans forward and appears intent on hearing your message; and (4) prospect begins to study sales brochures, handle the product, or show other tangible interest.

When you observe buying signals, don't hesitate to attempt gaining commitment. These signals may occur anytime during the demonstrating capability step. If they occur during the step itself, then a trial close is appropriate. If they occur at the end, then other methods are appropriate. We will discuss these methods next.

Methods to Close or Gain Commitment

The following methods are the most commonly used in gaining commitment. There are generally two times to attempt to gain commitment: during or after the demonstrating capability process. Sales literature often presents many creative variations that can usually be reduced to these broad categories.

Minor Closing or Gaining Commitment *During* Demonstrating Capability

There is one method used *during* the demonstrating capability step. It is used as a test to see if the prospective buyer is ready to buy before the salesperson has completed the entire presentation. If the salesperson senses the buyer is ready to buy, he/she will move to any of the *major* closing methods discussed next. An attempt to gain commitment early in the demonstrating capability process is commonly known as a *trial close*. It is a *minor* close since most *major* attempts to close or gain commitment are found at the end of the demonstrating capability process.

The trial close is very similar to a confirmation question first introduced in Chapter 9. During the process of demonstrating capability, a salesperson often asks questions that result in an affirmative answer by the prospective buyer. After several of these affirmative responses, it becomes clear to the salesperson that the buyer has a positive attitude toward making a purchase. Thus, the salesperson might immediately skip several steps in the demonstrating capability process and move to a major close (asking for the order). The *trial close* is a **minor closing** attempt made at an opportune time during the sales presentation to encourage the customer to reveal readiness or unwillingness to buy.

The trial close is most appropriate after obtaining sufficient agreements to buy *and* getting buying signals. For example, after matching needs with features/benefits and asking the confirmation question "Do you think your attendees will be happy with these junior suites?" you might ask, "Would you like to formalize these arrangements?"

Minor Closing or Gaining Commitment *After* Demonstrating Capability

There are six major closes or methods of gaining commitment that usually occur at the end of the process of demonstrating capability.

Summary-of-the-Benefits Close. A summary-of-the-benefits close is a reemphasis of the benefits that will help bring about a favorable decision. It summarizes the most important buyer benefits already discussed earlier that will produce a favorable decision.

This close is used after the salesperson has overcome all buyer concerns and objections and there simply are no more. This is a logical conclusion to the presentation. It becomes obvious that there is nothing left to do but ask if the buyer wants to purchase.

This type of close may be worded, "Let's review all of the benefits that we have discussed, benefit #1, #2, #3, and so on." This summary would be followed by, "Can we get the ball rolling by signing this letter of agreement (contract)?" This last statement combines a **direct-appeal close** with the summary-of-the-benefits close.

Assumption Close. An **assumption close** assumes that the prospect is going to buy. The salesperson begins to act and talk like the prospective buyer has already purchased the product or service. This talk and action are focused on what takes place next (since the sale has already been made).

This close comes near the end of the planned demonstrating capability process. It comes after all genuine needs have been identified, solutions/benefits have been presented, and all concerns and objections have been negotiated or answered in a satisfactory manner.

For example, you might ask one or more questions regarding a minor point or begin writing up the order: "Shall I indicate *master billing* on the letter of agreement?"

Special-Concession Close. The special-concession close offers the buyer something extra for acting immediately.

Use this close carefully because some buyers are skeptical of concessions. Use it to push the prospect who seems to be on the edge of a decision.

For example, offer a special price reduction, a more liberal credit plan, or an added feature that was not anticipated by the prospect. "As an added bonus, we can host (provide as a comp) your group's reception party on the night of arrival."

Single-Problem Close. The single-problem close deals with a single concern or objection that stands in the way of gaining commitment from the prospective buyer. The buyer himself/herself comes to the conclusion that there is only one concern left. The salesperson had already eliminated all concerns or objections during the presentation but this last one.

It will generally surface on a "trial close." Handle it immediately when you recognize it.

For example, you might say, "Mr. Prospect, it seems that you like all of the benefits that we have discussed except this one. Is that right? If I could take care of this, would you sign the letter of agreement?"

Limited-Choice Close. A limited-choice close uses a series of increasingly narrow product or service choices offered to the prospective buyer as a way of helping the buyer to make a decision. This is similar to the single-problem close, but this comes at the *end* of the demonstrating capability. At this point, the prospective buyer still is undecided about several concerns. The salesperson helps to narrow the concerns. In the single-problem close, the salesperson answered all concerns *during* the presentation and the prospective buyer only has one concern left at the end of the presentation.

This close may be used after the prospect seems unable to decide but the salesperson knows that the benefits have already been accepted or sold to the buyer. The following describes a way to implement this method: (1) allow the prospect to examine several different "choice packages" and try to assess the degree of interest; (2) cease showing new choices when it appears that the prospect has been given ample selection; (3) remove a product in which the prospect seems uninterested; and (4) concentrate on products in which the prospect seems to be definitely interested.

For example, you might say, "It appears that these two choices are your primary interest. Is that right? The pluses and minuses of each are these: . . . Which one would you like?"

Direct-Appeal Close.   The direct-appeal close involves asking for the order in a straightforward manner.

It is used after all benefits have been presented and agreed to. Don't use it too early.

For example, you might say, "Can we formalize our agreement with your signature on this letter of agreement?" or "Can I send you the letter of agreement?"

Negotiating Additional Concerns at the Gaining Commitment Step Using the Seven Negotiating Methods

Generally, when the potential buyer again raises a concern or question at the gaining commitment step, it should be obvious that the prospect did not have all concerns clearly answered earlier during the matching statement discussion. Since the salesperson gave the prospect many opportunities to have all questions answered (asked confirmation questions after each matching statement) why would the prospect have more questions or concerns?

There are several possible explanations.

Prospect Raises Rational Concerns

A rational concern can be one that is connected with reason or with emotion. For example, a rational reason related to price may be that the prospect really does not have the money to pay for the purchase. An example of a rational emotion might be an inexperienced buyer who is feeling fear of a decision or is feeling the stress of uncertainty.

At the earlier part of the negotiation discussion, the prospect may have believed that the prospect's concerns were answered, but after more information is presented by the salesperson, an earlier concern becomes more magnified. Similarly, more information might cause different concerns to arise at the gaining commitment step.

Usually, rational concerns can be addressed by a rational approach. A consultative salesperson attempts to use effective interpersonal skills to continue to question and listen to the prospect in order to address rational concerns.

Prospect Raises Irrational Concerns

An irrational concern appears to have no foundation in reason. Yet, often there is a reason. The prospect may simply be using a *stall*. A stall is a way to postpone making a decision, while using a concern that sounds rational. In this case, they are stalling for an irrational reason, perhaps a subconscious fear of failure as mentioned by Brian Tracy (1995). A stall is difficult to handle because it cannot be rationally addressed. Sometimes a salesperson resorts to win-lose strategies to address the stall, perhaps using a strong appeal to emotional motivators such as fear or greed.

For example, the prospect might have a concern with price. As discussed previously, the prospect has a concern about price being too high. But, in this example, is he/she simply raising this concern to see if the salesperson will give him/her a deal? Is this a trial balloon to test the salesperson? Is this concern real or a stall? Or, it may be that the prospect habitually says no to any request. Believe it. There are people who have these characteristics.

So, what can a salesperson rationally do when encountering prospect concerns during the gaining commitment step? As you learned in Chapter 11, there are seven methods to negotiate concerns: indirect denial, direct denial, superior benefit, demonstration, trial offer, third-party testimony, and questions. And, there is an effective sequence to deliver these seven methods. Let's briefly review.

1. Recognize the concern.
   a. Verbal and nonverbal signals
   b. What type of concern is it (of the five common types)?
2. Validate the concern—Use reflective listening.
3. Answer the concern—Use one or a combination of seven methods to respond.
   a. Decide which of the seven techniques or combinations will answer the concern.
   b. Use feel/felt/found statement.

For a more in-depth review of how to negotiate concerns, revisit Chapter 11. Let's now turn our discussion to the focus of gaining commitment. We are asking the prospect to give us a commitment by signing the proposal that we have been discussing. When he/she signs the proposal, it is transformed into a legal contract or letter of agreement.

The Letter of Agreement or Contract

Revisiting Document Flows

In Chapter 8, Table 8–2, we introduced the concept of *suspects, prospects,* and *customers,* each associated with different probabilities of becoming an actual buyer or customer. As consultative salespeople, we want to work smart. We only want to expend our valuable time and resources on approaching qualified potential buyers. Thus, we used a series of increasingly more complicated communication documents (see Table 8–2) when we approached each of the various levels of suspects to prospects to customers.

In Chapter 9, the first face-to-face appointment that the salesperson made was with a prospect for the purpose of investigating needs and thoroughly discovering the prospect's wants, needs, desires, and problems to be solved. After these needs were discovered through in-depth questioning, the salesperson returned to the office to develop a proposal. This document is the salesperson's best estimate of how the product or service can solve the prospective buyer's problems or satisfy needs.

In Chapter 10, the second face-to-face appointment was for the purpose of presenting the developed, but estimated, proposal. During this session, the buyer and seller negotiated the appropriateness of the proposal's ability to solve the buyer's needs or problem. If there were no changes to the original proposal, the prospective customer signed it and it became the basic contract or letter of agreement. Of course, in most cases there are changes from the proposal; thus, the original will be rewritten and modified to reflect negotiated changes. Signatures are again obtained. Many times it takes a third, fourth, or more negotiation sessions in order to gain the buyer's commitment and agreement, complete negotiations, and close the sale. The signed and official letter of agreement outlines the basic understanding between the buyer and the seller.

In the lodging industry, the major services sold by salespeople are conventions, conferences, and group business. Usually a buyer purchases or signs a basic letter of agreement far in advance of the actual dates of the conference itself. In the case of corporate meetings and conferences, the letter of agreement might be signed up to one year before the actual meeting. In the case of association meetings and conventions, the letter of agreement might be signed as far in advance as three to five years. Thus, the basic letter of agreement certainly will be expanded and revised during the time between first signatures and actual meeting. So, how does the letter of agreement evolve with these inevitable changes? The answer is that all new additions and subtractions are agreed to between buyer and seller and evidenced by separate documents. These separate documents are added to the original basic letter of agreement as an appendix and become a legal part of it.

Contract or Letter of Agreement Defined

Webster's Encyclopedic Unabridged Dictionary defines a contract as follows:

> *An agreement between two or more parties for the doing or not doing of something specified. An agreement enforceable by law. The written form of such an agreement (Webster's 1996, 441).*

The word *contract* usually causes people to think of lawyers and may cause potential buyers to have concerns about signing. In sales, we use a friendlier term, *letter of agreement*. While most people know that this term clearly indicates a contract, we recommend that you use *letter of agreement*.

The Basic Letter of Agreement Contains Only Essential Components

The basic letter of agreement should contain only the most essential components of the agreement between the buyer and the seller. In fact, all the components of even a complex meeting, conference, or convention can be contained on the front and back of a single sheet of 8-1/2 by 11 paper. There are two major reasons for keeping the letter of agreement pared to its essential elements.

First, most meetings and conventions will have changes between the date the letter of agreement is signed and the dates of the actual meeting itself. There is no way at the date of signing of the contract or letter of agreement that either the customer or salesperson can know all the final service needs that will be required at the actual meeting. Due to this first reason, only major meeting needs and understandings should be included in the letter of agreement. These are usually financial and blocking of lodging and meeting space needs.

Second, a more subtle reason, both the seller and the buyer want to finalize an agreement quickly once it has been reached. Complex contracts are bait for corporate attorneys whose job it is to protect their organizations. If a letter of agreement or contract contains complex estimates of contingencies and changes that may or may not occur over the period between the requested date of signing and the dates (often years into the future) of the actual meeting, convention, or conference itself, these complexities are almost certain to cause serious delay. Corporate attorneys will scrutinize and rewrite complex clauses. The salesperson and the buyer will be seriously delayed in proceeding to implement the sold product or service as discussed in the buying/selling exchange process, Phase Three—Post-Negotiation Strategy, Step One—After-Sale Implementation.

What Are the Essential Components of a Basic Letter of Agreement?

As mentioned earlier, when a salesperson makes a sales presentation or demonstrates capability, the salesperson is simply explaining a prepared proposal. This document essentially looks very similar to the final letter of agreement. In fact, if the buyer signs the proposal as written and/or with minor initialed changes, the proposal is formally transformed into a basic letter of agreement. Most of the time, the buyer has more significant changes to the proposal; thus, the final letter of agreement is rewritten and modified to reflect these changes.

We now turn to our discussion of the essential components of a basic letter of agreement. The following is modified from Astroff and Abbey's excellent treatment of the topic of letters of agreement (Astroff and Abbey 1998).

Identity Items. *Names of Organization and Hotel.* The correct names of both contracting organizations must be clearly indicated on the letter of agreement.

Official Dates. Along with the dates, the time of arrival and departure should be indicated. For example, "February 2–5, 2003" would indicate arrival on Sunday and departure on Wednesday and check-in at 4 PM on the day of arrival and checkout at 12 noon on the day of departure.

Meeting Attendee Arrival Patterns. Some meetings have the same number arriving and the same number departing over the official dates of the meeting or conference. Other meetings have a lesser number of attendees on the first day, a greater number over the next few days, and fewer numbers on the last day. Make sure that the letter of agreement is exact.

Warranty of Authority. A warranty of authority clause states that the signers have been granted authority by their respective organizations (both buying and selling organizations) to enter into an agreement that binds their organizations to the letter of agreement. This clause is especially important considering turnover of both lodging industry personnel and meeting planning personnel and given the length of time from the date a letter of agreement is signed to when the meeting is actually held.

Sleeping Rooms. *Number and Kinds of Sleeping Rooms.* Numbers of single and double occupancy in suites, standard rooms, or other must be indicated.

Sleeping Room Rates. List the rate that will be charged for each type of room.

Complimentary. Often a lodging facility has a policy that provides complimentary rooms *(comps)* for, say, every 50 contracted. If this has been negotiated, be sure to indicate it in the letter.

Meeting/Exhibit/Banquet Rooms. *Number and Setup Styles of Meeting/ Exhibit/Banquet Rooms.* Along with meeting rooms, include any needs for banquet rooms. Make sure that the number of meeting rooms is indicated along with the times they are needed. Include the number of attendees to the meeting or banquet function. Be sure to indicate the style of room set-up. Theater style for 150 requires a smaller room than a room set up classroom style for 150. Different room set-up styles regardless of purpose (meeting/exhibit/banquet) will determine the size of room needed.

Meeting/Exhibit/Banquet Room Rates. Generally, there is no charge for the use of meeting rooms when a conference and/or convention is spending sufficient revenue on food and beverage and sleeping rooms. However, be ready to refer to a meeting room price list, if necessary.

Audiovisual Equipment. Provide a price list of equipment for which you charge, and reference the published price list in the letter of agreement where applicable.

Union Regulations. If applicable, provide a list of the basic workday rates, and overtime charges. Reference this list in the letter of agreement.

Food and Beverage Functions. Generally there are four types of food and beverage functions that are planned by meeting planners: breakfast/lunch/dinner; special banquets; cocktail parties with food; and refreshment breaks. Make sure that the contract specifies all policies applying to any of these four: (1) prices along with tax structure and any inclusive gratuities or applicable service charges, (2) advance notice of number of guaranteed attendees to functions, (3) description of items included in terms like *refreshment break,* and (4) regarding liquor, do you charge by the bottle, the hour, or the drink, and what becomes of unopened bottles; does your lodging property charge an add-on corkage fee for liquor purchased off-property but consumed on-property?

Financial Items. *Master and Individual Accounts* (Folios) *and Credit Procedures.* What will be billed to the master account, and what will be billed to individual accounts? Be sure to specify this and who is authorized to encumber the master account.

Before extending credit to a corporate group or association, especially for the first time, it is customary to request a completed credit application.

Method of Payment. How will the lodging facility be paid? One common method is payment in thirds: (1) one-third as a deposit when the contract is signed, (2) one-third paid before the convention/conference or meeting departs, and (3) one-third paid at a later date. Corporations generally have the ability to comply with this payment structure, whereas associations and SMERF (social, military or medical, educational, religious, and fraternal) businesses generally can't comply with the rigorous one-third deposit up front. The contracting lodging facility must be sensitive to the characteristics of their customers, but whatever the method of payment used, amounts and due dates should be clearly specified.

Miscellaneous Charges. Some lodging facilities ensure that their service personnel will receive additional compensation for services. Thus, bellperson charges per bag both in and out are often specified in the letter of agreement. Also, daily housekeeping charges per room per day are specified.

Legal Items. *Nonperformance Clauses.* **Nonperformance clauses** are the specification in the letter of agreement that compensate either the seller (lodging facility) or buyer (meeting organization) if one or the other party does not perform according to the terms of the letter of agreement.

1. Termination/Cancellation. What happens when either party has to cancel because of circumstances beyond its control?
   a. If the customer cancels, the lodging facility commonly has included a sliding scale of penalties that the customer would have to pay. The first date of the scale indicates that there is no penalty if the meeting is cancelled prior to that date. A second date closer to the official meeting dates might be 25 percent of the full value of the contract. A third date even closer to the official meeting dates might be 50 percent of the full value of the contract. Dates increasingly closer to the official dates would be set on this sliding scale with increasing monetary cancellation fees up to 100 percent of the full value of the entire meeting.
   b. If the lodging facility cancels, the customer may or may not have recourse. In the past, letters of agreement were one-sided. Only the lodging facility negotiated cancellation clauses to take care of their risks. Today, sophisticated meeting planners are likely to insist that a clause be placed in the letter of agreement to protect them.
2. Penalty Clauses. What happens when either party does not fully live up to the terms of the letter of agreement? This is not an outright cancellation of the meeting, but failure to live up to parts of the agreement. For instance, the lodging facility might oversell its room inventory and have to shuttle some of the meeting attendees to another hotel. Or, the meeting organization might not pick up the number of rooms that it contracted for. What to do? There is recourse in the legal system, but the question is whether or not this remedy is practical. Some solutions are various clauses in the letter of agreement itself:
   a. The lodging facility already protects itself with room reservation *cut-off dates*. Cut-off dates are various dates, 90-day, 60-day, and 30-day dates prior to the official meeting dates at which contracted room blocks are released and sold to walk-in hotel guests if the meeting organization does not fill them. This is common with

association markets where individuals make their own reservations (credited to the contracted room block). Corporations make reservations for the individual attendees; thus, the cut-off system doesn't apply.

As added protection with the above cut-off system, another protection clause, an *attrition clause,* protects the hotel against sleeping room block *slippage*. Essentially, this is a provision that allows the lodging facility to charge for any rooms contracted for but not picked up.

Also, the lodging facility protects itself through 48- to 72-hour banquet guarantees. In both of the above lodging protection systems, the customer is responsible for any room or banquet guarantees made.

    b. The customer or meeting organization often has little protection. But, the customer can insist that a clause be placed in the letter of agreement. For example, the hotel agrees to arrange for and pay for accommodations at other hotels if it overbooks.

The reality of the situation for both parties is that little can be done without a specific clause in the letter of agreement and, even if it is there, legal action may be necessary to enforce it. Generally, people of good faith should ensure that they contract with other people of good faith.

Insurance and Indemnification. It is common for the lodging facility to stipulate that the meeting organization agree to carry adequate liability insurance that protects the lodging facility against claims arising from the group's activities conducted in the facility during the conference or meeting.

Legal Jurisdiction and/or Arbitration Clauses. It is preferable and more advantageous for a party to legal litigation to be subject to the legal jurisdiction where it is located. Thus, the lodging facility might provide a clause to specify in which state's court system legal conflicts might be resolved.

Arbitration is a means for settling disputes outside the court system and is less costly. It is usually in the best interests of both the meeting planner and the lodging facility to use arbitration instead of the court system.

The Convention Liaison Council (CLC) has an alternative dispute resolution (ADR) procedure as an alternative to either lawsuits or arbitration. The CLC and its ADR procedure allow hotels and meeting planners to submit a written statement of claims and to present their case at an oral hearing before a three-member panel composed of individuals from within the hospitality industry. A hearing is held within 30 days after statements are filed.

All rulings by the panel are nonbinding unless agreed as such by the parties (Astroff and Abbey 1998, 312).

Although CLC decisions are nonbinding, if a specific clause is initially placed in the letter of agreement to use the CLC in disputes, people of good faith generally will abide by such ruling.

After Obtaining a Signed Letter of Agreement, What Next?

As was discussed earlier, customers sign a letter of agreement one to several years in advance of the actual dates of the meeting or conference. They often ask as soon as they sign, "What happens next?" What they are asking is how the meeting will be implemented. Additionally, they are asking if the salesperson and their organization will make sure that the intangible service they just purchased will be adequately managed. At this point, the salesperson must give the new customer reassurance and a general plan of implementation. The salesperson might say something like this:

> *As soon as you signed the letter of agreement, it became the "marching orders of the house." We will immediately assign you a Conference Service Manager (CSM) who will call and let you know about various time lines and things needed to detail the meeting.*

In Chapter 13, we will thoroughly address after-sale implementation and how to manage the customer's uncertainty between signing the letter of agreement and the time the meeting is actually held. We will illustrate the concepts and methods described in this chapter with a role-play model script at the end of this chapter.

The Demonstrating Capability Appointment with Negotiating Concerns and Gaining Commitment

Let's look at the logical steps of systematically discussing the proposal by magnifying Phase Two of the buying/selling exchange process. In Table 12–1 we will look at the details of the demonstrating capability step when the prospective buyer has questions, objects, or resists some of the matching statements in the salesperson's proposal presentation. Remember, we have already investigated needs during the first appointment of this multi-call negotiation session. Therefore, we have a different purpose for this second appointment: *gaining commitment* by making a sale or having the prospective buyer agree to continue working with the salesperson to complete the sale.

Table 12–1   Objectives in the Demonstrating Capability Negotiation Session with Negotiating Concerns and Concerns at Gaining Commitment

PHASE TWO – NEGOTIATION PROCESS STRATEGY

Step One – Approaching the Buyer (Chapter 8)

Objective #1–Approach and Reestablish the Relationship

1. Effectively reestablished relationship that was strengthened in the first appointment of this multi-call negotiation session (make enthusiastic comments about information from last meeting and what commonalities are now known). This is the social conversation.

2. Communicated positive *body* language (good entrance, carriage, handshake, and seating posture).

3. Communicated positive *verbal* language (used positive words, showed enthusiasm with a well-modulated voice).

4. Used customer's name effectively (at least three times).

Objective #2: Transition from Social to Business Conversation

Made transition statement from social conversation to business purpose. Communicated sales appointment objectives (shared why salesperson was calling).

Step Two – Investigating Needs (Chapter 9)

Objective #3–Question to Investigate Customer Needs

This step was completed in the first appointment of this multi-call negotiation session (Chapter 9).

Step Three – Demonstrating Capability (Chapter 10)

Objective #4–Summarize and Confirm Needs

1. Showed clear understanding of each of the customer's needs (from investigating needs role-play).

2. Ended this summary of needs with, "Is there anything else that I have not covered?"

Objective #5–Give Brief Differentiation Statement

1. Communicated something unique about your facility (this is a type of "headline" that puts the customer on alert to look for something special). The salesperson can state this differentiation statement a second time if it was also used in the first appointment. Simply reword it.

Objective #6–Match Each Need with a Product or Service Feature/Benefit

1. Make need/product matching statements. The components of a matching statement are

   a. Restate need (do one need at a time with a full matching statement for each).

   b. Match needs with a feature.

   c. Support feature with a proof device. This could be a picture or other visual proof such as a report document, map, property schematic, and so on. You should have a brochure (paper or electronic on your laptop computer) with you if you are presenting at the customer's office. The best way to offer proofs is to present as you were giving the customer a site visit of your hotel: real experience is better than pictures.

   d. Use translation words to convert features to benefits.

5. End each matching statement with a confirmation question or statement. (*Note:* The confirmation question will either receive an affirmative or a negative answer that would indicate a *buyer's concern* or *objection*.)

Step Four—Negotiating Concerns (Chapter 11)

Note: The salesperson will normally encounter buyer concerns when presenting matching statements in the demonstrating capability step. Specifically, the prospective buyer will show this concern when the salesperson asks the confirmation question.

Objective #7—Recognize and Negotiate Concerns As They Arise

1. Recognize the concern.

    a. Verbal and nonverbal signals

    b. What type of concern is it (of the five common types)?

2. Validate the concern—Use "reflective listening."

3. Answer the concern—Use one or a combination of seven methods to respond.

    a. Decide which of the seven techniques or combinations will answer the concern.

    b. Use a feel/felt/found statement.

Step Five—Gaining Commitment (Chapter 12)

Objective #8—Select an Appropriate Closing Method

1. Recognize buying signals through verbal and/or nonverbal language.

2. Select one of six common closing methods.

Objective #9—Ask for the Buyer's Commitment

1. Summarize the benefits that were discussed in the matching statements in Step Three. Although *summary of benefits* is a type of closing method, it is *always* a good idea to summarize here even if the salesperson also used a different closing method in Objective #8.

2. Asked for the order or purchase in a clear and direct way. (Be sure that there is no mistake that you are asking for the order.) Some salespeople become wishy-washy here. Since so much time and effort have been invested up until this point, avoid a common salesperson's weakness of getting cold feet at this step.

Objective #10—Negotiate Any Customer Concerns about Making a Commitment

Generally, a concern here is addressed the same way as a concern in Step Four. Obviously, the prospective buyer did not have all concerns answered earlier.

1. Recognize the concern.

    a. Verbal and nonverbal signals

    b. What type of concern is it (of the five common types)?

2. Validate the concern—Use "reflective listening."

3. Answer the concern—Use one or a combination of seven methods to respond.

    a. Decide which of the seven techniques or combinations will answer the concern.

    b. Use a feel/felt/found statement.

Objective #11—After-Sale Service Statements

1. Thank the customer for the business.

2. Give the customer an idea of what actions will take place after the order is placed. (This keeps the customer from feeling that the salesperson is only interested in making this sale, and assures him/her that implementation will be taken care of.)

◈ SUMMARY

Gaining commitment is the step in the buying/selling exchange process at which the salesperson asks the potential buyer (prospect) to make a purchase. When he/she signs the proposal that transforms into a letter of agreement, he/she is now considered to be a customer.

The gaining commitment step is often a stressful and seemingly difficult moment for both the prospect and the salesperson. It need not be. If a salesperson is well prepared and is an effective negotiator, then the gaining commitment step should be the logical conclusion of a systematic negotiation session.

In this chapter, we discussed issues related to the gaining commitment step:

1. why gaining commitment is difficult
2. guidelines for gaining commitment
3. the methods used to gain commitment
4. how to negotiate additional buyer concerns
5. the letter of agreement or contract

We illustrate our discussions with a model role-play script.

Consultative salespeople are very conscious of after-sale implementation and service of this first sale. Why? Because they will build on their existing relationship with this first buyer to gain repeat business and referrals. These referrals are usually to other divisions within this first buyer's organization. So, this first buyer is a gatekeeper to the eventual penetration and development of the entire organizational account. After-sale implementation, relationship management, and continual improvement are the subjects of Chapter 13.

References

Astroff, M. T., and J. R. Abbey. 1998. *Convention sales and services*. 5th ed. Cranbury, NJ: Waterbury Press. Also distributed by Orlando, FL: The Educational Institute of the American Hotel and Lodging Association.

Manning, G. L., and B. L. Reese. 1997. *Selling today*. 7th ed. Upper Saddle River, NJ: Prentice Hall.

Tracy, B. 1995. *Advanced selling strategies: The proven system practiced by top salespeople*. New York: Fireside, a division of Simon & Schuster.

Webster's Encyclopedic Unabridged Dictionary. 1996. New York: Random House Publishing.

◈ DISCUSSION QUESTIONS

1. Often new salespeople find that the most difficult stage in the sales process is the gaining commitment or closing stage. Why do you believe this is so? What advice would you give to a salesperson to overcome his/her anxieties?

2. Compare and contrast a trial close with an assumption close. How are they similar but at the same time distinct from one another?
3. A sales proposal for a meeting contains what types of information? Why is it important to receive the signature of the customer on such a document once an agreement has been reached?

ROLE-PLAY: Demonstrating Capability with Negotiating Concerns and Gaining Commitment—Model Script

---

Model scripts in previous chapters have built on Jim and Erin's negotiation session to provide consistency in our illustrations. In Chapter 10, we saw Jim address Erin's six primary needs.

In Chapter 11, Erin voiced some concerns to Jim. Jim addressed each of Erin's concerns (by validating and answering each concern individually) and finishes by summarizing the ways the Hotel Park Plaza could meet the Erin's upcoming meeting needs. For the purpose of illustration in Chapter 11, Erin was convinced and did not voice any additional concerns at the gaining commitment stage. In this chapter, the role-play will unfold in a more realistic manner; Erin will balk at the gaining commitment stage. We pick up after Jim has received a clear buying signal from Erin. He is now going to attempt to gain commitment (refer to Chapter 11 for preceding dialogue in role-play).

Objective #9—Ask for the Buyer's Commitment
Jim's attempt here will fail as Erin will voice concerns.

Preface with Summarized Benefits
Briefly summarize benefits that were discussed in the matching statements in Step Three. Even though summary of benefits is a type of closing method, it is always a good idea to summarize here even if the salesperson used a different closing method in objective #8.

Jim makes this summary loose and free flowing. Jim summarized *needs* at the beginning of the presentation. Now *benefits* are summarized. These benefits are associated with each of the six matching statements.

Jim makes his first attempt to gain commitment.

JIM: Let's review where we've been: We have your dates available *(benefit #1)* and we have provided spacious accommodations for both the meeting and trade show *(benefit #2)*. Our oversized and newly renovated sleeping rooms provide comfortable accommodations for your seminar presenters *(benefit #3)*. The chicken luncheon prepared by our award-winning chef will be artistically presented and delicious *(benefit #4)*. Easy access to our downtown location and our free adjacent parking garage will provide your guests convenience *(benefit #5)*. And, most important, all of this is within your budget range *(benefit #6)*.

Can we formalize our agreement to host your meeting by signing this letter of agreement?

Jim places the proposal in front of Erin with a pen.

Objective #10—Negotiate Any Customer Concerns about Making a Commitment

Jim attempts to negotiate each concern as it arises and then attempts to gain commitment each time.

Erin's First Concern

ERIN: Well, Jim, even though you can give me free airport transportation and this saves me $400 and helps me get close to my budget, I can get the same free transportation at the Marriott. I need a better price. What can you do?

Jim makes a second attempt to gain commitment, using a special-concession close.

JIM: Erin, I understand your need to obtain the best cost/value for your meeting, but I have a tough time reducing the rates much further. I'll tell you what: You indicated that your meeting is the first of a series and that it needs to have a "special feel" *(need)*. As an added bonus, we can host *(comp)* a special reception party for your 40 seminar leaders on the night of arrival *(feature)*. What this means to you *(translation statement)* is that they will feel especially pampered. I can assure you that positive word will get around about how you and the YWCA handle meetings *(benefits)*. How does this sound *(confirmation question and trial close attempt)?*

Erin's Second Concern

ERIN: That would be wonderful and would really add to the tone of the meeting, but I wasn't planning on a reception. Though it would be nice, Jim, what I really need is a lower price.

Jim makes a third attempt to gain commitment, using a single-problem close. He will be successful with this third attempt.

JIM: Erin, what I think you are saying is that you absolutely need the charges on this proposal to total exactly $10,000. Is that right?

ERIN: That's right.

JIM: Well, it seems that you like all the benefits that we've discussed except the total price. If I can get this number to $10,000, can I have your commitment to meet at the Hotel Park Plaza?

ERIN: Yes.

JIM: Here's what I can do. I am authorized to reduce the price of the sleeping rooms by another $10 per night. For 40 rooms this will save you another $400 in addition to the savings on airport transportation *(feature)*. This means to you *(translation statement)* that the original proposal of $10,800 will be reduced to meet your budget of $10,000 *(benefit)*. What do you think? *(confirmation question and trial close)?*

ERIN: I like it. From everything you have told me, it sounds like my meeting will be a success.

Jim receives a clear buying signal that indicates he can again return to objective #9, having negotiated concerns (objective #10 several times).

Objective #9—Ask for the Buyer's Commitment

Directly Ask for the Order (Gain Commitment)

Ask for the order in a clear and direct way. Be sure that there is no mistake that you are asking for the order. Some salespeople become wishy-washy here. Since so much time and effort have been invested up until this point, avoid a common salesperson's weakness of getting cold feet at this step.

JIM: Can we formalize our agreement with your signature?

Jim places the written proposal along with handwritten changes that were negotiated in the negotiating concerns step in front of Erin with a pen.

The *signed proposal,* even with handwritten changes, is now a formal and legal contract or letter of agreement. Of course, a clean copy will be retyped and re-signed. The salesperson should always get a signature. If massive changes are negotiated, it is best to make another appointment to go over a clean revised contract with the buyer and have him/her sign it.

ERIN: *(while signing the letter of agreement)* Jim, what happens next?

Objective #11—After-Sale Service Statements

Give the customer an idea of what actions will take place after the order is placed. This keeps the customer from feeling that all the salesperson is interested in is making this sale.

Also be sure to thank the customer.

JIM: Thanks, Erin. We at the Hotel Park Plaza want to make your meeting a very successful one. As soon as you sign the letter of agreement, this becomes the marching orders of the house. We will immediately assign you a conference service manager (CSM) who will call and let you know about various time lines and meeting details. Of course, I am always in the background and watching over your meeting to make sure that everything runs smoothly.

ERIN: This sounds great. Having a person to help me with my meeting sure takes a load off my mind. Jim, it's been great working with you.

JIM: Erin, I am enjoying working with you and helping you to have a successful meeting. I appreciate your time and look forward to working with you. We'll stay in frequent contact. Thanks again for your business.

CHAPTER 13

Phase Three—Post-Negotiation Strategy:

After-Sale Implementation, Relationship Management, and Continual Improvement

After reading this chapter you should be able to

- ◆ explain the importance of maintaining after-sale contact with clients
- ◆ list strategies useful in avoiding confidence collapse on the part of buyers

- ◆ explain the importance of relationship management
- ◆ identify strategies and tactics useful in account penetration
- ◆ describe a framework of continual improvement for the sales professional

KEY TERMS & CONCEPTS

confidence collapse
relationship management
account maintenance
account penetration
referrals

W. Edward Deming
Total Quality Management
Continuous Quality Improvement

The core strategy of consultative selling is to target customers with a high potential for repeat and referral profitable business. Repeat and referral business is only possible with superior after-sale service.

This chapter is, in a way, a capstone of the buying/selling exchange process from the consultative salesperson's perspective. Here we will fully discuss Phase Three—Post-Negotiation Strategy: After-Sale Implementation, **Relationship Management**, and Continual Improvement. Our discussion is concerned with new activities that are mandatory when using a consultative selling strategy. By now the reader should be convinced that the old ways of selling, transactional selling strategy, are clearly being replaced by the new way of selling, consultative selling strategy, in those cases where the buyer needs customized solutions to complex needs and are willing to pay for them.

Before we proceed to discuss Phase Three, let's remind ourselves of where we have been from Chapter 7 through Chapter 12. Let's briefly review the entire buying/selling exchange process that we first introduced in Chapter 7 (see Table 13–1).

Through both Phase One and Phase Two, we have discussed specific steps that will lead to the prospective buyer making his/her first purchase from this salesperson, and, by doing so, being redefined as a *customer*. Step Five, the close or gaining commitment, is only the beginning for a consultative seller. The task now is to continue to develop the relationship with this first "gate-keeper" customer and thereby obtain repeat business and **referrals** within his/her organization. The goal of a consultative seller is to generate revenue by penetrating select customer accounts. This is accomplished in the post-negotiation strategy phase, where effective implementation leads to strengthening relationships. Additionally, the consultative seller continually monitors his/her performance and adjusts for improvement in his/her selling and general performance skills.

Phase Three—Post-Negotiation Strategy

So, you think that you can relax after the contract is signed? You believe that at a minimum, all that is necessary are periodic "feel-good" check-ins with the customer to maintain a mutually pleasant relationship? Think again! Unfortunately, this is one of most common strategic errors in selling, especially to major accounts and complex sales. It's tempting for a salesperson to think that he/she can put less effort into the account now that the sale has been made, but a good sales strategist knows that immediately after the sale more effort, not less, is the best move. In fact, initially obtaining a

Table 13–1 Comparison of the Buying/Selling Exchange Process and the Negotiation Process

THE BUYING/SELLING EXCHANGE PROCESS	THE NEGOTIATION PROCESS
Phase One – Pre-Negotiation Strategy: Negotiation Planning and Preparation (Chapter 7)	**Phase One – Pre-Negotiation Strategy: Negotiation Planning and Preparation (Chapter 7)**
Step One – Understanding Sales Process	**Step One** – Understanding Negotiation Process
Step Two – Research Potential Customer	**Step Two** – Know Your and Your Customers' Interests
Step Three – Sales Tactics	**Step Three** – Negotiation Tactics
Phase Two – Negotiation Process Strategy	**Phase Two – Negotiation Process Strategy**
Step One – Approaching the Buyer (Chapter 8)	**Step One** – Opening
Step Two – Investigating Needs (Chapter 9)	**Step Two** – Exploring
Step Three – Demonstrating Capability (Chapter 10)	**Step Three** – Proposing Agreement
Step Four – Negotiating Concerns (Chapter 11)	**Step Four** – Clarifying Proposal
Step Five – Gaining Commitment (Chapter 12)	**Step Five** – Gaining Commitment
Phase Three – Post-Negotiation Strategy (Chapter 13)	**Phase Three – Post-Negotiation Strategy**
Step One – After-Sale Implementation	**Step One** – Implementing Agreement
Step Two – Maintenance and Development	**Step Two** – Conducting Self-Critique
Step Three – Continual Improvement	

customer is only the beginning of maximizing the "lifetime" value of the customer account.

Why do salespeople commonly make this error? Because complex consultative sales accomplished through the buying/selling exchange process require persistence and hard work. This success is often followed by a rush of emotional elation. The lengthy multiple sales call of relationship building, needs assessment, presentation, and resolution of concerns (meeting buyer resistance and closing resistance) is difficult and draining. A successful close or buyer commitment leads to a sense of relief . . . and a natural human tendency to "take a brief vacation" and celebrate (mentally if not actually) the final closing of the sale. This is a danger: reducing involvement in an account immediately after a sale is made can jeopardize all of the hard work that has been done.

Up until this point, in the *pre-negotiation strategy* and *negotiation process strategy* phases, the salesperson has diligently worked to acquire the customer. The salesperson must work as diligently, if not more, in the *post-negotiation strategy* phase to *maintain* the initial customer and then to *develop* or penetrate the total account. Note the distinction between the two words in the preceding sentence: *maintain* and *develop*.

The post-negotiation strategy phase is composed of three primary steps: (1) implementation, (2) **account maintenance** and development, and (3) self-critique and continual improvement of the consultative seller's skills. Most successful complex consultative product or service sales pass through these steps.

Step One—Implementation of Product or Service

Implementation can be viewed both through the eyes of the product or service seller and through the eyes of the product or service customer. Consultative salespeople are generally focused on the customer's view of what is important regarding implementation concerns. To better understand how to add value, let's put ourselves in the buyer's shoes. From the customer's point of view, implementation goes through three distinct stages: (1) the novelty stage, (2) the learning stage, and (3) the effectiveness stage (Rackham 1989).

The Novelty Stage

In the case of a corporate, association, or other type of organizational meeting, immediately after the sale, customers are usually excited and interested because something new is happening. The initial exploration of the product or service seems to be superficial because of the lack of immediate demands for results from the purchase.

If the meeting organization is relatively unsophisticated at holding meetings, people may be unrealistic in their concerns about the difficulty of holding a complex meeting. Sophisticated meeting planners, on the other hand, recognize the many problems that are associated with implementing a successful meeting and will be fully aware of the necessity of using the "planning window" to start the implementation phase. In both situations, the seller has an opportunity to build confidence in the correctness of the buying decision. For example, a hotel can immediately assign a conference service manager (CSM) to the account. The CSM immediately communicates important time lines and procedures to the customer, and then both the CSM and the salesperson maintain periodic contact and communications.

In the novelty stage, the customer's confidence is usually the highest. This confidence may be a result of lack of focus on the meeting. This stage usually lasts until the meeting date begins to draw near and deadlines approach. At this time, changes and glitches seem to appear as the meeting date approaches and focus intensifies.

The Learning Stage

This is usually the most difficult stage of the implementation process. Here the customer's confidence may fall to crisis levels as his/her concerns about the meeting intensify. And the stakes appear to loom larger on the horizon as the meeting dates approach. After the more superficial exploration of the novelty stage, the customer has to begin the more difficult process of learning how to achieve full potential from the product or service. The learning process begins toward the end of the novelty stage and continues through the period within which the meeting is held.

In the case of a complex organizational meeting, this learning process continues through the meeting itself since a service such as a meeting changes and evolves around the initial meeting plan. In the delivery of services, especially complex services that are delivered by a large number of coordinated people, even careful plans can go wrong. What customers expect of the *learning stage* and how the service provider and the customer interact to rectify evolving meeting problems will determine the perception of successful customer service.

In the learning stage, the customer has to produce greater effort. This effort comes from increased focus and attention on the performance of the product or service as well as becoming familiar with operations. Generally, unsophisticated customers will underestimate the effort and difficulty of the learning stage. These unrealistic expectations may lead them to expect instant results and they may feel cheated if they don't get them. On the other hand, more sophisticated customers normally have less trouble in the learning stage.

The Effectiveness Stage

As the customer gains a full understanding of the product or service, the effort that the customer must invest in learning is dramatically reduced. Product outcomes and results materially increase at the same time and, thus, the customer has a positive feeling that things are getting easier. The meeting planner has become familiar with the hotel's operational staff and how they work. The meeting has commenced and, therefore, the initial "butterflies" have dissipated. Additionally, the daily routine and flow of the meeting are established. The meeting planner and the hotel service personnel are familiar with each other. The more smoothly a salesperson and CSM can help the meeting planner reach the *effectiveness stage,* the more successful the implementation is.

Graphically, implementation stages from the customer's perspective appear as illustrated Figure 13–1, "The Confidence Collapse." Initially, in the *novelty stage,* the customer's enthusiasm for and confidence in the product are high. This level then dramatically falls during the *learning stage*. Finally, if the product or service is successfully implemented and provides the buyer a satisfactory solution, confidence rises in the *effectiveness stage* and then levels out.

Sellers must be aware of and have strategies to manage each of these stages. The most important stage to manage is the *learning stage*. This is when the customer develops a condition called the **confidence collapse** (see Figure 13–1). In essence, the confidence collapse is the customer's perception of a *gap* between his/her *expectations* of the product or service performance and *actual performance/results* of the product or service. Of course, the customer often hasn't given the product or service enough time to fairly judge actual performance/results, but human psychology, being what it is, leads to this response.

In summary, the consultative salesperson can add value for the customer during the implementation step by understanding that the customer will generally experience uncertainty during the process. This added value will strengthen the relationship bond. If this uncertainty is not resolved, then the customer may be predisposed to dissatisfaction.

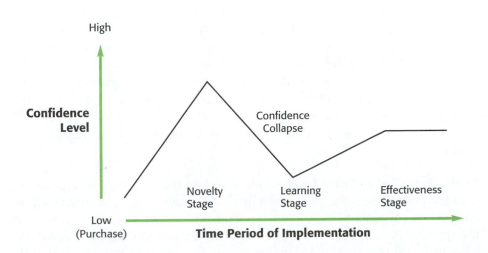

FIGURE 13–1

The Confidence Collapse

Source: McNeill, R.G. 2001. The successful salesperson of the future: A master of complex consultative selling. *Marketing Review* 18(1): 24–31.

Three Maintenance Tactics for Handling the Confidence Collapse During Implementation (Step One)

These tactics (*tactics* are specific actions) are specifically designed to ensure a satisfied initial customer.

Tactic One: Start Before the Contract Is Signed. In the implementation or installation of the product phase, an anxious customer will look for any sign that things are going wrong and may overreact to minor difficulties. The salesperson can look to the buying/selling exchange process to guide this tactic.

The salesperson can begin during the *demonstrating capability* step (Chapter 10) in the buying/selling exchange process. The salesperson can make sure that the customer genuinely feels that the product or service matches customer needs. In other words, ask enough questions and clearly and honestly demonstrate the product or service as compared to the competitive offerings.

During the *negotiating concerns* step (Chapter 11) in the buying/selling exchange process, the salesperson can make sure that the customer fully recognizes and sees *all* potential consequences or concerns. These must be *fully* resolved or they will become a potential future concern that will exacerbate and accelerate the confidence collapse. For example, if the customer feels nervous about the reputation of the salesperson's company, it is important to resolve the issue *before* signing the contract, so it won't resurface in the form of negative reactions during the implementation of product or service phase (Rackham 1989).

Tactic Two: Involve the Customer. Regardless of how careful the installation and implementation of a new product or service, something will go wrong. While a detailed step-by-step installation plan is essential, it will not guarantee success or protect against unexpected problems. Building a detailed implementation plan will increase the customer's comfort level. Making sure that the customer is involved in the construction of this plan will ensure his/her loyalty and satisfaction should any unexpected problems occur. After all, it's hard to "point the finger" at yourself.

Implementation is successful when salespeople get the customer to play a central role in the development of the implementation plan. Here the salesperson does not take the lead in designing the plan and plays the role of a "facilitator" who helps the customer improve on his/her own implementation plan ideas.

Tactic Three: Put In Effort Early. Understanding that the customer generally goes through three stages during the implementation phase can help avoid the confidence collapse. Salespeople who don't understand make the mistake of interpreting the customer's enthusiasm during the novelty stage as a signal that all is well and that this "high" will continue in a positive way. Consequently, they give the customer less attention and fail to detect the confidence collapse occurring in the learning stage.

It's easier to anticipate and prevent problems before they occur than to deal with something that is quickly deteriorating at a rapid rate (accelerating confidence collapse). It's easier and takes less time to prevent a fire than to fight one. Early effort will not prevent the confidence collapse; however, it will minimize the steepness and severity of the decline (Rackham 1989).

An unsatisfied customer is not a candidate for achieving repeat business and referrals, which are the focus of Step Two below.

Step Two—Maintenance and Development of Customers

Phase Three—Post-Negotiation Strategy continues after the salesperson has guided the customer through Step One, Implementation, and has successfully created a satisfied customer. Step Two has two distinct objectives: (1) *maintenance*—continuing to nurture the initial buyer through relationship strengthening while attempting to generate repeat business and (2) *development*—extending and developing more *internal* business (referrals) from the initial buyer's organization and obtaining *external* referral business to industry associates and friends of the initial buyer. These tactics and activities build on getting off to a good start with successful implementation accomplished in Step One.

There are two categories of maintenance tactics: (1) confidence collapse maintenance tactics discussed earlier as pertaining to implementation and (2) maintenance tactics specifically focused on relationship building. These maintenance tactics are aimed at the *initial* buyer. The salesperson wants to maintain him/her by doing a good job during the confidence collapse stage of implementation, and the salesperson must continually strengthen the relationship with the initial buyer after implementation. The purpose of maintenance is twofold: first, it creates a satisfied customer during implementation and, second, it systematically works to strengthen the relationship with this initial buyer. Why? Because the initial buyer is a source of repeat business as well as a "gatekeeper" to development and penetration of the organizational account through referrals.

Development tactics are applied primarily in Step Two of the model. Development tactics focus on systematically obtaining referral business by using the initial account customer as the gateway to *other* decision makers within the account. As you can logically see, once the salesperson is referred to another decision maker within the account and is successful in making a sale, he/she must revisit the confidence collapse once again and recycle as if this referred buyer were an initial buyer. Can you envision this continual referral activity snowballing?

During Step Two, both maintenance and development tactics are simultaneously executed. While the salesperson is strengthening the relationship of his/her initial buyer, development of the account is also taking place. Let's look at practical maintenance and development tactics. We will first discuss maintenance tactics that strengthen relationships with the initial buyer. Second, we will look at development tactics that are designed to penetrate the account.

Maintenance Tactics for Relationship Building

Maintenance tactics actually begin during Step One, implementation of the product or service. In Step Two, we are concerned with both maintenance and development tactics. However, the maintenance tactics of Step Two deal with relationship strengthening rather than the confidence collapse of Step One.

Once the product or service has been successfully provided, it can be assumed that tactics addressing the confidence collapse have been successfully applied. The salesperson now needs to focus on the goal of continuing a good relationship with the customer: relationship-building tactics. A good and continuing relationship with the initial customer will serve as a foundation for: (1) obtaining repeat business from the initial customer (maintenance) and (2) obtaining referrals from the initial customer for new external and internal potential customers (development). Two types of *relationship-building maintenance tactics* are discussed below: (1) *repeat business tactics* and (2) *external referral tactics*. Internal referrals will not be discussed in this section. Internal referrals (referrals for new business within the same organization) are the basis of account development and penetration and are discussed in our discussion of development tactics. Let's closely examine the two major categories of relationship-building maintenance tactics.

Repeat Business Tactics. The goal of repeat business tactics is to have the initial customer make repeated purchases from the same selling company. This means that the initial customer "recycles" back to the first step of the buying process and a new sales cycle begins. As previously discussed, an essential step of the buying/selling exchange process is the investigation of needs (Chapter 9). Obviously, with successful implementation in place and a strengthened relationship with the customer, the salesperson should have more familiarity with the customer this second time around. Dialogue with the customer during the crucial discovery of needs phase is likely to be more open.

Often, after a first purchase, the customer doesn't seem to have immediate additional buying potential. Unsuccessful salespeople simply play a passive waiting game until circumstances change. Successful salespeople, on the other hand, actively stay in front of the customer by having reasons to contact the customer. They continue to make periodic "presentations." The most familiar type of presentation associated with selling is the *persuasive presentation*. As discussed earlier, there are two other types of presentations that are used for maintaining relationships: the *reminder presentation* and the *informative presentation*.

Along with active social (general goodwill) tactics, the successful salesperson uses tactics that deliver real benefits to the existing initial customer. The following are the primary maintenance tactics used to generate repeat business:

1. *Tactic One: Common Sense Courtesies and Pleasantries.* The salesperson can make *social sales calls*. This strategy has traditionally been the mainstay of relationship building. Make no mistake: people buy from people that they like; thus, this strategy sets the stage for repeat and referral business. This strategy is often carried out by visits, lunches, and social chats. However, without other more beneficial strategies, this alone is usually ineffective.

Good information about the customer powers these social contacts. The salesperson should know a lot about his/her customer, both personally and professionally. This information can be warehoused in a database. The salesperson systematically and periodically finds a reason (birthday, anniversary, family related, and so on) to contact the customer. Using the database with a calendar or any computerized contact program makes this process simple and effective.

2. *Tactic Two: Actively Maintain and Simultaneously Actively Develop.* As mentioned earlier, the initial customer is not always ready to repurchase (repeat business) immediately. But, salespeople can continue to make new *persuasive sales calls*. The goal of these persuasive sales calls is not always to make a repeat sale to the initial customer, although this can be the goal. The goal of the persuasive presentation can be to advance penetration into the larger company account—obtain internal referrals. This type of persuasive presentation is called a *lead-generation sales call*. This type of call can be used for both external and internal referrals. The idea here is that the salesperson must adopt a philosophy that active maintenance of the initial customer actually is an important strategy that not only leads to repeat business, but also strengthens the referral capacity and potential of the initial customer.

Successful salespeople not only maintain their existing customer accounts (seek repeat business), they actively look for new opportunities either for new potential external business or internal business within these accounts. Their objective is not only to *protect* the existing initial customer but to *project* or to *sell*. By having an objective of developing during the course of maintaining their existing customers, successful salespeople not only will protect the account but also will obtain internal referrals resulting in more sales from the account.

3. *Tactic Three: Document the Good News.* Salespeople can make *reminder sales calls*. Most of the time, the salesperson is in contact with the customer

when things are going wrong. A better strategy is to remind the customer of the benefits that have come from the sale. Stay in contact with the customer when things are going right. Remember that customers keep a file of correspondence with the selling company. Imagine what a file full of bad news would look like to a new decision maker at the customer company. Shouldn't the good news be recorded?

Reminding the customer of the successes that have come from buying from the seller is a powerful way to have the customer remember the seller when the opportunity to purchase comes again. Successful salespeople track their customer's industries and know which companies are rising and which are falling. Did the seller's product result in more profitable results for the buyer? If so, the salesperson should bring this fact up. Does the buyer always know how successful the product is? Not always, often feedback comes from sources not available to the buyer. The point is to make sure that the buyer is reminded of the successful business relationship. This is not always easy to accomplish tactfully; however, creativity can be applied.

Good news such as that of other satisfied customers can be forwarded "FYI" (for-your-interest/information) to your existing customer. Additionally, the salesperson can write to the customer outlining the positive and successful impact his/her product has had and offering any further help and assistance.

What is the outcome of this strategy? First, it helps with repeat business from the initial customer. Second, the initial customer becomes a stronger referral agent who is the salesperson's foundation to obtain potential new internal customers—**account penetration**.

Note that in the process of maintaining the initial customer, the salesperson is further strengthening this customer as a *referral agent* to assist with *account development* and penetration. Successful salespeople use the following strategies to maintain their existing initial customers:

4. *Tactic Four: Educate the Initial Customer on New Developments.* Salespeople can make informative sales calls. This strategy maintains the initial customer and simultaneously enhances customer account development. Here the salesperson informs the customer of new products or services and changes within the industry or selling company.

Educating the customer means bringing new information to his/her attention. This can be in the form of professional interests, new product or service developments from the selling company or from the industry. Or, the salesperson might "leak" the names of prominent competitors who have also purchased his/her products. Often, this is public information available through press releases or other sources; people like to buy from popular sellers and they also justify and strengthen their own purchases from popular sellers. Education can also be connected to the customer's personal interests such as hobbies. Successful salespeople look for meaningful opportunities to stay in front of the customer, and educating or informing them is one way to accomplish this.

In addition to maintaining the initial customer and encouraging potential repeat business, the outcome of this strategy is to inform the customer of potential new products or services that might be of interest to other internal potential customers. Certainly giving the initial customer a solid and rational reason to give an internal referral is better than asking without a reason. Additionally, this open sharing of information further strengthens the long-term relationship between the initial customer and seller.

5.   *Tactic Five: Educate the Initial Customer on Decision Criteria.* The salesperson can make *decision criteria sales calls.* Salespeople can help educate or refine the process and criteria by which the customer makes decisions. Perhaps the customer's level of sophistication is relatively low. Here the salesperson can facilitate the customer's learning of methodologies that help decide on optimal product or service solutions. If the customer is sophisticated, the salesperson can openly discuss decision criteria. The salesperson can then glean useful information from the customer while serving as a sounding board to help the customer refine his/her ideas. In all cases, the customer will see the salesperson as a consultant and partner in the relationship. This bond should lead to a stronger long-term relationship and increased repeat business, external referrals, and internal referrals that lead to account development.

6.   *Tactic Six: Revisit the Initial Customer's Needs.* Salespeople can make *initial customer need reassessment sales calls.* The salesperson initially obtained his/her existing customer's needs during the pre-negotiation phase (see Table 13–1); however, needs change over time. The salesperson should call on the customer periodically to reassess his/her understanding of the customer's needs. Remember that competitors are regularly assessing your customer's needs. They can take an existing account away by uncovering and developing needs that the salesperson has neglected. After all, didn't the salesperson also take away this existing customer from someone else?

External Referral Tactics.   Salespeople can be very creative here, but we will address this category of tactics in a general way and provide only one example to illustrate a *flavor* of the category. The salesperson can make *external lead-generation sales calls.* Although the initial customer may not be ready to make a repeat purchase immediately, one maintenance tactic is associated with having the customer refer new but *external* potential customers to you. As noted earlier, *internal* referrals will be discussed later as a primary account development activity.

Traditionally, salespeople have been taught to ask for referrals from satisfied customers. This strategy helps the salesperson to gain access to new potential customers. An existing satisfied customer's introduction helps the salesperson get in front of a new but previously unknown person. Additionally, the salesperson carries additional credibility if the referring customer also has a good reputation. Although obtaining a sale from the new referral is no guarantee, access to the new referral is almost certain. The most common strategy for external referrals is the "endless-chain" method, whereby the salesperson directly asks his/her satisfied customer, "Is there anyone else you know who could benefit from my product?"

External referrals have been discussed as a maintenance tactic. Why? People generally like to help others out. They like to give their opinions and they like to be in a position of influence. The salesperson actually compliments the satisfied buyer by asking for his/her help. Thus, the relationship is further strengthened.

The discussion now turns to the heart of the post-negotiation phase. Today, consultative sellers cannot survive by obtaining only one new customer in one new company after the other. Success comes from development of or penetration of the initial customer's account. The goal is to use the initial customer to obtain other new buyers within the same company. The salesperson must acquire new internal referrals and effectively turn these people into new customers. In the process, the account is penetrated and total sales revenue from a single company account is increased.

Development Tactics

Two categories of development tactics are internal referral tactics and proactive account prospecting tactics.

Internal Referral Tactics. Successful salespeople take an active and dynamic approach by using their initial successful sale and satisfied customer to penetrate or develop the customer account. They look for more areas within the account (internal referrals) where their product or service may offer a solution. Generally, they use the following strategies (Rackham 1989).

1. *Tactic One: Actively Generate Internal Referrals.* Salespeople can make *internal lead-generation sales calls.* This type of sales call is actually a form of persuasive presentation. The salesperson's goal is to obtain internal referrals. Ironically, the more that the salesperson has satisfied the initial customer's needs, the less there is a need for immediate repeat business from the existing customer. The salesperson needs a rational reason to call on the existing customer along with the potential of a payoff. So, this type of persuasive sales call has the goal to obtain internal referrals.

Satisfied customers are often delighted to help the salesperson. They can give contacts and introductions. Remember that the confidence collapse occurs during the second stage (learning stage) of the implementation step, so referrals must be obtained early in the novelty stage or late in the effectiveness stage.

2.   *Tactic Two: Understanding Customer Account Needs.* Salespeople can make *account needs assessment sales calls.* The salesperson can use his/her existing initial customer to obtain needs that exist within the total account. Sales opportunities arise only from the existence of needs. If the salesperson's goal is to penetrate or develop the total account, he/she must have a solid grasp of the various account needs. The existing initial customer can be the first step in understanding these needs. Having a strong relationship with a key person in the account (the existing initial customer) is a gateway into account penetration.

3.   *Tactic Three: Understanding Customer Account Decision Process.* Salespeople can make *decision process sales calls.* Complex sales are usually associated with products that cannot be standardized for the customer; they require customization. Additionally, complex sales are usually high-ticket sales. Conventions and conferences usually are complex sales.

With complex sales, the decision-making process becomes complex. Often the salesperson sells not to one person, but to a buying committee. Often the salesperson does not have the opportunity to make a persuasive presentation directly to the real decision makers but must sell to gatekeepers and influencers who, in turn, sell to the real decision makers. Obviously, the salesperson who is aware of the account decision process and structure is in a powerful position to penetrate the account. Having an ally, the satisfied initial customer, to help navigate the account is a benefit. Thus, making decision process sales calls to the initial customer is aimed at understanding the structure of the total account as well as obtaining assistance in penetrating it.

Proactive Account Prospecting Tactics. The development tactics described previously are dependent on having an existing initial customer within the customer account. Salespeople do not always have this *gatekeeper* as an ally. First, the salesperson may not yet have sold to anyone within the account. Second, the initial customer may not be an active supporter. The successful salesperson does not let lack of an active supporting ally within the account stop him/her. There is one systematic tactic approach that can be implemented and is very effective.

1.   *Tactic One: The Salesperson Becomes an Internal Referral Agent.* The salesperson can make a *permission sales call.* This method was proven successful during one author's long career as a sales and marketing executive in the hotel business.

To become an internal referral agent, a salesperson must "map" the corporation and then internally refer decision makers to each other. Before the salesperson begins to pursue this goal, he/she must *gain permission* from his/her existing initial customer, if any, to implement this strategy. The strategy works as follows:

a. *Map the Company Account.* Most major corporations have many operating divisions and subsidiaries. Often these divisions have separate presidents, departments, and even names that do not indicate that they are part of the corporation. For example, Johnson and Johnson has many operating divisions or subsidiaries with names such as Surgikos, Extracorporeal, and so forth. As separate operating companies, they tend to make their own purchasing decisions. In such a large and diverse corporation, often decision makers within each of the divisions or subsidiaries do not know one another. This is the opportunity for the salesperson to become an *internal referral agent.*

To map the company account, the salesperson must obtain one or several of the many publications and directories such as *Directory of Corporate Affiliations, Standard and Poors,* and so on. These directories only provide a starting point. They do not list decision makers but do provide addresses and phone numbers. The salesperson systematically draws a relationship diagram. First, connect divisions and subsidiaries with the parent corporation. Second, connect the functional areas (that make buying decisions) with each division or subsidiary. Third, connect titles and names within the functional areas.

How does the salesperson obtain this information? Hard work! If proprietary information is sought, published lists of decision makers are a waste of money and time. The salesperson gets this information by directly calling the company and inquiring. Over time, a database is built.

b. *Internal Referral Agent.* All account development or penetration must have a starting point: an initial sale within the account. As mentioned, the salesperson may or may not have an active ally from the initial customer who helps penetrate the account. So, the salesperson must operate with the initial customer's permission as opposed to his/her active assistance. Simply stated, the salesperson is a "name dropper."

At this point, the salesperson has mapped the corporation, so he/she knows the names of the many prospects (potential but, as of yet, unsold customers). Additionally, one division of the larger corporation has already been a satisfied customer. And, remember that in large corporations, the many divisions or subsidiaries do not know each other.

So, when the salesperson makes his/her first call on one of these un-sold prospects, it is imperative that a discussion of the successful meeting held by another division or subsidiary be brought up. Additionally, the salesperson mentions the initial customer's name (remember that permission has been obtained) and requests that the new prospect call the initial customer.

Thus, the new prospect is given reassurance that the salesperson's product or service is generally acceptable since his/her company has already purchased it once. Additionally, the new prospect has a name and number within his/her company to provide detailed information. This is a powerful source of credibility for the salesperson.

One other benefit of the salesperson's display of knowledge about the targeted corporation is that customers want to deal with sellers who know them well and understand their needs. A salesperson that knows a lot about the customer's company has a head start in this area.

For the consultative salesperson, the post-negotiation phase is a time when relationships are strengthened to generate repeat business and referrals, the organizational account is penetrated in depth through development activities, and the salesperson improves his/her professional selling skills. We now turn to Step Three of Phase Three—Continual Improvement.

Step Three—Continual Improvement of Selling Skills

In the late 1980s, **Total Quality Management** (TQM) principles were actively discussed and implemented by industry. TQM or **Continuous Quality Improvement** (CQI) principles inform us that given time, persistence, and a desire to continually improve ourselves, each of us can realize the success and benefits that come from being recognized as a true *expert*. Whatever your choice of career or endeavor, whether you will seek a career in hospitality operations or revenue activities such as sales and marketing, you should be concerned with the process of CQI and through its practice achieve success in life.

Continuous Quality Improvement is fundamentally a business philosophy focused on customer satisfaction. We apply this process to the personal and professional activities of consultative salespeople. The process begins and ends with the customer—it is reflected in the products and services being delivered. For consultative salespeople, CQI is about continually assessing one's professional performance to please customers on a regular basis and facilitate innovations. To stay on top, quality is the overall factor in determining a salesperson's and their organization's competitive advantage.

Making quality an integral part of a salesperson's personal and professional aspirations takes hard work, a great deal of time, and a dedication to change. Salespeople must be willing to look at different ways of doing things. They must secure the resources, training, and time necessary to implement quality. Quality in its raw form is a new personal and professional management technique that people must learn. It means not being afraid to take chances to try new and innovative improvements.

Continual quality improvements result in reduction of costs and wastes, and in greater productivity. This results in increased customer satisfaction, stronger relationships, and increased competitive advantage for the salesperson and his/her organization.

The father of CQI, W. **Edward Deming**, speaking of Continuous Quality Improvement in industry, suggested *14 Points* to guide the CQI process. Additionally, Deming offered a simple tool as a checklist for implementing this process: the *plan, do, check, act* cycle (PDCA).

The 14 Points Adapted to Guide Selling Quality

Deming's (2000)14 Points are designed as a philosophical guide to implement quality. In effect, adoption of these points provides the salesperson with a philosophy guiding the practice of his/her profession.

1. *Create constancy of purpose for improvement of product and service.* Create a unified purpose toward improvement of selling skills and customer satisfaction.
2. *Adopt the new philosophy.* Every member of the sales and marketing system must learn new skills that support the quality revolution affecting their profession. People must learn to work toward improving the quality of products and services, and operate more productively and efficiently.
3. *Cease dependence on inspection to achieve quality.* Reduce the need for external inspection or *overseeing* sales management direction. Take personal responsibility by incorporating quality into one's own sense of pride of quality performance.
4. *End the practice of selling business on the basis of price alone.* Understand that customers will pay for genuine value delivered.
5. *Improve constantly and forever.* Improve quality and productivity by instituting a "plan, do, check, act" cycle. This process would identify problems and areas for improvement, implement the changes, and assess and measure the results. The cycle repeats itself to ensure quality at continually higher levels.
6. *Seek training on the job.* Quality begins and ends with education and training. When salespeople need to change the way they do things, they must also be provided the tools necessary to implement those changes. Training is that tool.

7. *Adopt and institute leadership.* Salespeople can provide leadership to others though modeling. Demand excellence of yourself and "walk the talk." Salespeople must develop a vision and mission statement for themselves. The focus and mission must be shared and quality must be incorporated.

8. *Eliminate fear.* Historically, sales organizations have been managed by fear, especially of being fired. Personally target excellence and perform. Excellent people are employable anywhere.

9. *Break down all barriers between staff areas.* Historically, sales and operations have been like oil and water: they don't mix. Today, successful organizations must operate as a team. Competitive advantage goes to organizations that can harmonize all of their human resources and focus them on achieving customer satisfaction.

10. *Eliminate slogans, exhortations, and targets for the sales force.* Instead, influence your sales management to involve everyone in the CQI learning process. Tie learning to real-life experiences and learn from mistakes in order to improve. Slogans are a temporary Band-Aid that do not solve underlying problems such as the need to improve. Creating a quality learning culture is everyone's responsibility.

11. *Eliminate numerical quotas.* Quotas are common in managing the sales force. Unfortunately, a singular reliance on sales quotas as a measure of sales effectiveness is not wholly compatible with the age of the new consultative salesperson. Building relationships is very important for today's salesperson. Should traditional sales quotas be substantially augmented with qualitative measures indicating performance toward building these relationships and/or account penetration? Influence your sales management to rethink the importance of objectives that they reward or punish.

12. *Remove barriers that rob people of pride.* In a typical sales force, high achievers are openly glorified whereas average performers are treated as second-class citizens. Often an actual list ranking performers is posted in the office. Some old-school sales managers believe that one can motivate by embarrassment or other demeaning actions. Actually, this is a lazy way of managing. Could an alternative approach be to coach or mentor an underperforming salesperson? This clearly takes more time and ability on the part of the sales manager. The question is, are today's sophisticated consultative salespeople valuable assets to be nurtured and developed or expendable commodities? Again, influence your management to reconsider habitual old-school management practices.

13. *Engage in a vigorous program of education and self-improvement.* Only by committed discipline can CQI be implemented. The rewards are great: expertise and success. But, be aware: these rewards will not come without effort. As the old saying goes, "Successful people do what unsuccessful people are unwilling to do." Which are you?

14. *Model for everyone in the organization to accomplish a CQI transformation.* Modeling presents an example for everyone. It encourages others to take personal responsibility for their success and paves the way for quality within the entire organization. Put everyone in the system to work in trying to accomplish a quality transformation of the entire organization. CQI is everyone's task.

It might appear to you that Deming's 14 Points are idealistic and require a lot of effort. You are right in your assessment. After all, only a small percentage of people strive with diligence throughout their lives and leave a legacy of excellence. Some things are harder to do than others. We all have free will and make choices that will significantly affect our futures. If you want to attempt to begin this difficult journey toward success and excellence, how can you do it? Deming offers a method.

PDCA—A Guide for Salespeople to Implement CQI

Organizations and salespeople begin the improvement process with a *plan, do, check, act* cycle (PDCA). With a desire to make changes that will improve how they sell, they design a *plan* of action. Then they *do* by taking action to implement the plan. By keeping notes and measuring their progress during the implementation of the plan, they *check* the results and study them after the plan is completed. Then they act to correct and improve any gaps found between the plan and actual performance.

After completing the buying/selling exchange process, the effective consultative salesperson reviews each phase and step of the process. Should improvements be made? Sensing that the path toward excellence always requires constant adjustment, the salesperson *plans* for improvement. This plan is shaped by the steps in the process itself. To *do* means that, armed with a plan of action, the salesperson encounters his/her next prospective buyer with an improved planned approach. During each phase and step of the buying/selling exchange process, the salesperson makes notes and measures his/her actual performance. "Did my performance match my plan?" the salesperson asks himself/herself. This is *checking*. "How can I improve my performance?" the salesperson asks. Armed with new information, the salesperson creates a revised and improved plan and *acts* to implement it with another prospective buyer.

As the salesperson continually cycles through PDCA, over time he/she gets better and better at his/her profession. He/she is well on the way to success and recognition as an expert. This is Continuous Quality Improvement. It requires effort and discipline, but the rewards are tremendous.

SUMMARY ◇

This chapter concludes the discussion of the phases and steps of the buying/selling exchange process. We have presented and discussed the new world of buying and selling using a consultative selling strategy along with win-win negotiation tactics. This approach to our discussion was for illustrative purposes. As we learned in Chapters 4, 5, and 6, today sellers must practice situational selling. The specific buying/selling exchange process is dependent on both the buyer and seller's perception of value. Thus, whereas our buying/selling exchange process model is accurate for all situations that require negotiation, the way that it is applied depends on the *situation*.

This chapter discussed the final phase in the buying/selling exchange process, Phase Three—Post-Negotiation Strategy. This phase is the most important for the new sellers practicing consultative and alliance strategies. Why? Because these strategies depend on repeat and referral business resulting in organizational account development and penetration. To this end, we offered specific and practical tactics on how to accomplish account penetration results.

Finally, the post-negotiation strategy requires that each salesperson take personal responsibility for Continuous Quality Improvement (CQI) of their selling skills and performance. We presented W. Edward Deming's philosophy and implementation guidelines as a way for a salesperson to achieve professional success and excellence. Although Deming designed his message for quality improvement for organizations, it is equally applicable for salespeople and other professionals.

The text now turns to Section 4, "Managing Your Future." We will present specific tools and information that might be applied in your CQI just discussed.

References

Deming, W. E. 2000. Out of the crisis. Boston: MIT Press.

McNeill, R.G. 2001. "The successful salesperson of the future: A master of complex consultative selling." *Marketing Review* 18(1):24–31.

Rackham, N. 1989. *Major account sales strategy.* New York: McGraw Hill.

DISCUSSION QUESTIONS ◇

1. What is meant by the term *confidence collapse?* When is it likely to occur? Why does it occur?
2. Consider for a moment that you have booked a meeting for a new company that will for the first time be bringing its stockholders together. From the client's perspective, a lot is riding on a successful outcome of this meeting. Outline a series of steps you could take to avoid confidence collapse on the part of your client.

3. Comment on the need to maintain contact with existing accounts. Why is it important? How often should you follow up with them? Discuss potential tactics you believe would be useful in maintaining a client's goodwill.

4. Suppose your hotel has successfully served a large manufacturing company's human resources department for a series of training meetings. Create a map of the company highlighting the other divisions of the company that may be a source of meetings and rooms bookings. Discuss a strategy you would use to solicit this new business.

Section 4

4

Managing Your Future

CHAPTER 14

Sales Professionalism:

Ethical and Legal Responsibilities

After reading this chapter you should be able to

- ◆ discuss the legality of various selling strategies and tactics
- ◆ explain the importance of seeking win-win outcomes in sales negotiations
- ◆ recognize the deceptive bargaining tactics of others and know how to defend against them
- ◆ understand the ethical responsibilities of the salesperson

rule of law
fraudulent misrepresentation
business defamation
tying arrangements

reciprocity
bribes and gift giving
BATNA

Have you ever found yourself pressured to act one way but felt ethically you should act another? How often have you told a "white lie"? Are there times when it is appropriate to do so? Everyday life confronts us with ethical dilemmas, and selling professionally will be no different. Whereas some acts in the selling process are clearly unethical and perhaps illegal, others are less clear and present dilemmas for the salesperson.

In this chapter we discuss the ethics of selling. Ethics are broadly applied societal standards for what is right and wrong in particular situations, as well as a process for setting ethical standards. They differ from morals, which are personal beliefs about what is right and wrong. Ethics advance from particular philosophies that purport to define the nature of the world we live in and prescribe rules or standards for living together.

Hitt (1990) has summarized four standards of business ethics. They are making decisions on the basis of

- what gives your firm the greatest return on investment
- what the law requires
- the strategy and values of one's organization
- one's own personal convictions and conscience

Each of these standards reflects a fundamentally different approach to ethical reasoning. The first may be called the *ends justify the means* in that what is right is determined by the benefits minus the cost of its consequences. The second may be called the *rule of ethics,* where the **rule of law** defines what is right and wrong and where the line is. The third may be called *corporate ethics* in that the appropriateness of an action is based on corporate norms. Last, the fourth may be called *personal ethics* in that the appropriateness of an action is based on one's conscience and moral standards.

Often we see evidence of salespeople who perceive that their duties to their firm are inconsistent with their responsibilities to others (for example, the customer), and must therefore select one ethical standard over the others. To illustrate, ValuJet's employees knew that shipping flammable materials as cargo was against the law, but rationalized that it was a legitimate hazard, accepted the orders, and changed the packing slips. The result was that a plane crashed in the Florida Everglades and the company was driven into bankruptcy. Were the company and these specific employees inherently unethical? We argue that this is a case of good people who did a bad thing. Salespeople who are looking for guidance in ethical decision making should refer to guidelines by their professional associations such as Hospitality Sales and Marketing Association International (HSMAI) (see Figure 14–1). However, it is the responsibility of management to set benchmarks and draw the line well short of ethical and legal standards since corporations can ill afford to err.

Each of the four approaches to moral reasoning need not conflict with one another where the organization and its salespeople set out to execute their sales

FIGURE 14–1

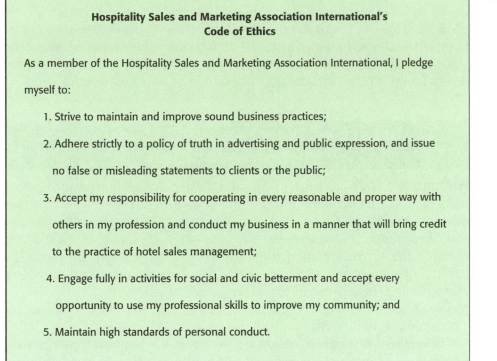

**Hospitality Sales and Marketing Association International's
Code of Ethics**

As a member of the Hospitality Sales and Marketing Association International, I pledge

myself to:

1. Strive to maintain and improve sound business practices;

2. Adhere strictly to a policy of truth in advertising and public expression, and issue

   no false or misleading statements to clients or the public;

3. Accept my responsibility for cooperating in every reasonable and proper way with

   others in my profession and conduct my business in a manner that will bring credit

   to the practice of hotel sales management;

4. Engage fully in activities for social and civic betterment and accept every

   opportunity to use my professional skills to improve my community; and

5. Maintain high standards of personal conduct.

and marketing plans. It is hard to imagine that any business or salesperson would intentionally set out to deceive their customers and expect long-term success and continued existence. Unethical activity on the part of the seller may result in a single transaction, but the development of a true relationship requires complete honesty and integrity. According to Marks (1996), "The best policy for a salesperson—and the most profitable—is to be honest and forthright with customers. The ones buyers continue to do business with are the ones they trust. Good ethics are good business" (Marks 1996, 71–72).

The Law and Selling

What is the legality of various sales tactics and strategies? Is there a difference between a salesperson offering opinions and providing statements of fact in educating the customer about the unique features and benefits of his/her product? Is it appropriate to offer disparaging comments to a customer about the competition? Is it proper to discuss with one's competitors ways in which to stabilize prices and avert a price war? Is it permissible to offer discounts to one customer and not to others? Failing to understand the legality of various selling practices can entangle you and your firm in costly lawsuits.

Marks (1996) and Clarkson et al. (2000) have highlighted several legal issues about which all salespeople should be knowledgeable. Although it is beyond the scope of this chapter to address these laws in detail, the following are issues that sales and marketing professionals should be aware of. Links to resources available on the Internet where one can explore these issues further can be found at http://www.ftc.gov/ and http://wbl.westbuslaw.com.

Breach of Warranty and Fraudulent Misrepresentation

Warranty is an age-old concept. In sales a warranty is an assurance by one party of a fact that the other can rely on. Warranties can be verbally expressed during the negotiation process or communicated to the buyer in the salesperson's brochures, advertisements, and promotional materials. When a customer relies on information provided by a salesperson in purchasing a product or service, only to find later that it fails to perform as promised, the customer has the legal right to sue for breach of warranty. Generally, salespeople should never make statements of fact without irrefutable evidence and a commitment to back them up.

Fraudulent misrepresentation occurs when a salesperson intentionally deceives a customer into believing in a condition that is different from the one that exists and causes financial harm. In general, cases of misrepresentation are decided on an individual basis based on two criteria: (1) whether factual statements were made concerning the product or service's performance and (2) the level of knowledge of the customer in the trade. The salesperson should clearly understand the difference between offering an opinion and making statements of fact and warranty particularly in cases in which the customer is less than knowledgeable in a product or service that is highly complex or technical in nature. "Our product or service is second to none" and "we are the best in the business," are statements of opinion and generally will be viewed by the courts as puffery or sales talk that should not be relied on by customers. However, when the salesperson begins to make statements of a factual nature such as "Our HVAC system will reduce your hotel's energy consumption by 10 percent" or "Our firm can design an incentive travel program for your firm that will improve your bottom line by 5 percent" are statements of fact and warranty. Often firms will solicit testimonials from customers willing to share such facts or commission independent researchers to produce such evaluative evidence. However, the salesperson must guard against making claims that all customers will experience the same results. The courts have ruled that customers experienced in the trade have a duty to look beyond the assertions of the salesperson and perform their own investigation of the product.

Business Defamation and Misrepresentation

Companies have been sued under the Federal Trade Commission Act for the following:

◆ unfairly accusing competitors of engaging in illegal or unfair business practices
◆ telling a third party (customer) that a competitor fails to live up to its contractual responsibilities when the allegation is untrue
◆ making false statements about a competitor's financial health
◆ making false statements that a principal executive of a competitor is unreliable, dishonest, or incompetent

These and other statements fall under the category of **business defamation** and include: (1) *business slander* (making unfair or untrue statements verbally to a third party construed to be damaging to a competitor's reputation); (2) *business libel* (unfair or untrue statements provided in writing to customers that damage a competitor's reputation in the form of brochures, letters, and advertisements); (3) *product disparagement* (providing false or deceptive comparisons concerning a competitor's product or services); and (4) *unfair competition* (providing statements that misrepresent the characteristics or qualities of one's own product or services).

The Federal Trade Commission Act also considers it wrong if a firm substitutes without approval goods that are different from what the customer ordered; misrepresents delivery dates; or does not fulfill an order within a reasonable time frame. These are unfair methods of competition.

Tying Arrangements

When a seller conditions a sale of a product on the agreement that the buyer will purchase another product or service produced or distributed by the seller, a tying arrangement results. **Tying arrangements** may be illegal, particularly if it can be shown that an arrangement is for the purpose of reducing competition. A tying arrangement may also require that in order to receive an order, the seller must be willing to buy products or services from the purchasing organization. Tying has been proved to be in violation of the Clayton Act (for products) and the Sherman Act (for services) where franchisees are required to purchase the franchiser's products and equipment exclusively as a part of the contractual franchise agreement. The Justice Department and the Federal Trade Commission also closely scrutinize the offering of *requirement contracts,* in which buyers are required to purchase a specified percentage of their needed supplies and services from a buyer, typically in a specified period of time. Such an agreement is considered illegal since it bars or limits the abilities of other vendors to compete for the business. Firms should be mindful that the FTC will closely examine any strategic alliances that serve to create monopolistic concentrations of economic power (lessen competition) through tying arrangements and requirement contracts.

Reciprocity

In the hospitality industry, a firm can be both a buyer and seller in its relationship with other firms. When these relationships evolve to the form of alliances, the firm may establish a rule that customers should be given preferential consideration when it comes to buying. This is known as **reciprocity**. However, the practice can get out of hand when a salesperson hints, "If you do not buy from me, we will not buy from you." The recipient of this statement will interpret it as a form of commercial blackmail and it will likely backfire on the salesperson. The FTC has been known to issue cease-and-desist orders to stop the practice. The perpetrating salesperson and firm can also be prosecuted under the Clayton Act if the practice serves to significantly impact competition.

Bribes and Gift Giving

In the hospitality industry, there can be a thin line between good business and **bribes and gift giving**. Buyers who ask for kickbacks, cash, and gifts in return for an order have obviously crossed the line of what is legal. In the mid-1990s a number of Asian tour operators in New Zealand were prosecuted for their practices of requiring kickbacks from duty-free shop owners in return for stopping their motor coaches at these shops. The practice can escalate to the point at which it is no longer profitable for the seller, let alone the individual guest who is provided an opportunity to shop with the highest bidder—not the firm with the highest value.

Gifts are not categorically unethical or illegal. Often a salesperson and his/her firm use gifts to express their regards to a friend who also is a buyer. Gifts are also a way to express to a customer that you care and appreciate their business. However, gifts can easily begin to resemble bribes, particularly when companies begin to compete with one another to give their customers better gifts. Some firms have instituted no-gift policies for the employees. The rule of thumb for the salesperson is if the buying company has a rule prohibiting gift giving, don't do it. If gifts are acceptable, keep the dollar amount within reason. An acceptable limit in many cases may be $25, the limit set by the Revenue Act of 1962 for tax-deductible gift giving to any one individual per year. However, the value of gifts may need to be much higher in an international context. The highly ritualized practice of exchanging gifts in Japan is paramount to cultivating long-lasting relationships with other businesses. However, even gifts in this context should never exceed $150 in value.

Relations with Competitors

It is unlawful to discuss with competitors means to fix or stabilize prices, or to enter into an agreement that has even a remote or indirect effect on prices. Today's Global Distribution Systems, or GDS for short, provides instantaneous access to competitors' prices in the hospitality and tourism industry. As a result, airline executives never meet with one another for fear of inviting the scrutiny of the FTC.

Relations with Customers and Distributors

Salespeople must be careful not to favor one group of customers over others to avoid violating the Robinson-Patman Act. This vague and often confusingly worded act is intended to protect small businesses from unfair competition of large chains. In effect, the law requires that manufacturers and distributors who provide price breaks or extra cooperative advertising expenditures to one customer must provide the same program to all others. There are two exceptions. Some price discrimination is allowable if the seller can demonstrate that the cost of doing business varies between firms due to transportation costs or production costs. Second, a seller may discriminate in price between customers if the price is lowered to the one in order to respond to the low price of a competitor. Discriminatory pricing is a fundamental aspect of all hotels' and airlines' revenue management systems under which consumers are offered different prices based on forecasted demand and various rules and restrictions. Such practices fall outside the purview of the Robinson-Patman Act. However, salespeople who market products and services to organizational buyers must be careful to make sure they treat all customers equally, except under the two circumstances outlined above.

Dealing with Customers' Adversarial Behaviors

The selling environment is loaded with customers who are low bidders and use hardball and deceptive tactics. All salespeople would rather avoid doing business with such customers, focusing instead on those who seek cooperative win-win relationships. However, survival often means that you attempt to get orders from all types of customers. In reality, most sales negotiations have both integrative and distributive dimensions to them. All customers are interested in gaining value at the least possible cost, and likewise for the salesperson for his/her organization. The central insight of this view is that selling almost always involves a tension between giving value and claiming value. Effectiveness in sales requires balancing this tension, finding ways to create value for your customer while still claiming value for your firm. In short, sales is best seen as a tough balancing act between giving and claiming value, involving both integrative and distributive negotiations. The best salespeople can recognize hardball tactics, how they work, and how to respond appropriately to each with a focus on pulling the customer back toward a reasonable win-win deal.

The best news is that negotiation is a game like tennis or golf. Any person can learn the skills to become better at negotiating. The key is being prepared. Once you accept that and begin playing, you will start to improve. First, realize the game is played by people, not companies. You are negotiating with Jane or Joe, not MegaCorp. The game is won only when both players—and the firms they represent—win. There are only four possible endings to a game:

◆ I win, you win (game is won and relationship continues)
◆ I win, you lose (game over)
◆ I lose, you win (game over)
◆ I lose, you lose (game over)

A win-win outcome ensures that both players have a sense of accomplishment. They are satisfied with the exchange and willing to play again. The win-lose results mean the game is likely over. If, however, it does continue, the loser is now playing with a sense of getting even. This results in an adversarial relationship of one-upmanship that should be avoided. Win-lose deals are a virus in that they grow inside the loser and eat at his/her self-esteem. It is better to walk away and play again later than to have guilt, grudges, and a burning desire to get even.

The most successful salespeople prepare to win long before they ever step into the game. It is absolutely vital that you be prepared for the game of negotiating. Although you may be aboveboard and ethical, you never know whether the other player might be.

Typical Hardball Tactics

We now turn to a discussion of hardball tactics, or win-lose maneuvers. The point of this discussion is not to encourage you to use them. Instead, the intent is to help you recognize the tactics and ways to avoid getting backed into a corner.

Good Guy/Bad Guy

The good guy/bad guy tactic can be seen in virtually all movies and television shows about police. The first police officer (the bad guy) puts the subject under a spotlight, pushes him/her around, threatens him/her with the fullest extent of the law, and then leaves the room to take a telephone call or to cool off. When that officer leaves the room, the second police officer (the good guy) apologizes for the behavior of his/her partner, and tries to reach a quick agreement before the bad guy returns and makes life difficult for everyone.

In a sales negotiation, two people on the same side can stage such a quarrel. Assume you are in an appointment with a meeting planner and his/her client. The client takes a tough stand: "We won't pay a cent more than $75 per guest room and expect the meeting rooms to be thrown in for free." The meeting planner chimes in, "Frank, be reasonable. Given the time of year and the quality of the resort, a $95 rate is quite reasonable and we certainly cannot expect the hotel to give its meeting rooms away." Turning to you, the meeting planner may ask, "Could you compromise by waiving the cost of the meeting rooms?"

The most obvious weakness to this tactic is its transparency, particularly if it has been used before. The smart salesperson will ask for a rationale as to why his/her offer is unreasonable and requires additional concessions. Another tactic is to openly describe the tactic they are using by humorously responding, "That is the best good guy/bad guy routine I have seen in years. Did you plan it or was it just coincidence? Now seriously, let's see if we can establish a fair price and provide you the best meeting you have had to date."

Lowballing

The lowball tactic begins with the buyer opening with a ridiculously low offer they know you cannot accept. The theory is that the extreme offer will cause you to evaluate your own counteroffer and move closer to the buyer's ideal price. If you give in to your natural tendency to serve the customer, you may also begin making concessions toward the outrageous bid. To defend against such tactics requires good preparation. The best way to deal with such a lowball tactic is not to make a counteroffer. Instead, share with the buyer a general understanding of your product's market value. Something to the effect of, "The April time frame you have given me for your meeting is truly the most beautiful in our city. Demand is high, and as a businessperson I am sure you can understand that we do not offer discounted rates during this period. I would be happy to provide you the names and numbers of mid-level properties that may have rooms available. But if you are willing to pay our normal rate, I am sure we can provide you a meeting that will exceed the expectations of your group."

A variation of lowballing called *rock bottom pricing* is when a buyer calls up and says, "I don't have much time. What's your rock bottom price for an order of . . ." Intentionally or not, the buyer who employs this tactic is attempting to evoke from you a quick response eliciting your lowest discounted rate. The buyer will often indicate that he/she is calling two or three of your competitors for their best price. The salesperson must avoid giving too quick a response, leaving no room for negotiation. If the customer is insistent on receiving a price quote with no further discussion, provide him/her a reasonable rate and have the confidence to stick to it. However, first attempt to learn more about the customer's needs in an effort to identify the ideal way to present your property's features and benefits. Attempt to deflect the conversation from price for the moment by stating, "I can appreciate that price is important to you, Mr. Jones. If you can provide me a few moments to learn more about your group and its specific needs, I will be in a better position to find you the best possible price."

Bogey

Customers who use the *price bogey* tactic state a fixed dollar amount beyond which they will not go. The seller who falls victim to the tactic feels constrained to reduce his/her price in order to fall within the buyer's price constraints. Often meeting budgets are more flexible then they appear because money can be shifted from one line item to another. A salesperson who responds to a buyer who asks for some approximation of the costs well before the details of the meeting are discussed often brings this tactic on himself/herself. The seller, anxious to please, states a range of figures that essentially boxes him/her in before the final details are settled.

Another form of a bogey is when the buyer keeps the salesperson blind to his/her real needs and interests. Assume for a moment that the events planner is flexible with his/her dates but wishes to gain as many price concessions as possible. The buyer might indicate that he/she has little to no flexibility in terms of dates and proceed to negotiate the best deal on what is known as high-demand dates. Once the salesperson has invested a significant amount of time in the negotiations and is on the verge of losing the sale, the buyer offers a "what if" offer to move to a low-demand period. Having thrown off the salesperson with the bogey, the buyer is in a better position to demand a better deal. Bogeys of this nature are difficult tactics to defend against, and the salesperson should be suspicious that they are being used when the buyer makes a sudden reversal in his/her position, particularly late in the negotiations. One should question the buyer carefully about why the sudden reversal is suddenly acceptable and not concede too much too soon.

The Nibble

Customers using the nibble ask for a small concession that has not been previously discussed to close a deal. Imagine negotiating with a meeting planner. A large amount of time and effort have been spent in planning a complex meeting and reaching a final price. The agreement is close, but the meeting planner asks you for a final concession that will cost you relatively little (for example, free upgrades). The buyer assumes you will agree because the amount is too little to jeopardize the deal over. The major flaw with the tactic is that its recipient will feel that the buyer did not bargain in good faith, and the tactic will invite retaliation.

There are two basic ways to confront a nibble. First, the salesperson should respond to each nibble with the question "Is there anything else?" Once all of the buyer's issues are in the open, both parties can discuss all the issues together. Second, the salesperson could counter with his/her own nibbles ready to offer in exchange.

How to Respond to Hardball Tactics

Up to now our strategy has been to recognize the hardball tactic being employed and attempt to negotiate over it. Negotiations are not, however, limited to the exchange of offers and counteroffers. Another important source of power in negotiations is what Fisher, Ury, and Patton (1991) coined **BATNA**, which is short for Best Alternative To a Negotiated Agreement. You should never agree on something in a negotiation unless it exceeds the value of your best available alternative or there is a strategic value in doing so. For example, it would be unwise to offer a discounted room block on high transient demand days. In such a case it would be appropriate to offer regrets to the buyer that the discount rates are unavailable and risk losing the business. On the other hand, attempting to understand the buyer's BATNA, particularly when he/she is employing hardball tactics, provides you an advantage. Assuming in the case previously that you know there is little availability in your facility during the dates in question, the low BATNA of the buyer gives you little reason to give in. Research suggests that sellers with an attractive BATNA should tell buyers about it if they expect to receive its full benefits. By way of explanation, the seller can point out that most people in business can understand that during high-demand periods discounted prices are closed, leaving only the standard rates. On the other hand, sellers with an unattractive BATNA should be careful about communicating it because it may weaken their position.

SUMMARY ◈

In this chapter we have taken a look at the ethical and legal responsibilities of the salesperson. In particular, we have discussed how business ethics contributes to long-term profitability and survival. In contrast, we know that treating customers unethically not only will doom repeat business but will invite your customers to seek retribution in the court system. Good ethics is good business.

We also turned our attention to dealing with customers who attempt to game the negotiation process. The give-and-take in the exchange process leads even the most ethical customers to attempt to gain the best deal possible in a negotiated exchange. Tactics and strategies are involved in all negotiations, either knowingly or unknowingly, and the wise salesperson will be committed to seek win-win outcomes for both parties. You can't be in sales more than a week before you realize profits come from repeat business and referrals.

However, the salesperson should never be surprised that customers at times are only too willing to engage in hardball or deceptive tactics in their attempts to maximize their share of the value pie. The best salespeople will recognize the various hardball tactics, how they work, and how to respond appropriately to each in attempting to pull the customer back toward a reasonable win-win deal. There is an 80/20 rule that says the ill-prepared negotiator will make 80 percent of his/her concessions in the last 20 percent of the negotiation. Knowing your BATNA, as well as that of your buyer, can help in determining when to offer concessions, when to hold firm, and when to walk away. Your BATNA is the only protection you have from playing lose-win.

References

Clarkson, K., et al. 2000. *West's business law.* 8th ed. Albany, NY: Thomson Learning.

Fisher, R., W. Ury, and B. Patton. 1991. *Getting to yes: Negotiating agreements without giving in.* New York: Penguin.

Hitt, W. 1990. *Ethics and leadership: Putting theory into practice.* Columbus, OH: Battelle Brown.

Marks, R. 1996. *Personal selling: A relationship approach.* 6th ed. Upper Saddle River, NJ: Prentice Hall.

◆ DISCUSSION QUESTIONS

1. What are the four types of ethical standards that influence the salesperson?

2. Why do ethical people at times do unethical things? What ethical boundaries should never be breached? Cite examples from your own experiences in which you have seen this happen in a sales environment. Comment on why you believe it happened.

3. What are the similarities and differences between *sales hype* and a *statement of warranty?* On what criteria will a court base a verdict in regard to discriminating between the two?

4. In what circumstances can a gift to a valued client be considered a bribe? Discuss what standards you believe are appropriate for a sales professional.

5. Define what is meant by BATNA. What is the BATNA for a hotel sales professional?

CHAPTER 15

Sales Management

After reading this chapter you should be able to

- describe the career advancement opportunities for hospitality sales professionals
- list the major responsibilities of a director of sales
- identify techniques and strategies for determining a sales force size and structure
- explain how best to select, train, organize, and motivate a sales force

DOS (director of sales)

DOSM (director of sales and marketing)

key accounts

initial call reports

continuous call reports

coaching

Why study sales management? After all, few students who pursue a career in hospitality sales will land their first job, right out of the gate, as a sales manager. Then again, few future captains of industry start their careers as CEOs. That doesn't mean that the time they spend preparing themselves for that goal is wasted. According to Marks (1997), the reasons for studying sales management are quite simple.

◆ Sales management is a worthy career goal for ambitious salespeople.
◆ The skill set required of sales managers is quite different from that for personal selling.

If you are interested in the benefits that accrue to excellent sales managers, think about this: an understanding of sales management issues will not only help you in your communications with your superiors, it can help you get promoted to the high-level position you desire . . . due to your understanding and appreciation of the subject. Just as the ambitious are told, "Dress for the position you want," you may find it profitable to "Train for the position you want."

If this is your goal, you may accept as your first sales position a job such as conference service manager or sales administrator. This is your first move onto a lily pad that may give you the jumping-off point you need to edge out the competition when a first hotel sales position opens up. The conference service management—or events management—position is important. This person is an intermediary who deals with the

◆ promises made by the hotel sales staff
◆ needs and expectations of the meeting planner
◆ necessary interface with the hotel's operations team, which is responsible for executing the event

Does it sound like a tall order? It can be. But, such experiences give you valuable insights into the product (the what) and the processes (the how) of event sales and management. On the other hand, you may take a sales administration assistant position, which can give you invaluable insights into how sales departments are organized and how they function. The administration assistant helps senior sales staff maintain detailed records, collects and analyzes data on a prospect's conventions or events activities, and assists in the follow-up with clients. In addition, sales assistants are asked to work with walk-in prospects in the absence of sales personnel, which is another opportunity to further develop their sales skills (Astroff and Abbey 1998).

Figure 15–1 depicts not only the career advancement opportunities within hotel sales departments, but also the skills needed to advance. Figure 15–2 shows the traditional organization of sales and marketing at the full-service-property level and the corporate level.

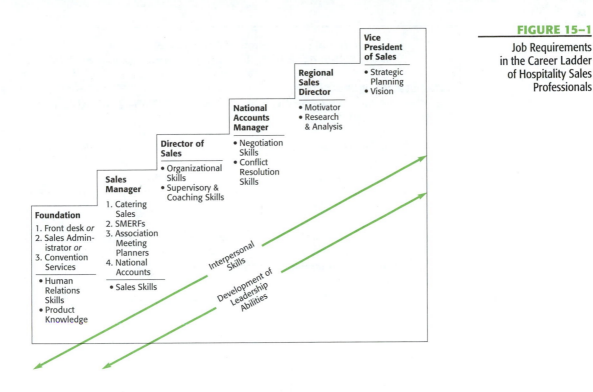

FIGURE 15–1

Job Requirements
in the Career Ladder
of Hospitality Sales
Professionals

Often your first sales management position will start off in banquet or catering sales, and from there advance to the SMERF market, association meetings, and then onward into corporate accounts. The clear progression from relatively modest to high-valued accounts provides the salesperson with a proving ground on which his/her selling abilities can be further developed and proved. From a monetary standpoint, progression from selling to the SMERF markets to association meeting planners is one very worth pursuing.

For the ambitious salesperson with the right interpersonal skills and willingness to develop supervisory, negotiation, and leadership skills, the pursuit of a **director of sales** position (or **DOS** for short) is the next career step. This is the position we will emphasize in this chapter. However, the opportunities do not stop there. Reachable steps beyond DOS include national accounts manager, regional sales director, and vice president of sales. To achieve any of these advanced positions will require that you develop strategic-planning, motivational, and leadership skills of the highest order.

First, we will briefly outline the major responsibilities of a hotel DOS and discuss five of their principal duties. These are

- ◆ determining the sales force size and structure
- ◆ recruiting the sales force
- ◆ selecting and training the sales force

Traditional Organization of Sales and Marketing at the Full-Service Property Level and Corporate Level

FULL-SERVICE PROPERTY LEVEL

There are three primary hotel sales positions at the property level, according to HVS Executive Search. They are

1. **director of sales and marketing** (usually the DOM as DOSM oversees both sales and marketing functions)
2. **director of sales** (this DOS reports to the DOM or DOSM)
3. **sales manager** (focused on group business; called managers in that they manage their customer accounts)

Additionally, an individual full-service property will have specialist sales positions such as
1. **tour and travel sales manager**
2. **corporate transient sales manager**

These dedicated salespeople are often supported by
1. **sales assistants**
2. **telemarketers**

CORPORATE LEVEL

There are nine positions identified at the corporate level.
1. top senior executives (corporate)
   a. **senior VP sales and marketing**
   b. **VP marketing**
   c. **VP sales**
2. national level executives
   a. **director of sales and marketing**
   b. **director of marketing**
   c. **director of advertising/PR**
3. regional level executives and sales
   a. **regional director of sales**
   b. **regional sales manager**
4. major or alliance account salespeople
   a. **account executive/sales representative**

◆ organizing the sales office
◆ motivating and evaluating salespeople

The Director of Sales

The director of sales is responsible for executing those aspects of the hotel's marketing plan related to going after group business and meetings, and meeting revenue objectives. According to a study by Laventhol and Horwath (2000), some 50 percent of all lodging revenue is derived from group sales. Though the actual percent of group versus transient demand will differ from property to property, the director of sales position will exist in only those properties where group sales contribute significantly to the top-line revenue of the firm.

Major responsibilities of the director of sales of a hotel are to

◆ manage those aspects of the marketing plan related to group sales so as to achieve the marketing plan's objectives
◆ meet or exceed budgeted REVPAR for the hotel
◆ accurately forecast revenues
◆ analyze and adjust the sales plan on a continual basis to reflect market conditions
◆ know the hotel's demand segments as well as the principal competition for each demand segment and be able to take advantage of the hotel's relative strengths in these areas
◆ produce sales reports for the executive team as well as for corporate headquarters
◆ work with the executive team to reposition the hotel when needed

To execute these responsibilities effectively, the director of sales handles duties at several functional levels. When the DOS is charged with creating a new sales department from scratch—as in the case for a new hotel, he/she will probably follow a series of steps: (1) designing and organizing the sales force, (2) managing the sales force, and (3) improving the sales force (see Figure 15–3). Within each of the steps is a series of functions, but for the purposes of this chapter, we will confine our discussion to the five principal areas described earlier.

◆ determining the sales force size and structure
◆ recruiting the sales force
◆ selecting and training the sales force
◆ organizing the sales office
◆ motivating and evaluating salespeople

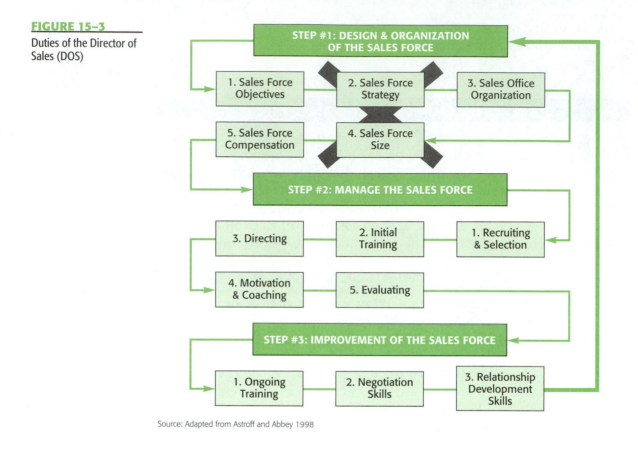

Source: Adapted from Astroff and Abbey 1998

Determining the Size of the Sales Force

A sales force is one of the more expensive assets of a firm. Determining the number of sales staff needed and organizing them into the most effective and efficient structure is one of the responsibilities of the director of sales. If there is a need to increase the size of the sales staff, the DOS will have to make a persuasive case to the owners and executive committee to demonstrate the need for new positions.

A general guideline for determining the size of a sales staff requires a few simple calculations. Assume that the sales quota of group sales for last year was $12 million and that the sales office employs five full-time sales representatives. Further assume that next year's marketing plan calls for increasing the group sales quota to $15 million—or a 20 percent increase. Following this logic, the number of sales staff needed should correspondingly increase by 20 percent—or at least one new sales representative.

An alternative approach put forth by Kotler, Bowen, and Makens (1998) is the *workload approach,* which suggests the following steps:

1. Clients and prospects are grouped into A, B, C, or D categories according to their annual sales volume.
2. The DOS and staff establish a standard for the number of sales calls per account per year for each category of accounts.
3. The total workload for sales is calculated by multiplying the number of accounts in each group by the corresponding frequency of sales calls.
4. The DOS and staff determine a "doable and desirable" average number of sales calls a sales manager can actually make per year.
5. The DOS determines the number of sales representatives needed by dividing the total workload (total number of sales calls required) by the average number of calls a salesperson can realistically make.

To illustrate, assume that there are 30 'A' accounts, 75 'B' accounts, 200 'C' accounts, and 300 'D' accounts in your market (see Figure 15–4). Assume that

- ◆ A accounts warrant two personal sales calls per month (24 per year) and three telephone contacts per month (36 per year)
- ◆ B accounts merit one personal sales call per month (12 per year) and two telephone contacts per month (24 per year)
- ◆ C accounts warrant one personal sales call every other month (6 per year) and two telephone calls per month (24 per year)
- ◆ D accounts require one contact per month by telephone (12 per year)

This means that the firm needs a sales force that can make 3,720 personal sales calls and 11,280 telephone sales calls per year. If the average salesperson can make 15 personal sales calls per week (780 per year) and 43 telephone sales calls per week (2,256 per year) then the company would need five full-time sales representatives to successfully manage the workload.

FIGURE 15–4

Key Account Management: Prioritizing Accounts Based on Their Profit Potential

A accounts—established accounts that generate a high level of business. These accounts warrant greatest attention in the form of understanding the client's full range of business needs through personal sales calls and telephone contacts that emphasize consultative sales strategies.

B accounts—high-potential accounts. They may be established accounts that are already providing a good level of business but have a potential to provide more (for example, by winning other pieces of their business away from competitors). These may warrant your attention at the same frequencies as 'A' accounts, perhaps even more.

C accounts—potential new accounts or established accounts with medium potential.

D accounts—potential new or established accounts with low potential. Follow-up on these accounts comes last—after all other accounts have been handled.

Source: Adapted from Astroff and Abbey 1998

Determining the Structure of the Sales Force

Once the size of the sales force has been established, the director of sales must organize the sales staff into an effective structure.

Assigning by Territory

One of the simplest sales organizational forms is assigning sales representatives to an exclusive geographic territory in which they will represent the firm's full line of products and services. Organizing the sales force by territories is the preferred organizational form of cruise ship companies, airlines, food and wine wholesalers, and several corporate hotel chains. The approach has a number of advantages because it can reduce travel time and costs, since the salesperson is traveling in a limited geographic area. Assigning sales representatives to specific territories encourages sales staff to develop strong ties within the community and industry, which is a foundation of relationship marketing.

Assigning by Market Segment

Often a hotel will assign its sales staff to specific market segments such as the association/conventions market, corporate meetings, SMERF groups, and group tour markets. Each market has specific needs and expectations and often requires a consistent and long-term approach to win business. Assigning sales staff to specific kinds of accounts helps them develop the understanding and relationships necessary to penetrate and grow new accounts in each market segments.

Assigning by Key Accounts

At the corporate level, firms will often assign their most senior salespeople to **key accounts** or national accounts. These key accounts are singled out for special attention because of their enormous buying power. For example, a number of sectors in the economy have experienced considerable consolidation through mergers and acquisitions. This creates significant revenue potential for national hospitality firms that can win their business. Another factor influencing the formation of national accounts management is the trend of many organizational buyers to participate in *supply chain collaborations,* whereby they combine their purchases with other firms to achieve greater bargaining power (see Chapter 16). Restaurant chains like Applebee's and Pizzeria Uno, as well as independents (such as Main Street's New York City restaurants), today use e-procurement systems to combine their purchasing power not only to achieve greater cost savings but also to gain a tighter control of the supply chain. Hilton, Marriott, Hyatt, and Clubcorp have similar relationships with many of their suppliers. For the suppliers, winning such key accounts generates increased volume of business at reduced marketing and accounting costs. If a company has several such accounts, it has likely evolved its national sales force into a national accounts division.

Recruiting the Sales Force

The next task of the director of sales is to recruit, select, and train the sales staff. Sales positions can be filled either from inside the organization or from outside. If suitable internal candidates are available, they are preferable for a number of reasons.

◆ They know the product. It's difficult to sell something you do not fully understand. Promoting a person to sales from conference services or sales administration ensures that the candidate will show up on the first day of the job with not only a knowledge of the property and its services, but the relationships with people in other departments that can make him/her more effective.

◆ They are a known quantity. The candidate's performance has been observed and evaluated and his/her strengths and weaknesses are known. More important, such candidates have shown loyalty to the company by seeking to "grow where they're planted"—by seeking new responsibilities and challenges with their current employer. Solid people from within the organization have another advantage: what you know about them is real. With external candidates, it's well to remember that some people have a knack for interviewing well—but their post-hire performance may not reflect their interviewing performance. There is more uncertainty when hiring externally.

◆ Promoting from within motivates others to strive for excellence. Rewarding employees with advancement opportunities sends a clear message that the firm values hard work and service excellence.

When internal people are advanced into a sales position from operations, they should anticipate that their first position will be in catering sales or serving the SMERF markets. As we have stated earlier in this chapter, selling to these smaller, less complex accounts provides a new sales manager with a good opportunity to develop his/her sales skills. Often, when a senior salesperson with responsibilities for national accounts or national associations leaves, the DOS will fill the vacancy by promoting intermediate or junior salespeople. This creates room at the bottom.

This is not to say that every sales position can be filled successfully by an internal candidate or that it is always wise to do so. External candidates are preferred when the skills needed in a salesperson are unavailable or when a new viewpoint or perspective is needed in the sales department. External candidates often bring fresh perspectives, ideas, and skills gleaned from their previous experiences.

Searching for External Candidates

Several search strategies for external candidates exist. You may be able to recruit salespeople who work for other properties in your chain or franchise. These individuals already have some knowledge of your product and have a sales performance track record within the context of your organization. Often, their portfolios will include an advantage: fresh ideas learned from other locations that can easily be adopted at your property.

You may also be able to recruit from the sales professionals working for local competitors. Like salespeople from within your chain, they will have knowledge of the product as well as have established relationships with local buyers. However, it's not generally a wise tactic to solicit them directly—what some call *raiding*. This tactic can backfire in several ways.

◆ You may sour your relationships with their employers and invite retribution, that is, they'll respond with counterraids.
◆ Bidding for competitors' salespeople can escalate salaries to unrealistic ranges.
◆ Hiring pirated talent at high salaries can shatter the morale of your existing salespeople, who feel devalued when they see their salaries in comparison.

As a rule it is not appropriate to seek out a competitor's salespeople unless they approach you first. Nor do we recommend the formal use of employee referral programs (where you provide incentives to your sales staff to solicit salespeople away from competitors). That, too, should be avoided.

Advertising in the local newspaper may generate a number of applicants, but many will not have the sales experience in the hospitality industry or your niche within it. Although you may have heard that "someone who can sell can sell anything," research suggests that sales skills are not transferable across all sectors. Surprisingly, even professionals who have been successful in other fields (such as selling automobiles or real estate) may find their experience of little value in selling conference services. Ideally, when a technically qualified salesperson is needed, it is best to advertise in a trade magazine (for example, *Hospitality Sales and Marketing Association International*) or on a listserv focused on hospitality sales (for example, http://LTaverna@Hospitality-1st.com).

Universities that teach hospitality sales courses are also rich sources of recruits. Insiders who need to fill one or two positions (rather than recruiting many) often use two alternatives to setting up interviews with a college placement office.

- ◆ contacting an appropriate faculty member who can refer top candidates
- ◆ gaining permission to come speak to classes, since the brightest and most motivated students will step forward with questions as well as introduce themselves after class

Selecting Sales Staff: Interviewing Concerns

An extensive discussion of the selection process is beyond the scope of this chapter. However, directors of sales must be aware that asking certain types of interview questions can quickly get you into legal hot water. Some prehire questions are simply not acceptable because they seek information about federally protected characteristics—either by asking directly or by trying to indirectly ferret out such information. For example, advertising that your firm is seeking recent graduates may show a discriminatory attitude toward hiring older workers. Similarly, asking a female job applicant for her maiden name indirectly asks her for her marital status, which is not relevant for any employment decision. This tactic has also been used as a route to determining an applicant's national origin or ethnicity, which likewise should not be considered. As a general rule, it is inappropriate to ask any questions regarding an applicant's age, race, religion, and disabilities. The wise DOS will consult with the director of human resources and get a firm grip on what questions are permissible in the application and interview process—and which must be avoided at all costs. Your property's human resources department can be a valuable ally. If you ask for assistance, they will help you design a well-written ad that will attract qualified applicants. The information they capture on application forms is essential to the selection process. Beyond providing insights as to the applicants' overall qualifications, they provide the names of previous employers and of references. It is important to attempt to verify each "short-list" applicant's data by contacting the references and former employers.

The Interview

Interviews often are the crux of the selection process since they provide the only means to gauge a candidate's personality, poise, motivation, and ability to converse articulately. Ron Marks (1997) warns the DOS not to dominate the conversation but to use open-ended questions to encourage the candidate to talk. Examples of good open-ended questions for sales candidates include

◆ What is the single most important thing that has happened in your hospitality career to date?
◆ What goals did you set in your last job?
◆ Walk me through the steps you took in achieving those goals.

The candidate's responses can help you to decide if he/she has the attributes you need for the job opening. It is common to use a rating sheet or matrix for each candidate for later review. Ethics and good business sense should be applied to such sheets, however. In the 1990s, at least two hospitality companies were sued for unfair hiring practices when it was found that they commonly "coded" rating sheets to discriminate based on race or perceived gender preferences.

More Than Words

During the interview, it is important to pay attention to the candidates' body language and gestures. Psychologists have taught us to watch for particular "attending behaviors," which provide insights as to the candidates' abilities to establish and maintain rapport as well as their willingness to actively listen to others. Interviewers should take note of the following body language signals, all of which are important attributes of successful customer-oriented salespeople:

◆ the position of the candidate's body
◆ the tone of voice
◆ head movements
◆ the level of eye contact

There are no universal norms of how polished a person's verbal and nonverbal demeanor needs to be in order to be successful in sales. In fact, individuals who appear overly rehearsed and polished may put you—and if you hired them, your clients—on guard. When conducting an interview, the DOS should judge the candidates' ability to come across credibly and persuasively in the way they dress, speak, and behave. If someone does not come across as credible and persuasive during the interview, what in the world would make you think he/she will do so when communicating with your customers?

Poets have often claimed that "the eyes are a window to people's souls," and it is surprising how annoying most people find it when those eyes, along with someone's attention, wander during interactions. Though it is quite possible to listen well even when one is not giving good eye contact, that really is not the point. When someone speaks without looking at us, we doubt that he/she is listening. We may feel unimportant or even disrespected. Nor do we want to be stared at. Good salespeople, and good professionals in general, know how to show they are listening and are attentive by giving a sufficient level of eye contact.

Body posture is important too. Virtually all parents have advised their children to "Sit up!" followed by ". . . and pay attention." Parents are teaching their children another cultural reality. Most people believe that body language is a good indicator of whether we are paying attention. For salespeople, holding one's body erect, leaning slightly forward when seated, and facing the other person directly are important attending behaviors customers expect. Look for these in the interview. One last tip: fair or not, many customers and employers judge a professional by the condition of his/her shoes. A polished shoe, even if it is not new, shows a concern for appearance and respect for the "ritual" of a meeting or interview. Don't let your first impression stop at the knees. The poets might also agree: "Shoes are the window to a person's sole!"

Organizing the Sales Office: The Filing and Call Report System

Once the sales staff is in place, it is the responsibility of the director of sales to organize them into an effective unit. Identifying and calling on potential customers is a major part of a hotel salesperson's efforts. It is the responsibility of the director of sales to set up a system of tracking sales activity. The system can be designed around sales automation software (the subject of Chapter 17) or can be as simple as a filing system.

A good sales call report system is composed of the following:

- ◆ two essential sales call reports—an initial sales call report and a **continuous call report**
- ◆ account files to hold reports for high-potential accounts
- ◆ two filing systems—one standard file drawer to hold high-potential accounts (A, B, C accounts), one accordion file to hold **initial call reports** for low or no-potential accounts (D accounts)
- ◆ a trace card system to remind the sales manager to follow up on all accounts at an appropriate time

Here's how the four elements work together. Let's look at this from a **coaching** perspective; we'll talk you through it.

1. When you make the first sales call to a potential customer, fill out an initial sales call report (see Figure 15–5). At the same time, create a trace

FIGURE 15–5

Sample Trace Card
System

Initial Sales Call Report

Organization   XYZ Corporation   Contact Mr. John Wade

Address   701 Parkway Drive   Title _____
                    P.O. Box 4711   Tel _____
                    Atlanta, GA 37424   Fax _____
                                         Email _____

Room Nights Per Year   1,500 _____
Current Rate $84.00
Relocation Needs   not at this time
Meeting Needs   Quarterly operations.   Monthly sales _____
Individual Needs   Periodic
Hotel(s) Currently Used Radisson
Summary of Discussion   _____
                        _____
                        _____
                        _____
                        _____

Salesperson   _____

3" by 5" trace cards
filed in index card box
by month and dated

XYZ Corp   HIGH
701 Parkway Drive
P.O. Box 4711
Atlanta, GA 37424

12/04/04
1/14/05
2/16/05

Continuous Call Report

Organization _____

Date _____ Call Type _____ Contact _____
Objective _____
Discussed _____
          _____

Date _____ Call Type _____ Contact _____
Objective _____
Discussed _____
          _____

Date _____ Call Type _____ Contact _____
Objective _____
Discussed _____
          _____

Date _____ Call Type _____ Contact _____
Objective _____
Discussed _____
          _____

card for each high- or low-potential account and place it in a card file box under the future date on which you will contact the account again.

2. If you determine from your first sales call that the account has high potential, then place the initial sales call report in the file drawer alphabetized by the company name. If you decide that the account has low or no potential, then place the initial sales call report in an accordion file alphabetized by the company name.

3. Check your trace cards each day to see which accounts need to be contacted the following day.

4. If a high-potential account is listed on the card, pull the file folder from your sales account file drawer. Use a continuous call report (see Figure 15–5) to note activity and comments on that account. This report is left in the file folder for the purpose of maintaining a running record. Once the account has been recontacted, cross out the old trace card date and write a new date for follow-up. Refile the trace card in the card file box under the new date.

5. If a low-potential account is listed on the trace card, pull the initial sales call report from the accordion file for contact purposes. If once you contact the account you determine that it has current potential, complete a continuous call report and make a sales file for it. Again mark a new date on the trace card for follow-up.

Motivating and Coaching Salespeople

Meeting revenue goals requires a motivated and well-trained sales staff. Keeping a sales staff at peak performance is a challenge, to say the least. According to Marks (1997), a salesperson can experience wide emotional swings between the elation of landing a large new account and the frustration of losing one. In addition, hospitality salespeople whose positions require extensive travel sometimes develop feelings of isolation, which can be de-energizing and demotivating. The wise director of sales will recognize when a salesperson is experiencing a slump in his/her performance, and offer appropriate assistance and support. The job of the director of sales requires not only the structuring and monitoring of a manager, but also the insight, sensitivity, and coaching vision of a leader.

This can be a fine line to walk. When does a challenging goal become an impossible and stressing one? What is an acceptable level of pressure to place on salespeople? Should a DOS establish sales quotas when the sales staff is being encouraged to establish long-term relationships with clients? If so, at what level should the sales quotas be set? Should sales quotas be set at a level that salespeople have only a 50/50 chance of reaching? The director of sales is responsible for reaching revenue targets, so it is only natural that he/she place pressure on the sales staff so the overall goals can be reached. Many DOSs have learned ways to motivate their staff to produce at high levels without applying unrealistic pressure on them.

Contrary to popular belief, a manager cannot motivate a person; the employee must motivate himself/herself (Kavanaugh and Ninemeier 2000). The director of sales creates the conditions that motivate employees by establishing goals and influencing employees to reach those goals. The recipe for success includes establishing realistic and obtainable sales goals, encouraging the sales staff to reach those goals; and providing the meaningful rewards, incentives, and support. According to Kavanaugh and Ninemeier, supervisors develop a motivated staff by creating a climate in which the staff wants to work *with*—rather than against—the goals of the department.

We have observed that the best DOSs are often the best *coaches*. Sales training teaches people how and why they should perform their jobs. **Coaching**, on the other hand, helps people learn *where* to apply what they have learned to specific situations. Studies have shown that in sales training without follow-up, 90 percent of what is learned in the classroom is forgotten. Good directors of sales make a continual effort to reinforce, teach, and reteach elements of good sales techniques to their staff each day.

Coaching can be informal as well as formal. Coaching informally is a routine part of supervision and occurs whenever the DOS communicates with an employee about his/her performance. A particularly effective coaching technique is "catching someone doing something right"—and then praising him/her immediately for it. Another effective coaching technique is developing an open-door and personally involved style so that members of the sales staff feel they can seek the DOS's advice and counsel about a situation or a problem. When coaching is done informally and trust is built, then pointers from the DOS are less likely to be perceived as threatening. With trust, a DOS may occasionally come along on a salesperson's call and be perceived as an ally. This creates a unique opportunity to observe sales techniques and provide supportive feedback to the salesperson afterward.

Formal coaching occurs in privately scheduled meetings or sessions. These meetings need to be held in private areas, away from potential distractions and interruptions, and conducted in a positive and caring way. They are designed to clarify issues, discuss problems that are affecting sales performance, and address other specific training purposes. The best coaches keep the focus on issues and never come across as blaming. They emphasize techniques that will build success and confidence, which are useful both to experienced salespeople finding themselves in a slump and to new sales staffers—who may need a few sessions on closing skills.

SUMMARY ◇

In the hotel industry, salespeople are commonly called sales managers (since they manage their customer accounts). These hotel sales managers are supervised and managed by executives called directors. In a hotel's sales and marketing department, these executives commonly are designated in one of the following ways:

1. director of marketing—manages the entire department and delegates the specific sales management duties to the directors of sales
2. director of sales
3. director of sales and marketing—in some hotels, combines both roles into one position

This chapter focused on the general functions of a director of sales and the responsibilities associated with these functions. The architecture phrase *form follows function* is applicable because we know that for a sales force to be effective it must be carefully designed, organized, and managed. Ultimately, the *form* the sales department takes mirrors the *function* the sales force is expected to achieve in the hotel's marketing plan.

For the ambitious salesperson with the right skills, taking the next step up the career ladder can be rewarding. But to do so, and to succeed thereafter as a director of sales, takes a commitment to personal mastery. A DOS is more than someone who has proven himself/herself an excellent and successful sales executive. An effective DOS must take on the mantle of leadership, which means caring about and guiding his/her staff members toward their own levels of personal mastery.

References

Astroff, M., and J. Abbey. 1998. *Convention management and service.* 5th ed. Lansing, MI: Educational Institute of the American Hotel and Lodging Association.

Kavanaugh, R., and J. Ninemeier. 2000. *Supervision in the hospitality industry.* Lansing, MI: Educational Institute of the American Hotel and Lodging Association.

Kotler, P., J. Bowen, and J. Makens. 1998. *Marketing for hospitality and tourism.* Upper Saddle River, NJ: Simon and Schuster.

Laventhol and Horwath. 2000. *The U.S. Lodging Industry/Annual.* Philadelphia, PA: Laventhol and Horwath

Marks, R. 1997. *Personal selling: A relationship approach.* 7th ed. Upper Saddle River, NJ: Simon and Schuster.

DISCUSSION QUESTIONS ◇

1. Comment on the skills and abilities needed to advance a career in sales as visualized in Figure 15–1. What skills and abilities need to be developed along each step of career advancement opportunities?

2. Describe the steps in determining an ideal size of a sales force using the workload method. Include in your discussion the concept of key accounts.
3. What are the advantages and disadvantages of deploying a sales force by territory versus by market segments?
4. Explain in detail how a sales office should ideally be organized in terms of a (manual) filing and call report system. Include how the elements work together.

CHAPTER 16

Sales Channels and Intermediaries

After reading this chapter you should be able to

- explain how competitive advantage can be achieved through the use of sales channels and intermediaries
- describe the assumptions and theory guiding leading firms to reach and serve their markets

- identify where it is appropriate to deploy one's own sales force, a sales intermediary, and the Internet
- describe what problems often arise in a multiple sales channel strategy

go to market systems
channel advantage
channel mix
intensive channel coverage

hybrid channel coverage
channel lift
channel shift

271

Not long ago, virtually all hospitality firms sold their products and services directly to the consumer, utilizing their own sales force supported by their own promotional campaigns. Hilton Hotel Corporation, for example, employed a large and well-trained hotel sales staff at each of its corporately owned and franchised properties. Supported by the Hilton brand name and advertising support, each property's sales force had the responsibility for all group sales (for example, meetings, corporate transient accounts, catering, and so forth).

Today, Hilton goes to market with multiple sales channels, a mixture of

- a hotel-specific sales force
- a national sales force
- the Internet
- telephone sales centers
- centralized reservation centers supported by national marketing campaigns
- sales intermediaries such as travel agencies and tour wholesalers
- strategic alliances with airlines and credit card companies

In this chapter, we discuss the reasons why firms are engineering such complexity into how they sell their products and services. Though it can be argued that the topic falls outside the purview of the salesperson, it is our contention that an understanding of channel design and management will help the individual salesperson understand his/her role in the increasingly complex **go to market systems** used by today's companies. As an aspiring salesperson, you may one day wish to become a national sales director or vice president of sales. If so, the ability to design a well-thought-out mix of sales channels that delivers results—the kinds of results that show up on income statements and affect stock prices—will be essential.

Sources of Competitive Advantage

The role of a sales channel is to connect products with markets. Today, leading firms are putting at least as much effort and creativity into how they connect with their target markets as they do in bringing their products to the market. Let's briefly explore why this has happened.

According to Friedman and Furey (1999), leading authorities in channel management, "For a business to be viable at all, it must do something well. For it to win in a competitive market, though, it has to do something better than its competitors" (Friedman and Furey 1999, 3). Therefore, to achieve competitive advantage—to make sales in a competitive marketplace—you have to be better than your competitors at something your customers consider important. That *something* could be a better product or service, a lower price, or providing customers what they want and how they prefer to acquire it. Let's discuss again each of these means of achieving competitive advantage in greater detail.

Hotel firms are always in search of *new products* or *amenities* they can add to their properties to deliver competitive advantage. A free breakfast, in-room entertainment systems, health and fitness facilities, and in-room workstations with Internet access have all provided the innovating firm a competitive advantage. The problem is that they yield the kinds of competitive advantages *that do not last*. In other words, these innovations are easily recognized and adopted by competitors and the competitive advantage is lost, often in just a few months. What is needed is one or more competitive advantages that are sustainable over the course of years.

Price is another way to gain competitive advantage. Offering the right product at the lowest price is another method companies use to achieve competitive advantages. The TQM revolution of the 1980s was all about ways to streamline business processes in order to please customers by delivering quality at the lowest possible costs, and thus, at the lowest price to the customer. Unfortunately, most of today's firms have already streamlined their processes and are finding it harder to find new ways to further improve processes so that they can reduce costs in any substantial way. Today, most firms have reached a level of parity (equality) with their competitors. We can see this in the eerie similarity of business structures and processes employed by most hotel companies. Competing on cost structures is possible, but most of the straightforward ways operations can be streamlined have already been done. In other words, everyone has made the obvious and relatively easy changes.

Companies can also seek competitive advantages not only in what they provide customers but in the ways they connect with them. New technologies such as the Internet, call centers, and customer relationship management systems are providing firms with a wide range of alternatives in how they reach and serve customers. These technologies can create **channel advantages**.

Traditionally, a hotel sales and marketing director's *go to market system* would be composed of a sales staff supported by an advertising and promotional budget. Today the go to market system is much more complex, involving a national sales force (provided by the chain, franchiser, or referral association), call centers, intermediaries such as WorldRez.com, retail travel agencies, and marketing partners and alliances. Instead of a sales force of four or five salespeople, the sales director now has literally hundreds and perhaps thousands of trained and motivated salespeople selling (albeit part-time) his/her products on his/her behalf. Moreover, the affordability of these sales channels lets firms generate sales from new markets they could probably not afford to reach with their own sales force.

The remainder of this chapter will focus on three important topics related to channel management.

◆ What channels are being used in the hospitality industry and why?
◆ What implications do these channels have for the hospitality sales professional?
◆ How should they be managed to make them an integrated go to market system?

As we have discussed all through this book, the sales profession is evolving. It is essential for both the director of sales and sales managers to understand and appreciate their role in a multi-channel go to market system.

Sales Channels in the Hospitality and Tourism Industry

You may be surprised to know that the hospitality and tourism industry has been in the forefront of pioneering indirect sales channels. Travel agencies and wholesalers have served as sales intermediaries driven by sales commissions and discounts, respectively. These sales intermediaries have afforded hotels, attractions, cruise ships, and airlines an expanded market coverage no one firm could afford on its own (see Figure 16–1). What is different today is that the number of such sales channels has grown, and so has the depth of relationships suppliers have with these intermediaries.

The theory behind the advantage of a channel-focused system is relatively simple. Sales directors now have a wide range of options for connect-

FIGURE 16–1

Types of Travel Agencies

vacation stores

commercial agencies

direct response agencies

cruise-only agencies (no airline accreditation)

consolidators

meetings, incentive, convention, and expositions (MICE)

tour operators

    1. preformed vs. free and independent Travelers FIT

    2. inbound (receptors) vs. outbound

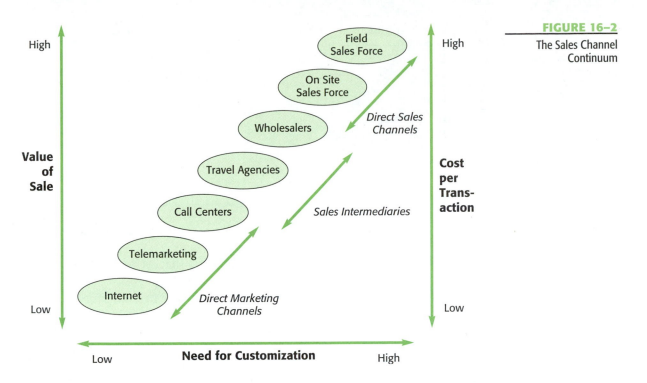

FIGURE 16–2

The Sales Channel
Continuum

ing their products and services with consumers via the Internet, a sales force, and everything in between. Each channel has its unique strengths as well as weaknesses. As Figure 16–2 illustrates, a direct sales force is most advantageous in circumstances in which the complexity of the product is high, face-to-face interaction with the customer is expected, and the high costs associated with a sales force can be recouped in the sale. On the other hand, the Internet works well for some types of products or services. Products or services that are relatively simple and seldom need customization can often be sold on the Internet at less cost for both the seller and buyer. The bottom line is that the use of a single sales channel will limit a firm's sales performance to whatever that particular channel is able to do well. If your firm uses only a sales force, you will be able to deliver excellent support and service but at a cost disadvantage to any competitor that decides to sell through almost any other channel. On the other hand, if you sell only on the Internet, you probably will be limited to selling relatively simple off-the-shelf products at a low price and will face significant challenges in developing customer loyalty. No single channel can do everything well or competitively.

Channel mix is a concept used by marketers to describe the multiple sales strategies they use to go to market. The purpose of a channel mix is to intercept a broad range of sales transactions in order to increase sales volume and market share. Channel mixes come in three forms: **intensive**, selective, and **hybrid**. Intensive channel mixes provide overlapping coverage of one or more markets where each channel competes with each other. Selective channel

FIGURE 16–3

Example of Intensive
versus Selective Channel
Coverage

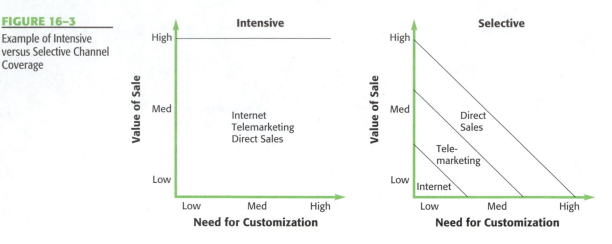

mixes assign an individual channel to one specific market without overlap or integration with the other channels (see Figure 16–3).

A hybrid of the two is much more common. A hybrid channel strategy involves the assignment of a single channel to one or more product markets. To illustrate, British Airways employs a hybrid channel strategy in order to keep all its flights flying with as many passengers as possible. It serves its broad base of individual and business travelers with multiple overlapping channels. Virtually all customers can use any channel; the goal is to intercept as many customers as possible by providing them with their preferred method of making a purchase. At the same time, the airline maintains a direct sales force to serve large corporate accounts that require specialized services. The purpose of the sales force is not to achieve total market coverage, but to reach, develop, and serve those high-valued accounts that need customized services. Note, too, in Figure 16–4, that those segments of the market that cannot be served profitably receive nonchannel coverage.

FIGURE 16–4

Example of a Hybrid
Channel Coverage

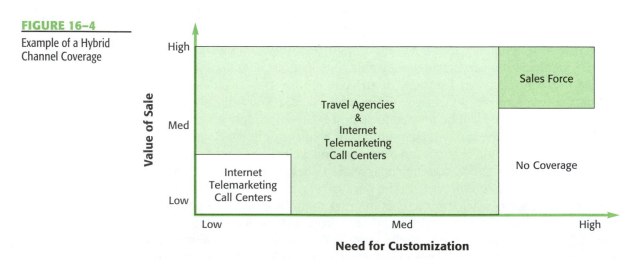

The foundation of channel strategy is a firm's understanding of the consumer behavior in each market segment. The channels added to the mix should be those that collectively reach and profitably capture a share of the transactions in each market segment. So why not take all that your firm sells, throw it out on all the sales channels available to you, and see what happens? In reality, that is what many firms are doing. They are chasing sales over profits. The problem with such an approach is that having more channels costs more money and inevitably leads to channel conflicts. You should always consider long-term profitability when you develop a sales channel mix. Take time to think about the following:

◆ *Multiple sales channels may end up chasing the same sales.* Coverage of a market by multiple sales channels may create **channel shift** (customers moving from one channel to another) without **channel lift** (new sales). Though difficult to estimate, one should assess how much new sales volume will actually be produced by adding a new channel to the product-market mix. If the answer is not a whole lot, it may make sense to defer channel expansion in order to hold down the cost of sales.

◆ *Not all channels will be profitable in every product market.* Each channel should focus on the product-market mix from which it can conceivably generate profits. It is unlikely, but still possible, to sell a large association meeting over the Internet. (Buyers usually expect considerable interaction with the seller before they feel confident enough to sign a contract.) It is highly unlikely that hotel companies in the market for a new property management system (PMS) or point-of-sale (POS) system would ever purchase one without interacting with a salesperson. Though any sales channel could theoretically be capable of handling either of the above transactions, the odds are against it if there is a poor alignment with how customers prefer to buy. On the other hand, a firm that sells relatively simple meeting services simply can't afford to have a highly paid salesperson make every sale.

A real-world example comes from SYSCO Food Systems. SYSCO wanted to create flexibility in how reorders are taken from its client base of small restaurant customers. The company realizes that though it may be profitable for a salesperson to personally take the order from a restaurant manager of a 4,000-room hotel in Las Vegas, the same is not true for orders from a small restaurant that purchases $200 to $300 twice a week. Imposing the big-customer model on the small customer is wrong-headed. Instead, SYSCO focuses its field salespeople on securing the initial business from these small accounts with the hope that they will "migrate" to placing their orders over the Internet (http://www.sysco.com) or by fax.

◆ *Manage the conflict where possible with channel members.* In a product market covered by multiple channels, competition between channel members for sales is inevitable and must be managed. Channel conflict is just another way of saying that customers are provided with multiple purchasing opportunities by the same service provider. A national sales team may "steal" a sale from the hotel sales manager (an example of channel shift), which means the firm experiences a net gain of zero. Such competition can be a good thing in that it keeps all channel members on their toes. However, it can be confusing for customers when they are provided different offers for the same product, often at different prices. A solution many firms find more advantageous is to encourage their competing direct channels to work together (a topic we will address in the next section). On the other hand, conflict between a firm's direct channels and its indirect channel partners is a completely different story. A firm that launches its own Web site or call center and focuses it on the same market as its retail, distributor, or wholesale partners does so at a risk of voiding the supplier-distributor relationship. For years, no airline wanted to be the first to reduce the commissions paid to travel agencies for every ticket they sold. The perceived risk was that travel agents would react to such a move by shifting their bookings to other airlines that maintained the normal commissions. Unfortunately for travel agents, all airlines have now capped their commissions, which has forced travel agencies to look for new products to sell.

Cruise ship companies and many hotel companies, in an attempt to expand their market coverage, have not only maintained but increased their commissions to travel agencies to maximize the channel's potential. The point is that multiple channels in a market are independent entities that are selling against each other. In a market that is growing, this may not be a problem since all channel members have room to grow. However, if every sale comes at the expense of another channel member, something has to give, be it fewer channel partners or fewer direct sales channels. Any realignment of channels should be focused on customer preferences and how they wish to buy.

Channel Integration

Another channel strategy that is gaining momentum in the hospitality industry is this: firms employ different channels in each stage of the sales process. As we have learned earlier in this book, the sales process can be thought of as a series of discrete tasks involving prospecting, account qualification, exploring needs and proposing, closing, and after-sale service and support (see Figure 16–5).

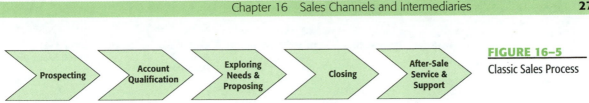

FIGURE 16–5

Classic Sales Process

Is it necessary to have one channel perform all these tasks? A more profitable and more effective solution would be to create a division of labor *within* the sales process—or in other words, assign different functions to each sales channel. For instance, as we have previously stated, we would expect very few sales to be made for expensive and highly complex hotel property management systems over the Internet. However, the Internet, *in combination with* a call center, may be an effective way to generate leads and qualify leads with a far lower cost and far higher quality than a higher-cost salesperson. The same is true for hotel sales. As Marriott has done, why not have lower-cost telemarketing representatives generate and qualify leads of group business, close the easy ones, and pass the complex ones off to sales managers at the property level? In addition, the after-sale fulfillment and support component can be passed to the conference service manager, who is a specialist at working with event planners on the execution of their events. Such reengineering of the sales process lowers the total cost of sales, improves after-sale service, and frees up sales managers to focus on what they do best.

In short, integrating the channels in such a way involves transferring tasks in the sales process to channels that are better skilled and trained to perform them at lower costs. Thus, a firm that starts off with sales managers handling all the tasks within the sales process could realign some of those tasks to other channels, thus allowing the sales manager to focus on the tasks where his/her skills count the most (see Figure 16–6).

Channel integration of this nature is profitable, but that does not make it easy. In reality, channel integration brings with it a number of complexities. Marriott's *Sales 2000* is a recent attempt to reengineer its sales process in a way that's similar to what we have previously described. Marriott's hybrid approach for its direct sales channels is composed of

- eight event-booking centers throughout the United States
- a direct sales force focused on alliance accounts, market cluster sales, and property sales (room and catering)
- event-management personnel at the property level

Before adopting such a hybrid model, firms need to think through two important considerations. For simple transactions involving relatively short sales cycles, will such a system be worth the effort? For complex sales with relatively long sales cycles, how will buyers react to a new hybrid system when they have come to expect a sales manager's involvement in every step of the

FIGURE 16–6

Multiple-Channel
Sales Model

process? Hospitality is at its foundation a "high-touch" industry. Companies that make substantial changes to the sales processes run the risk of getting too far ahead of what customers expect and want. However, when firms improve service at reduced costs, customers can be expected to reward them with loyalty.

Account "Ownership"

In order for an integrated channel system to work effectively, the account in question must be "owned" across all selling tasks. What does this mean? In the case of major accounts, a single sales manager (or sales team) should have ownership of an account from the first sales call to the closing of the first account and throughout the continuation of the relationship. No one else in the organization (upward or downward) should be ringing the account's doorbell or trying to gain entry through the back door. For smaller, less complex accounts, the sales manager may find himself/herself in competition with other (downward) channels in getting the sale, because the client may feel comfortable starting at that level. In still another variation of the hybrid model, the sales manager's efforts may be integrated with other channels. He/she may assign downward channels to tasks that are appropriate to their skills and to the client's needs. In the best hybrids, accounts are "owned" by the organization, not the sales manager. The sales team "works" the account, but no one member owns it.

If you remember your biology, you'll recall that the term hybrid refers to a blending of traits from different parents or species. Oftentimes, hybrids are more robust and adaptable than their original sources. Such hardiness will help innovative companies thrive in a competitive marketplace.

SUMMARY ◈

Most hospitality firms have realized that they cannot serve an entire market with a single channel anymore. Limiting sales to any one channel is either too limited in market reach and growth or too expensive. A hybrid channel model is often a better solution. Hybrid models that are well designed can provide impressive gains, efficiency, and profits. However, they add complexity to the sales process and need to be managed *as systems*.

For the student of hospitality sales, this chapter provides a glimpse as to what the future may become. The highly trained and compensated sales professional will be deployed to cover large high-valued accounts that are complex and require excellent customer support. Simple transactions will be pushed downward to less expensive channels where it makes financial sense to do so. In the team-based hybrid model, the account is not *owned* by one salesperson. Instead, the account is *owned* by the organization and *worked* by the team of professionals who create and manage it.

References

Friedman, L., and T. Furey. 1999. *The channel advantage.* Boston: Butterworth Heinemann.

DISCUSSION QUESTIONS ◈

1. How can a firm gain and sustain competitive advantages? How can sales channels contribute to a firm's financial success?
2. Explain the assumptions represented in Figure 16–2.
3. Compare and contrast the three methods of channel coverage as presented in this chapter. What method would you prepare to work under and why?
4. Discuss the evolution currently underway where firms are reengineering their sales channels as described in Figure 16–6. What are they attempting to accomplish and how?

CHAPTER 17

Information Technologies and Sales Force Automation

LEARNING OBJECTIVES

After reading this chapter you should be able to

- ◆ identify the significant boosts in productivity that can be achieved through the adoption of sales automation technologies (SAT)

- ◆ list ways in which SAT and the Internet can aid in the relationship development and management of key accounts
- ◆ explain how SAT can reduce costs and save the time of a sales professional

KEY TERMS & CONCEPTS

IT (information technology)

sales automation technologies (SAT)

Technology Acceptance Model (TAM)

property management system (PMS)

functional diaries

request for proposal (RFP)

banquet event order (BEO)

Is it worth it to introduce **information technology (IT)** into the sales process? Most will answer, "Yes!" since IT has been shown, on many occasions, to result in superior returns on investment for companies in terms of enhanced productivity, customer communications, and relationships. However, acceptance of such technology at both the corporate and sales force level is at best mixed in the hospitality industry. A long line of research in the information systems literature has been focused on explaining the acceptance of such aids. Perhaps the best model for predicting and explaining why some companies and salespeople readily accept technology while others do not is the **Technology Acceptance Model (TAM)** (Davies et al. 1989). According to TAM, the acceptance of software aids is determined by two factors: the perceived usefulness (that is, the extent to which the company and/or salesperson believes the system will improve his/her job performance) and perceived ease of use (that is, the extent to which a company and/or salesperson considers the system to be free of effort).

Over the years, research has supported the basic premise of TAM but has also added to it. Davies (1989) suggest that the following factors play important roles:

- ◆ competitive pressures
- ◆ customer influences
- ◆ personal innovativeness
- ◆ computer self-efficacy
- ◆ (We also believe that, until recently, price had also played a role.)

Because of these influences, young computer-literate hospitality sales professionals wishing to make their mark in the industry may be at an advantage. Technology and the Internet are changing the rules and landscape of hospitality and the meeting industries. So much business is being done through e-commerce that the technologically savvy have a strong edge over their technophobic counterparts.

We have organized this chapter as follows. First, we will describe hospitality **sales automation technology (SAT)** used in selling guest rooms. Then we will discuss catering sales and management systems. Though both processes are generally handled by the same software system, users tend to specialize in their areas of responsibility. For example, a hotel's group sales staff will use only those aspects that involve selling guest rooms and services to prospects, whereas catering will use the system to plan, monitor, and manage catering events. Woven into the chapter are figures that show the layouts of the two leading hospitality sales automation systems on the market: Newmarket International's Delphi system and Daylight's Enterprise system.

Sales Force Automation for Group Sales Time and Contact Management

On any given day, a hotel salesperson's schedule will have appointments, follow-ups, and other tasks to perform. Salespeople are also responsible for responding to inquiries and **requests for proposals (RFPs)**—and doing so quickly. All this *can* be performed with a manual system that is well thought out and well managed—perhaps by using day planners, ledgers, and both historic and teaser files. However, several firms offer a suite of software aids that not only automate the process but also offer features through which a salesperson can stand out from the competition. Chief among these firms are

- Newmarket International (http://www.newsoft.com/)
- Daylight Software Inc. (http://www.daylightsoftware.com/)
- Computer Sciences Corporation (http://www.csc.com/)
- MICROS (http://www.micros.com/) hotel and catering sales software

The Functional Diary

Functional diary software packages help a salesperson manage daily tasks (see Figure 17–1). By simply logging onto the system via the desktop, salespeople can schedule meetings and tasks months in advance with the assurance that they will be reminded of it at the pertinent time. In addition, the software also allows the salesperson to keep track of which client groups are on-property. This can be helpful for relationship management purposes as well as for monitoring the status of the hotel (for example, renovations or events).

The guest room control log (see Figure 17–2) gives the salesperson instant access to forecasts of transient demand and group commitments including target rates and room type availability. Prior to having such information technology, a salesperson could not predict availability very far in the future. If a meeting planner called to request preferred dates and rates, the salesperson would have to schedule a call-back time, then find out whether the needed meeting facilities were already booked and if the hotel showed guest room availability. Now the technology, through its interface with the hotel's **property management system (PMS)**, allows the salesperson to check availability and book the business while the customer is on the phone.

If a hotel cannot accommodate the business, the software provides a means to electronically refer the business to another more suitable property within the chain or franchise. Moreover, innovations involving the Internet have created a single database for multiple properties. Now the salesperson with an appropriate security clearance can instantly check availability and book business within the chain or management company. Such a feature has enabled chains like Hilton-Direct, Opryland Hospitality, Orient Express, and

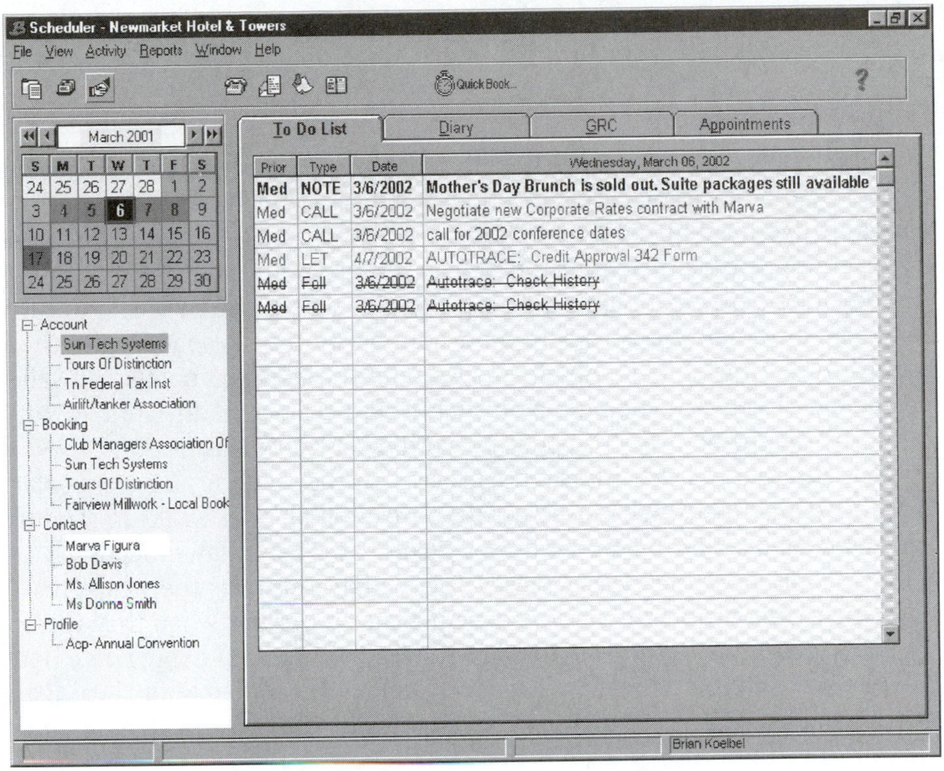

FIGURE 17–1

Scheduler Screen

Reproduced with the permission of Micros Systems, Inc. (www.micros.com)

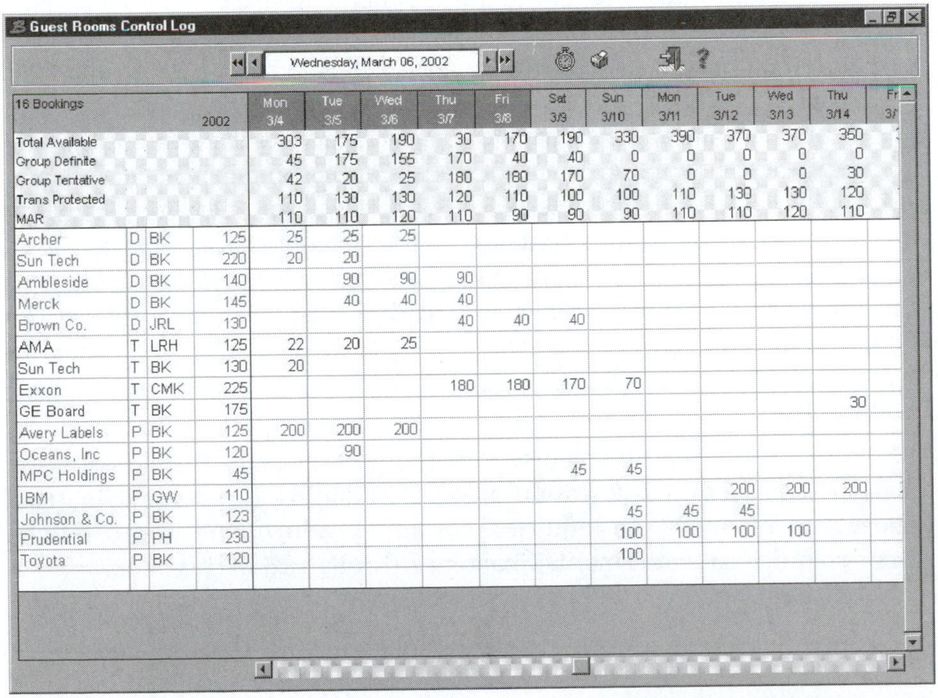

16 Bookings			2002	Mon 3/4	Tue 3/5	Wed 3/6	Thu 3/7	Fri 3/8	Sat 3/9	Sun 3/10	Mon 3/11	Tue 3/12	Wed 3/13	Thu 3/14
Total Available				303	175	190	30	170	190	330	390	370	370	350
Group Definite				45	175	155	170	40	40	0	0	0	0	0
Group Tentative				42	20	25	180	180	170	70	0	0	0	30
Trans Protected				110	130	130	120	110	100	100	110	130	130	120
MAR				110	110	120	110	90	90	90	110	110	120	110
Archer	D	BK	125	25	25	25								
Sun Tech	D	BK	220	20	20									
Ambleside	D	BK	140		90	90	90							
Merck	D	BK	145		40	40	40							
Brown Co.	D	JRL	130				40	40	40					
AMA	T	LRH	125	22	20	25								
Sun Tech	T	BK	130	20										
Exxon	T	CMK	225				180	180	170	70				
GE Board	T	BK	175											30
Avery Labels	P	BK	125	200	200	200								
Oceans, Inc	P	BK	120		90									
MPC Holdings	P	BK	45						45	45				
IBM	P	GW	110									200	200	200
Johnson & Co.	P	BK	123							45	45	45		
Prudential	P	PH	230							100	100	100	100	
Toyota	P	BK	120							100				

FIGURE 17–2

A Guest Room Control Log

Reproduced with the permission of Micros Systems, Inc. (www.micros.com)

others to cross-sell business within a cluster of properties in the pertinent geographic area.

Inquiry Management

The hotel sales process has traditionally been burdened with the inefficiencies caused by the numerous ways in which business opportunities arrive. Tour operators and meeting and event planners will often mail, fax, or telephone to a convention and visitors' bureau (CVB) a request for proposal (RFP) detailing their group's needs and requirements. The sales staff of the CVB will, in turn, mail, fax, or e-mail these leads to their member hotels. Responding to these inquiries is a time-consuming process for both the CVB and hotels, but salespeople have to be primed to jump on such RFPs because, in the world of hotel sales, the salesperson who responds first often books the business.

The Internet has streamlined the process for the meeting and events planner, CVBs, and hotels. What used to take a meeting planner weeks in sending, retrieving, and analyzing proposals now takes days. This allows meeting planners to book more meetings in less time, which improves their own firm's efficiencies and profitability. CVBs have it easier too. Now, when they receive an RFP electronically, they can forward the lead out to their appropriate hotel members without the need to manually rekey the information into leads sheets or faxes. The lead can also be saved into the CVB's own database for future prospecting.

Using software aids, a hotel can quickly merge documents into a proposal and e-mail it back to the planner in a matter of hours (see Figure 17–3). Instead of mailing a packet of the hotel's layout, a salesperson can attach schematics of meeting room dimensions and suggested setup diagrams. Once the business is booked, the catering/convention services department will have full details of the booking. This reduces a troublesome gap in communications that has often fallen between the sales arm and the operations arm. Now, a group's needs and requirements are automatically shared knowledge. All this is made possible through a travel industry consortium called the Open Travel Alliance, which has created specifications that allow meeting planners and hotels to exchange meeting data.

Prospecting

The ability to pursue leads and prospects is one of the skills that distinguishes a salesperson from a reservation agent. The ability to *create* demand as opposed to responding to inquiries is a highly valued skill in professional sales—so much so that it merits Chapters 7 through 13 in this book.

As a salesperson, you will be responsible for

- identifying sources of leads and prospects in your territory

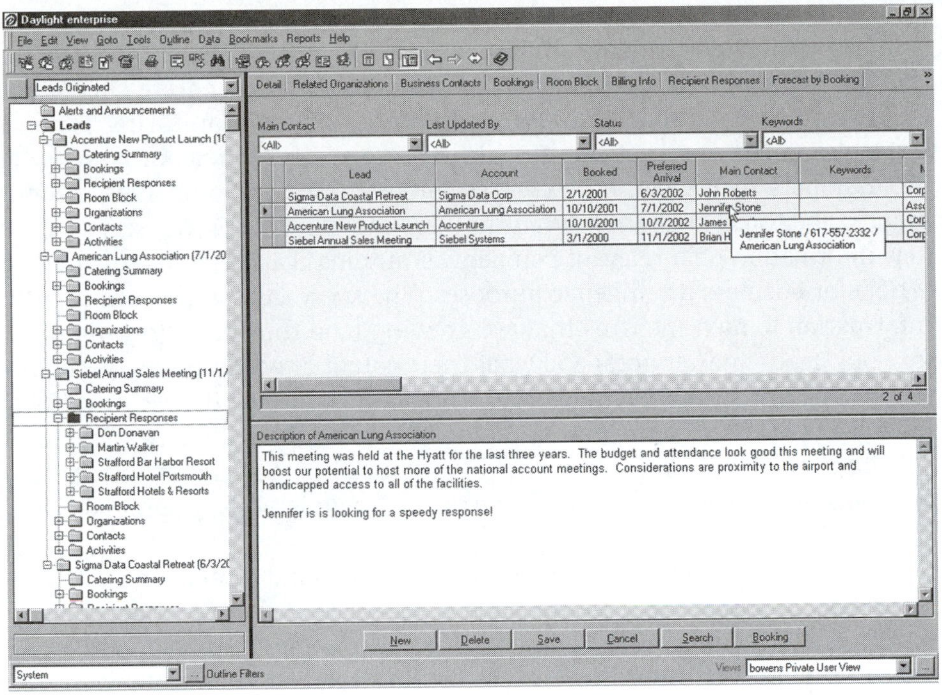

FIGURE 17–3

An Inquiry Management System Screen

Reproduced with the permission of Micros Systems, Inc. (www.micros.com)

- prioritizing them in terms of the quantity and value of their potential business
- determining the best method by which to contact them

Information technologies, including the Internet and databases, have improved and simplified the process.

Traditionally, the most productive way of generating leads was through networking, tradeshows, and making cold calls. Though these are still extremely valuable, a variety of information technologies have been added to the salesperson's arsenal. Software has provided salespeople a level of access to historical records unheard of in the old manual days. Prior to such software, the dominant feature of a sales office was horizontal file cabinets containing the histories of every group that had ever used the hotel. Often the files were arranged in a chronological fashion and color-coded for callback purposes. Many were also organized in terms of the potential for and value of the repeat business. Such systems worked well when disciplined sales staff systematically recontacted, at the appropriate time, selected meeting planners who had previously booked business at the hotel. Such information can now be stored in an electronic database, saving both time and space. Moreover, chains have often centralized the database on an enterprise-wide basis, providing a salesperson access to meeting planners who hold events throughout the country and world. Metaphorically speaking, the "file cabi-net" has expanded by a quantum leap.

The Internet provides a useful tool in monitoring corporate clients and identifying new prospects. Subscription-based media-monitoring services available on the Internet at sites like http://www.hoovers.com allow sales professionals to track the newswires for mentions of companies, people, brands, and topics that are relevant to their company. When the service finds new information on a relevant company, it automatically e-mails the full text article for business intelligence purposes. The savvy salesperson can use this information to identify firms that are growing (and thus have growing needs for your goods and services) and what their potential needs are. Research has shown that firms respond more positively to salespeople who have an in-depth knowledge of their company's products as well as their industry. The same subscription database can be also be a source of new leads for existing accounts by providing news of other divisions, acquisitions, promoted executives, and so forth.

Large corporations can require meeting spaces and rooms for a variety of purposes. To illustrate, pretend for a moment that you have developed a strong relationship with Brunswick Corporation's Mercury Outboard Motor Division, which periodically brings its field sales staff to your hotel for training. To further develop the account you may wish to explore other departments of the company for sources of new business. The investor relations department may periodically host potential investors; the CEO may meet quarterly with his/her board of directors; the corporation's five other divisions might have other needs. The savvy salesperson will use this information to identify other sources of business like these within the corporate account. The same database can also be used to research companies with whom your firm currently does not do business.

Hospitality Sales and the Catering System

The key difference between hospitality sales automation and virtually any other kind of sales automation (finance, pharmaceuticals, manufacturing, and so on) is that hospitality sales automates the whole process from prospecting . . . to selling . . . to delivering the product or service. In a hotel, that means ensuring that the customer gets the right guest rooms and, where necessary, that all the catering activities go off as planned. On the guest room side, the hospitality sales and catering system passes the inventory management task off to the PMS, but the catering side is managed within the sales and catering system.

"Catering," in this context, means everything from reserving the needed function space for a group to ensuring that the space is correctly set up and that the necessary meals, audiovisual equipment, computers, and everything else the group needs are there on time and properly charged for.

In many ways, this can be seen as the most complex part of a sales and catering system. The hotel must manage innumerable elements of a meeting, right down to the last detail, in an accurate and efficient way. The catering and conference services managers using this part of the sales and catering system are responsible for generating a high volume of extremely accurate work on a production basis every day. In addition, detailed forecasting and reporting on final results is of great importance to management. The efficiency of the sales and catering system is critical to productivity and profitability in this department.

There are five key components in the catering portion of the system.

1. The function diary—the efficient, automated version of the big physical book used to manage the function room inventory
2. Event management—the portion that manages all elements of an event to be held in a function room
3. The banquet event order—a dynamic contract with the customer detailing what the hotel will provide at the event and what it will cost
4. The banquet check—the final bill for an event
5. Various forecast and production reports that make it possible to manage the department profitably

The Function Diary

The automated function diary (see Figure 17–4) provides a real-time, up-to-the-minute function room inventory—for a single property or any number of properties in a cluster. (Soon automated function diaries will be available for the whole hotel chain.)

The function diary, sometimes called a scheduler, is used to display function space, functions, and guest room availability for a three-day period. The colors and symbols on the event bars vary and can display status, setup, combinations of rooms, and so on. If the cursor is placed over an event, the window shows a detailed view of that specific event. Events may be edited by clicking and dragging or double-clicking and opening an editable detail form. There are several key parts of any automated function diary: the function room display, the event display, and the guest room availability overview.

The Function Room Display. This is where you can review all the attributes of a function room, from ceiling height to capacity with various setups. You also select and sort sets of function rooms, showing just the rooms in a certain wing or specific hotel, perhaps. This is particularly important in a hotel cluster: where sales managers reviewing availability could quickly find suit-

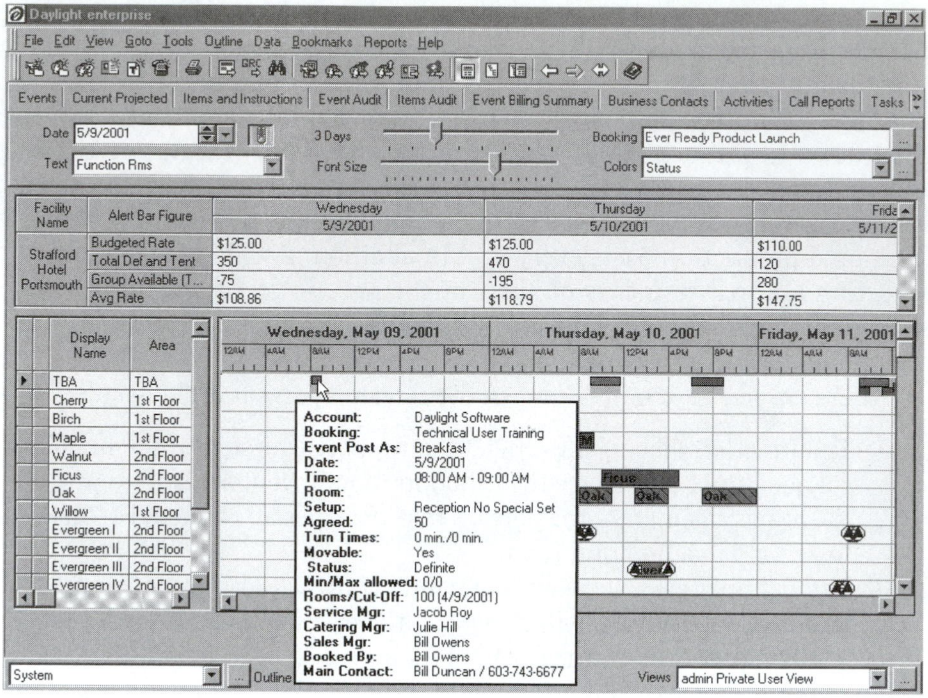

FIGURE 17–4

Function Diary

Reproduced with the permission of Micros Systems, Inc. (www.micros.com)

able space even though they may not know a specific hotel's function space characteristics. The ability to search for suitable space is further enhanced by features that offer access to room photos, layouts, and links to the corporate meeting planning Web site for the chain.

The Event Display. This is where users create and edit events, reserving the appropriate function room inventory as they go. The automated function diary allows the user to "draw" an event from start to end in the desired function room. If the event has a *definite* status, (usually an event with a signed contract on file) the space is firmly reserved and cannot be used by anyone for any other booking. A *prospect* or *tentative* event might not obligate the space: a *definite* event would be allowed to book over it. Catering managers can move an event or change the event start and end times by just dragging and dropping the bar for that event. Users can also view or edit event details from here. When changes are made here, there is no need to update information anywhere else. One change changes it in all places.

The event display also shows events with *an option* on the space if the current event is cancelled or moved and events which are still *TBA* (to be assigned). On a daily basis, the catering or function space manager checks the TBA queue using the on-screen or printed reports to properly assign the events.

Guest Room Availability Overview. When checking on whether the hotel can accommodate a group on a certain date, it is often necessary to check for guest room and function room availability at the same time. The function room diary optionally shows various guest room availability figures such as remaining availability.

Configuration Options—Views. Many kinds of users do many types of tasks in the function diary, from checking availability to managing function room inventory. Users can modify the diary as they go, to meet their needs. They can create named *views* of specific sets of function rooms for use as needed. They can change the range of dates being viewed. The colors and text can be changed to show the information considered most important at the moment (event status, conference name, which properties are visible, and so on).

Event Management

Each individual event in a group booking requires detailed attention to ensure that clients get just what they expect.

Effective event management starts with setting up the system at installation time. The director of catering establishes the item types (food, beverage, audiovisual, labor, computers, and so on) most appropriate for that hotel. These item types can then be grouped into the revenue categories needed by management and the accounting department for forecasting and production reporting. Finally, the DOC identifies the types of events most commonly needed at that hotel (meeting, breakfast, morning break, lunch, and so on) and determines the normal revenue pattern for each type of event.

When this initial setup is done with care, the property can always have a reasonable catering forecast. How? When a sales manager or catering manager creates an event of a certain type, the system automatically forecasts the income from that event. This is the forecast the hotel uses until the actual event details are added, which might be at a much later point.

When it is time to detail the events for a booking, key elements of the event will probably already have been defined.

◆ The *type* of event will have been established.
◆ A room will have been assigned.
◆ The attendance will have been estimated, though the catering services manager may later enter a more exact figure or even a guarantee.

So now, the catering manager will establish the setup and detail the other catering services to be provided, such as meeting materials, audiovisual support, coffee breaks, or full meals.

To catering, one of the most powerful benefits of automating is that all the catering items used by the hotel are stored in the system and can be efficiently selected for use in specific events. If the lists of catering items are built with

FIGURE 17–5

Example of a Banquet Event Order Generated by Daylight Enterprise Software

Reproduced with the permission of Micros Systems, Inc. (www.micros.com)

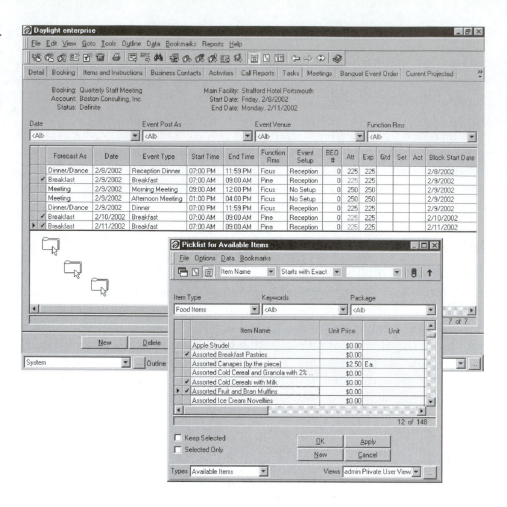

care, then they will be displayed as desired on **banquet event orders (BEOs)**, and an accurate forecast of future catering revenue can be created with a minimum of effort.

Throughout the planning period, while working with the client to determine menus and other needs, the catering manager can select, edit, and replace catering items as needed. When the time comes for the client to approve the BEOs, everything is close to being settled.

The software can make specific or universal changes. For example, suppose a group will be in-house for a meeting for four days. The catering manager created the event entries when the booking was confirmed. Now the group is finalizing their plans and has decided that for all of their breakfasts they will have the same items. Instead of entering this change four separate times, the catering manager can tell the software to change all breakfasts for the group. Once this is done, all items will be displayed on the merged BEO.

The Banquet Event Order (BEO)

The activity of the catering office revolves around creation of the banquet event orders (BEOs), which serve not only as the contracts with the client, specifying every detail, but as the internal communication about events, used by every department in the hotel. The four key tasks of successful BEO automation are

◆ making the BEO look *just right* for the client, with minimum fuss
◆ sending the BEO to the client
◆ making changes efficiently (since BEOs change constantly until the event actually happens)
◆ making it easy and efficient for the hotel staff to use

Looking Just Right. The BEO must be attractive and understandable to the customer. Some items will be priced a la carte, others on consumption, and others as part of an audiovisual package. Still other items will have no price at all. Some items will need a special annotation (*set up at the back of the room*). Others will need boldface type or some other special emphasis, such as highlighting.

An automated BEO provides the opportunity to create as many types of BEOs as might be needed—one for weddings, another for group meetings, and so forth. In addition, it allows the catering manager to create most BEOs without further editing, but still allows direct editing on the BEO to provide special notes and highlighting as needed. Then, as changes are made to the BEO and new data is merged into it, these edits are retained.

Sending It to the Client. It used to be necessary to print and fax or "overnight" the initial BEOs and each of the changes to the client—a time-consuming process. Now, in an automated BEO, the catering manager just e-mails the set of BEOs to the customer for review and comment and then, when each BEO is final, for printing and signature—a far more efficient process.

Making Changes Efficiently. After a BEO is created, it will change frequently. The catering manager can quickly substitute one item for another, quickly merge the BEO again, and see the result. A change log is often part of the BEO to track all of the changes, who made them, and when—resulting in an automated trail of changes.

Making It Efficient for the Hotel Staff. The property has the option of creating a different BEO laid out for the chef, banquet services, and other staff. This can be e-mailed or printed, depending on the state of automation in the hotel. It can also be posted to an internal Web site that allows the various departments to review and organize their BEOs online and print them as needed.

They can also see, either online or in reports, just the catering items of concern to them, making the whole process much more efficient than the paper-based process was.

Many of the managers that are part of BEO distribution are responsible for staffing departments like banquets, bartenders, and waitstaff. The automation of all items associated with a BEO offers an on-screen diary of events and corresponding items. This makes it easy for an audiovisual setup person, for example, to know how many staffers are needed and how many projection systems will be needed in the next seven days.

Banquet Check

The banquet check is the final bill for a specific BEO. At this point, the sales and catering system almost becomes an accounting system. After an event is completed, the banquet captain makes any final adjustments to the items the client consumed (how many bottles of wine, any additional audiovisual equipment, and so on) and prints a banquet check for the client to sign. When the group departs, all these banquet checks are combined with all other charges for the conference into a master bill for the client.

Catering Reports. Catering forecasting and production reporting have been among the most time-consuming tasks in the catering office. Data often got

FIGURE 17–6

Catering Report

Reproduced with the permission of Micros Systems, Inc. (www.micros.com)

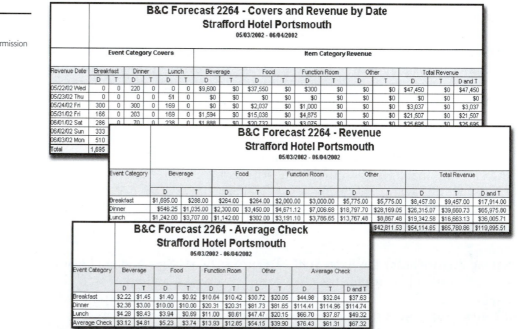

pulled from a variety of systems and reaggregated in a variety of ways for various purposes. Now, with the newer automated systems, all this reporting can be done with the push of a button (see Figure 17–6).

A sample of the types of reports that can be generated in the system just by entering accounts, contacts, bookings, and functions appears in Figure 17–6. Once information is entered, it may be accessed through a variety of both printed and on-screen reports. Another type of reporting is the ability to have private views of data. A private view of data is a screen or window containing information you need the way you want it—in the order you want, in the font you want, and filtered how you want.

The Future

The next advances in catering automation are likely to be in several important areas described below.

Web-Based BEOs

Currently, despite the ability to e-mail BEOs, the BEO management process still involves a lot of paper. The client sends back a signed copy; annotated copies of the BEO are passed around the hotel, and so forth. Soon, the BEO will be able to be posted to the Web for client comment and approval. Then the completed BEO will be available on the Web to hotel departments.

Wireless Catering

Vendors are on the verge of offering practical wireless catering applications that will allow catering managers to see everything they need from a hand-held device anywhere, any time.

Reporting

Traditionally hotel sales managers required their sales staff to set aside Friday morning to produce reports recapping their sales activities for the week. All this has been automated by the software, giving the salesperson back his/her most precious resource—time.

SUMMARY ◈

Technology provides several ways in which to improve the sales administration system. However, such software should be considered a sales *tool,* not a replacement of sales activity. In addition, for such systems to work effectively, they must be maintained constantly. Only you can decide if such a system makes the best use of your staff's time and resources. Look to the future to choose your best course of action.

References

Davies, F.D., R.P. Bagozzi, and P.R. Warshaw. 1989. User acceptance of computer technology: A comparison of two theorectical models. *Management Sciences,* 35, 982–1003.

◆ **DISCUSSION QUESTIONS**

1. Why do some firms lag behind others in the adoption of sales automation technologies? What advantages does this provide the technology-savvy hospitality sales student trying to gain his/her first job in sales?
2. What is a functional diary? How can it aid a sales professional?
3. Often it has been said that the first to respond to an RFP wins the business. How do SAT and the Internet streamline the process?
4. Describe the key component of a catering system of a SAT.
5. Explain in detail how a sales office should ideally be organized in terms of a (manual) filing and call report system as described in Chapter 15. Discuss what advantages software can provide in streamlining the sales process.

CHAPTER 18

The Future of Hospitality Sales:

A Situational World

After reading this chapter you should be able to

- describe the rapidly changing environment of sales professionals

- identify in which realms sales professionals will thrive and flourish and in which they will be displaced

- explain which sales strategy will remain the dominant selling mode and why

transactional selling

consultative selling

alliance selling

strategic partnerships

e-hubs

portals

vortals

key accounts

buyer-supplier alliances

Buyers purchase value—not just the satisfaction of needs. What research has shown is that providing satisfaction does not ensure a repeat purchase; providing value does. To illustrate, though most everyone would consider a stay at a five-star resort to be a very satisfying experience, only those with a significant income would consider it a good value and worthy of repeat purchase. On the other hand, consider for a moment the long lines often found at most quick-service restaurants. These customers may be only moderately satisfied with the core product and service but will return again and again because it is perceived as a good value compared to the alternatives. Value is defined as the buyer's "overall assessment of the utility of a service or product based on the perception of what is received versus what is given" (Zeithaml 1988, 14). This bears repeating.

> *Value is defined as the buyer's "overall assessment of the utility of a service or product based on the perception of what is received versus what is given."*

Thus, if what is received (product/service/quality level) is deemed appropriate for what is given (price), then the buyer perceives *value*. For a seller to provide value, he/she must deliver a product or service that meets the buyer's quality expectations at an appropriate price. Buyers judge and vote with their dollars among competitive product or service offerings and on the competitor's ability to deliver value.

Hospitality firms have traditionally created and competitively sold value to their corporate accounts in one of three ways. They offered their customers a product or service of

- comparable quality at a comparable price
- superior quality at a premium price
- low(er) quality at a low price

Today and continuing into the future, the concept of value is expanding beyond consideration of product and service. Along with the inherent and intrinsic characteristics of the product and service itself, value includes the acquisition process itself. The product or service is coming to comprise the actual offering plus the way it is bought and sold, as well as the reputation and support of the organization that produces it.

Product/service = actual offering $\times$ manner in which it is bought/sold $\times$ influence of reputation and support of the product

Under traditional thinking, there were no alternatives to the three ways to create value and to compete. As the twenty-first century opens, companies are redefining their business models, and we predict that hospitality sales in 2020 will have little in common with sales today. We are entering a period in which we, as salespeople, will be challenged to justify our contributions to our respective organizations!

The Continuum of Buyer-Supplier Strategies

The three buyer-supplier strategies we believe will conceptualize all hospitality sales into the foreseeable future can be thought of as points along a continuum (see Figure 18–1). On one end of the continuum is the **transactional selling** strategy, where competitive products are relatively simple and of comparable quality. Here, price is the principal issue for the customer. On the other end of the continuum are what we characterize as **strategic partnership** or **alliance selling strategies,** in which organizations form deep cooperative
relationships with their buyers and suppliers in exclusive and quasi-exclusive arrangements. In the middle of the continuum is the strategy that we predict will be the most prevalent: the **consultative selling** strategy, where buyers need complex products and services and work with their seller-suppliers in deep problem-solving relationships. Unlike with alliance selling strategies, the buyer does not wish to limit themselves by *single sourcing* or using exclusive procurement arrangements.

If *price* is the principal issue for buyers who do not need a great deal of technical support for their events, the hotel that can reduce the cost of the salesperson in the transaction can gain competitive advantage. The Internet, we believe, will help in the process. A number of **e-hubs, portals,** and **vortals** provide mechanisms that cut the costs of transactional selling by reducing the number of salespeople included. Some examples include

◆ http\\www.newmarketinc.com
◆ http\\www.plansoft.com
◆ http\\www.starsite.com
◆ http\\www.allmeetings.com
◆ http\\www.eventsource.com

This is especially true for corporate chains in the limited service category. Still, these Internet hubs do not completely eliminate the need for salespeople, since customers will always demand a choice in how they prefer to make a purchase and in how they prefer to connect and interact with the company.

FIGURE 18–1

Continuum of Buyer-Supplier Strategies

transactional selling strategy	*consultative selling*	*strategic partnership* or *alliance-selling strategies*

(They may prefer the Internet, a salesperson, or a combination of both.) We argue that organizations that successfully thrive in the price-sensitive conditions characteristic of transactional selling will need salespeople who can add value *and* work within the digital value-creating network. In this transactional selling environment, technology will become equally important as, if not more important than, salespeople. If so, the goal of transactional sellers must be to reduce selling costs (and, thus the price) of the product or service by reducing salesperson salaries and bonuses.

When products and services are complex and relatively expensive, most buyers are interested in and place a value on the advice and assistance the seller can provide. In fact, these buyers will frequently reject lower-priced alternatives in favor of one where the salesperson is actively helping them sort through the complexities and possible solutions. In these cases, the salesperson's assistance and expertise add problem-solving value within the sales process itself. We contend that this variation *(consultative selling)* will become the most predominant selling form for two reasons. First, when corporations downsize, they often lose internal expertise, which means they must then look to their suppliers for know-how and solutions to complex problems. The salesperson who takes the time to understand a client's real needs and to customize the hotel's offer responsively not only makes things easier for the buyer, but also delivers him/her more value from the exchange. The consultative selling process is therefore a source of competitive value. Since most firms place a great deal of value on preserving their freedom of choice, they will tend to prefer consultative selling over the more intense and less free strategic partnership selling. Keeping their suppliers at arm's length appeals to buyers who feel they must stay nimble (or unconstrained) to succeed in their own competitive environment.

We characterize the third buyer-supplier selling strategy that will continue to emerge as *strategic partnership* or *cooperative alliance strategies,* in which salespeople do not sell in the traditional sense but become relationship initiators and managers. Seller-suppliers often find it in their interests to seek out large organizational buyers who are seeking to consolidate their purchases through a single vendor. By streamlining procurement procedures, both the buyer and supplier can reduce the costs associated with the buying/selling exchange process. These savings, in turn, can be used to simultaneously increase product or service quality, sometimes within the same transaction! The benefits to both parties are clear. Buyers benefit when suppliers provide higher quality at lower costs, which suppliers are able to do partly because the guarantee of the buyer's business has reduced their need to advertise and market as intensely as before. Suppliers benefit through increased selling and production volume, better forecasting of demand, lowered marketing costs, and better facility utilization. In addition, the close working relationship provides the salesperson a unique opportunity to identify new needs and additional account penetration opportunities. It's a powerful relationship, but we don't see it taking hold on the meeting planner/hotel side of things. Instead, we contend that alliance selling strategies will grow among hotel companies (as buyers) with their vendors. Partnerships and alliances will rapidly become the norm in managing hotels' supply chain. On the other hand, alliance selling strategies by hotel companies (as sellers) to meeting planner end users will be less common. Here, consultative selling strategies will rule.

We also predict that major hotel companies will continue to advance the formation of alliances with other firms, not only as buyers and sellers, but also as strategic partners. These alliances will take many forms and will consummate with senior management being represented on each company's board of directors. Such representation at the highest strategic level makes sense when both firms realize that more value can be created through closer, more cooperative ties that go well beyond typical buyer-supplier relationships.

To illustrate, Marriott has created what it calls *alliance accounts* with a handful of firms, including Microsoft, Accenture, and AT&T. Marriott's alliance with these firms is centered on the sharing of core competencies more than on the driving of sales. When Microsoft decided to expand its Seattle campus's meeting facilities, it called upon Marriott to assist in its design and, ultimately, its management know-how. In return, when Marriott decided to create its own proprietary sales automation software to support *Sales 2000,* its pioneering redesign of its entire sales force structure in the 1990s, it called upon Microsoft and Accenture in its design and implementation rollout. Microsoft's core product is an operation system on which many software applications are based. Accenture, one of the world's leading management and technology consulting firms, designed the training module Marriott needed. Though it should not come as any surprise that Marriott receives a major share of its strategic partners' business (not to mention that Microsoft's and AT&T's products are in every Marriott property worldwide), alliances of this nature are *more than* buyer-supplier relationships. Their purpose is to create competitive advantages through the sharing of information and sharing of core competencies among firms with compatible strategic interests.

Is Deeper *Always* Better?

What prevents firms like Marriott from evolving all their major accounts to alliance accounts? If all these firms are both buyers and sellers of goods and services, wouldn't it make good sense to form more deep and committed relationships with all of them? The answer is no—for three reasons.

- ◆ First, recall from Chapter 14 that creating reciprocal buying and selling relationships with large accounts will invite the scrutiny of the Justice Department and the Federal Trade Commission as to the potential of illegal tying arrangements. No firm wishes to become embroiled in costly litigation.
- ◆ Second, and perhaps most important, one must understand that hotel companies are complex entities involving owners, franchises, and management companies, with each entity attempting to maximize its revenue and return on investment. Often it will make little financial sense for a hotel company to accept 100 percent of a **key account**'s business because the hotel could very well be selling its product or service to another buyer at a higher rate. Thus, companies hesitate to enter exclusive **buyer-seller alliances**. Becoming a vendor of choice is often quite sufficient in that it allows each hotel property to evaluate each potential piece of business in terms of profitability. Buyers themselves will often wish to preserve their freedom of choice and stay nimble or unconstrained in operating in their competitive environment.
- ◆ Last, not all buyers should be considered as candidates for strategic partnerships or alliances as previously described. Individuals—and the organizations they create and inhabit—encode and crystallize past experiences into routines that guide future behavior. Some people cannot be expected to suddenly change from playing poker with suppliers to now cooperating with them. Embarking on a cooperative relationship with another organization that retains an adversarial attitude will inevitably be a source of conflict that will keep the relationship from achieving its full potential for either party.

Alliances, regardless of the parties' level of commitment, cannot work unless both the buying and selling organizations view the business-to-business (B2B) relationship as a true business paradigm. Salespeople who have evolved to the role of managing alliance accounts should have no revenue goals. Instead they become full-time *relationship managers* responsible for creating value from the alliance by managing the interface between their firm's people and assets and those of their alliance partner. The most successful alliances are not created around precisely defined functional goals or within fixed periods of time. Instead, they are relationship exchanges whose functional goals are kept purposefully broad and imprecise in order to give the relationship manager and his/her team flexibility to deliver value across a variety of different circumstances. As such, they are built on a foundation of trust, the creation of value, and long-term commitment.

A Bigger Pie or a Bigger Slice?

Transactional selling, consultative selling, and alliance selling strategies are all hot topics in training circles as well as academic programs. Often, the traditional view is that selling exchanges need only one of these three distinct selling strategies—transactional. We suggest that such a prescription is not entirely correct. Instead, most buyer-seller relationships are a combination and a balancing of the three approaches. The central insight behind this situational prescription is the view that selling almost always involves a tension between "creating value" and "claiming value"—that is, trying to maximize the "size of the pie" (potential joint gains) and trying to maximize the size of one's own "slice of the pie" for both buyer and seller organizations (individual gains). That is, most buyer-supplier relationships have both competitive and cooperative dimensions, and a tension exists because the approaches called for by these dimensions are contradictory. If you focus on getting a bigger slice, it is harder to increase the size of the pie; and if you focus on expanding the pie, you risk having the other party grab a bigger slice. Effectiveness in sales requires balancing this tension, finding ways to create value while still claiming it, and vice versa. In short, consultative selling—which we believe will be the most prevalent form of selling in the future—is best seen as a very tough balancing act between creating and claiming value, between competitive and cooperative sales negotiations. Hospitality sales professionals today are venturing into a rapidly changing environment—but the basics of the personal selling process still apply. According to David Wilson (2000, 57), sales and marketing are "still about segmentation, needs generation, value creation, and the delivery of the promises that we make to the customer" and the salesperson who takes a broader view in the creation and exchange of value will be successful in either domain. Technology will play an enormous role in any sales approach, but according to Anderson and Narus (1998, 59), it "will never replace the salesperson's ability to establish trust with customers, respond to subtle cues, anticipate customer needs, provide personalized service, nurture ongoing relationships, and create profitable new business strategies in partnership with customers (Anderson and Narus 1998, 36).

References

Anderson, J. C., and Narus, J. A. 1998. Business marketing: Understand what customers value. *Harvard Business Review,* 76(6), 53–61.

Wilson, D. T. 2000. Deep relationships: The case of the vanishing salesperson. *Journal of Personal Selling and Sales Management,* 20(1), 52–61.

Zeithaml, V. A. 1988. Consumer perception of price, quality and value: A means-end model and synthesis of evidence. *Journal of Marketing* 52:2–22.

◆ **DISCUSSION QUESTIONS**

1. Hotels and restaurant companies as buyers often enter into exclusive buying relationships with their suppliers for items they purchase frequently. What factors are driving this trend?

2. Why would a hotel chain prefer to be a vendor of choice instead of evolving the relationship into a strategic alliance in which it accepts all of a buyer's business?

3. Technology will play an enormous role in the future. However, what aspects of the sales process can it never replace? Discuss.

Glossary

accommodative negotiation strategies   Bargaining strategies in which a seller's concern is maximizing the benefit to the buyer instead of one's firm. If repeated consistently over time, such a strategy will usually drive the selling organization into bankruptcy. However, it can be strategically applied where the long-term value of an account is more important than the short-term gains in a potential negotiated transaction.

account maintenance   Involves the servicing and regular follow up with business accounts assigned to a sales manager for purposes of earning new business from the existing customer. The frequency and depth of follow up varies if a key account system is employed.

account penetration   A sales task designed to extend and develop more *internal* business (referrals) from the initial buyer's organization.

active listening techniques   Oral and visual feedback techniques used by a listener that allow a check on accuracy and give the speaker the opportunity to confirm or amend the listener's perceptions.

AIDA   A sales and marketing acronym that stands for the stages in the consumer buying process: awareness, interest, desire, and action.

alliance selling   A synonymous term for *partnership selling* where buyer and seller have entered a formal, long-term, and on-going agreement to exclusively buy and sell from one another a specific product/service (example: meetings).

assumption close   A minor closing technique whereby the salesperson makes statements that assume that the prospect is going to buy. The salesperson begins to act and talk like the prospective buyer has already purchased the product or service. This talk and action are focused on what takes place next (since the sale has already been made). This close comes near the end of the planned demonstrating capability process.

authority   A term designating a prospect who has the authority to make a purchase decision for his/her firm.

BATNA   A term coined by Roger Fisher and William Ury that stands for "best alternative to a negotiated agreement." Any negotiator should determine his/her BATNA before agreeing to any negotiated settlement. If the settlement is as good as or better than one's BATNA, the agreement should be accepted. If the alternative is better, it should be pursued instead of the negotiated settlement. When one party's BATNA is good (or even if he/she just thinks it is good), he/she is unlikely to be willing to enter into negotiations, preferring instead to pursue his/her alternative option.

BEO   An acronym that stands for a banquet event order. The BEO can be a relatively detailed list of the goods and services agreed to by the buyer and seller and is useful in planning hotel events. The BEO serves not only as the contract with the client, specifying every detail, but as the internal communication about events, used by every department in the hotel.

BGC   An acronym for business growth cycle, BGC represents the stages a firm or enterprise theoretically goes through in the market, including introduction, rapid growth, maturity, and decline. The role of sales in each of these stages is fundamentally different.

breach of warranty   A legal term in sales whereby a warranty or assurance is extended by the seller that the buyer can rely on. Warranties can be verbally expressed during the negotiation process or communicated to the buyer in the salesperson's brochures, advertisements, and promotional materials.

bribes and gift giving   A bribe is something of value that is given or offered to a person or organization in a position of trust to induce that agent to behave in a way that is inconsistent with that trust. A bribe is considered unethical and illegal. Gifts are not categorically unethical or illegal. Gifts are a way a salesperson can express to a customer that he/she cares and appreciates their business. However, gifts can easily begin to resemble bribes, particularly when they are of high value and timed to influence purchase decisions.

business defamation   A legal term defined under the Federal Trade Commission Act whereby an individual representing a firm makes false statements about a competitor. Statements that fall under the category of business defamation include: (1) *business slander* (making unfair or untrue statements verbally to a third party construed to be damaging to a competitor's reputation); (2) *business libel* (unfair or untrue statements provided in writing to customers that damage a competitor's reputation in the form of brochures, letters, and advertisements); (3) *product disparagement* (providing false or deceptive comparisons concerning a competitor's product or services); and (4) *unfair competition* (providing statements that misrepresent the characteristics or qualities of one's own product or services).

buyer-supplier alliances   Buyer-supplier alliances, or *strategic alliances,* represent a new business model in which buying organizations intentionally form deeper, more cooperative relationships with fewer suppliers in an effort to improve quality and drive costs out of the manufacturing process. In such alliances, the consultative salespeople do not sell in the traditional sense but become relationship initiators and managers. By working in partnership to streamline procurement procedures, both firms can drive costs out of the exchange process that in turn can be used to increase quality at a reduced cost. The supplier can also reward the buyer by further lowering costs since the supplier has reduced its need to advertise and market as intensely as before due to the guarantee of the buyer's business. For a hotel chain, value is captured through increased volume, better forecasting of demand, lower marketing costs, and better facility utilization. For alliances of this nature to reach their full potential, each firm must view the business-to-business relationship as a true business paradigm, not a procurement technique.

buying motives   Determining buying motives is the process of finding out what problem(s) the customer has and offering your product(s) to solve their problem. These are the real reasons for a customer to buy; this is the key to the success of the sales process. There is no reason to go any further in the sales cycle unless the exact buying motives have been established. Without knowing what the customer's true buying motives are, the salesperson is merely guessing what the customer wants, or what may solve their problems. Taking the customer's buying motives into account, we should eliminate high-pressure sales because we are able to give the customer what they want, not what we think they want.

B2B   Short for business-to-business, a sales and marketing term that defines the consumer as another business rather than an individual customer. Developing B2B relationships with organizational buyers is a much more complex and time-consuming process for the sales professional than situations involving B2C relationships.

B2C   Short for business-to-consumer, a sales and marketing term that defines the consumer as an individual or social unit. From a sales perspective, retailing involves all business-to-consumer relationships.

channel advantage   A term coined by Friedman and Furey (1999) where selling firms use multiple sales channels to establish a larger base of customers, serve them in more flexible ways in order to improve customer satisfaction, and reduce selling costs.

channel lift   The foundation of channel strategy is a firm's understanding of the consumer behaviors in each market segment. The channels added to the mix should be those that collectively reach and profitably capture a share of the transactions in each market segment. When executed correctly the strategy lifts a firm's profitability through increased new sales with lower costs; this is known as channel lift.

channel mix   A concept used by salespeople and marketers to describe the multiple sales strategies they use to go to market. The purpose of a channel mix is to intercept a broad range of sales transactions in order to increase sales volume and market share. Channel mixes come in three forms: intensive, selective, and hybrid.

channel shift   A potential long-term effect of a firm's channel mix strategy whereby a firm's multiple sales channels end up chasing the same sales (customers moving from one channel to another) without channel *lift* (new sales). Though difficult to estimate, one should assess how much new sales volume will actually be produced by adding a new channel to the product-market mix.

coaching   A technique of cognitive apprenticeship whereby the director of sales observes sales managers as they try to complete tasks and provides hints, help, and feedback as needed. It can also include intensive on-the-job training through instruction, demonstration, and practice.

compensation   Represents the financial means by which salespeople in the hospitality industry are rewarded, including base salaries, sales commissions, and bonuses.

competitive differentiation   A strategy designed to create in the buyer's mind desirable differences, either tangible or intangible, between the product and service offered by the salesperson and the competitive alternatives.

complex goods and services   Goods and services that require a degree of customization to satisfying the unique needs and requirements of the buyer.

confidence collapse   A stage in the post-purchase process during which a customer perceives a gap between his/her *expectations* of the product or service performance and *actual performance/results* of the product or service prior to its delivery. It becomes the responsibility of the salesperson to anticipate and help the buyer who is experiencing such uncertainty prior to the implementation of the product or service.

confirmation questions   Questions that are useful in the demonstrating capabilities stage of a sales process. They help the salesperson to learn if the customer agrees that this "benefit" satisfies his/her needs. Here the salesperson is inviting the prospect to either agree with the matching statement or disagree. If the prospect agrees, the salesperson begins to select the next prospect need and starts a new matching statement. If the customer does not agree (with the confirmation question), "resistance" must be negotiated.

consultative selling   A sales strategy or mode targeted to buyers with a high potential for repeat and referral business. Consultative salespeople are generally focused on the buyer's view of what is important and how to increase value to the buyer in an effort to secure a long-term relationship with a profitable organizational buyer.

continuous call report   One of two initial sales call reports of a sales reporting system designed for high-potential accounts. Continuous call reports note the activity and comments on an existing or potential account. They serve as a reference tool for the salesperson in maintaining and developing accounts.

Continuous Quality Improvement (CQI)   Also known as Total Quality Management, CQI is a term coined by Edward Deming that reflects a fundamental business philosophy focused on customer satisfaction. This philosophy applies to the personal and professional activities of consultative salespeople. For consultative salespeople, CQI is about continually assessing one's professional performance to please customers on a regular basis and facilitate innovations. Continuous quality improvements result in reduction of costs and wastes, and in greater productivity of sales. This results in increased customer satisfaction, stronger relationships, and increased competitive advantage for one's firm.

customer   A buyer who has need for and ability to pay for the product or service the salesperson offers. Customers are high-probability prospects as well as actual buyers—90 percent to 100 percent. Most customers are not 100 percent because there is always a possibility that they might fail to purchase all that was agreed to on a signed contract and sometimes they even cancel contracts or letters of agreement.

customer choice   A sales and marketing philosophy based on the tenet that customers have and always will demand choice. Customer preferences will always be based on the perception of value; the perception of value can be enhanced not only by price and quality but also by the ease in which a buyer can connect and interact with the company.

customer objections   Concerns or objections of a buyer that the seller must answer or negotiate before an agreement can be made. They may be valid or not but require tactic appreciation in order to advance a sale.

demonstrating capability   The process of showing a product or service to a prospect prior to purchase and, if possible, letting them use it. In most hospitality selling situations, demonstrating capabilities involve the presentation of proof devices that demonstrates intangible service features and benefits matched to specific customer needs.

direct-appeal close   A close that involves asking the buyer for the order in a straightforward manner. It is used after all benefits have been presented and agreed to.

direct denial   A salesperson's response to a partially valid concern or an objection from a buyer. This involves directly refuting or denying what the prospect has stated. It's considered a high-risk method, but in some cases what the prospect has stated or believes may be very wrong or misperceived. In any case, if this misperception is left unaddressed, the prospect will probably not buy.

distributive negotiation strategies Distributive bargaining, also called "claiming value," "zero-sum," or "win-lose" bargaining, is a competitive negotiation strategy that is used to decide how to distribute a fixed resource, such as money. The parties assume that there is not enough to go around, and they cannot "expand the pie," so the more one side gets, the less the other side gets.

DOS An acronym that's standard for director of sales.

DOSM An acronym that's standard for director of sales and marketing.

e-hubs Today, business-to-business (B2B) e-hubs, e-procurement, and vortals are names for essentially the same set of e-commerce capabilities that are addressing companies' supply chain issues. They allow buyers to simplify the purpose process, saving their firms both time and money.

W. Edward Deming Generally considered the founder of the Total Quality Management movement. See Deming's *Out of Crisis* (2000), Boston, MA,.: MIT Press.

EQ Emotional quotient is a concept and personality test developed by Daniel Goldman. It is based on the assumption that there is no separation between how we think and our emotions. EQ shapes our interactions with others and our understanding of ourselves. It defines how and what we learn; it allows us to set priorities; it determines the majority of our daily actions. Individuals who choose to develop their emotional intelligence have been shown to be more effective in handling their feelings. EQ in part determines one's success and happiness in all walks of life, including business relationships.

exchange The act of obtaining a desired value (usually in the form of products and services) from someone by offering something in return.

extrinsic value The relative worth that a buyer places on a product or service that extends beyond its intrinsic value. For example, a meeting planner might place much value on a hotel whose salesperson offers him/her advice and solutions that save the meeting planner time, effort, and anxiety. In this case, value can be created by the salesperson.

fraudulent misrepresentation A legal term in sales whereby a salesperson intentionally deceives a customer to believe in a condition that is different from the one that exists and causes financial harm. In general, cases of misrepresentation are decided on an individual basis and are based on two criteria: (1) whether factual statements were made concerning the product or service's performance and (2) the level of knowledge of the customer in the trade. The salesperson should clearly understand the difference between offering an opinion and making statements of fact and warranty, particularly in cases where the buyer is inexperienced.

functional diary   A part of most hotel sales automation software packages designed to help a salesperson manage daily tasks. It simplifies and better organizes the process of scheduling meetings and tasks in advance with the assurance that the salesperson will be reminded of them at the pertinent time. In addition, the software also allows the salesperson to keep track of which client groups are on-property. This can be helpful for relationship management purposes as well as for monitoring the status of the hotel (for example, renovations and events).

gaining commitment   Commonly referred to as closing, gaining commitment is the point in the buying/selling exchange process when the salesperson asks the potential buyer to make a purchase.

go to market systems   Systems companies use to take their products and services to the market for purposes of reaching and serving customers as profitably as possible. Today they often involve complex mixes of sales channels and are designed to gain a firm competitive advantage.

hybrid channel coverage   A form of channel mix strategy involving the assignment of a single channel to one or more product markets. The purpose is to serve a firm's broad customers with multiple overlapping sales channels. Virtually all customers can use any channel since the goal is to intercept as many customers as possible by providing them with their preferred method of making a purchase. At the same time, the firm's direct sales force is assigned only those large corporate accounts that require specialized services. The purpose of the sales force is not to achieve total market coverage, but to reach, develop, and serve those high-valued accounts that need customized services.

imperfect competition   A term used to describe a competitive environment in which there are many suppliers of a product or service in the marketplace but the customer has limited information of these offerings. Salespeople have traditionally thrived in such environments.

implication questions   One of the four types of questions as coined by Neil Rackham whereby the seller heightens the potential buyer's awareness and concerns by having him/her consider the pluses and minuses (implications) if his/her stated needs (problems) are not met.

indirect denial   A salesperson's response to a partially valid concern or objection from a buyer. Here the salesperson will acknowledge that the prospect is partially right. This is a "soft" and "conditional" denial, as compared to a direct denial.

information technology (IT)   Software and technology systems through which a hotel reaches and serves its target market. In a hotel sales setting, IT often involves sales automation software, e-commerce, and catering management systems.

initial call report   One of two initial sales call reports of a sales reporting system. An initial call report is filled out after a first sales call and generally contains the names and contact information of the prospect's company, what his/her needs are, and his/her potential to become a customer. It is valuable when used in tandem with a continuous call report. These reports are usually filed alphabetically under the prospect company's name.

insurance and indemnification clauses   Since all events involve the assemblage of the public, which can range from less than a 100 to thousands, they create risk of injury for not only the public but the firms that put them on. Additional insurance and agreements to hold harmless the host facilities are inherent in any hotel sales contracts with the event sponsor.

integrative negotiation strategies   Integrative negotiations (also called "interest-based bargaining" or "win-win bargaining") is a negotiation strategy in which parties collaborate to find a "win-win" solution to their dispute. This strategy focuses on developing mutually beneficial agreements based on the interests of the disputants.

intensive channel coverage   A form of channel mix in which a firm intentionally provides overlapping coverage of one or more markets where each channel of a firm's sales channels competes with each other. It is based on the assumption that sales will best be generated through competition.

interests   Interests include the needs, desires, concerns, and fears important to each side in a negotiation. They are the underlying reasons behind positions of both the buyers and the sellers involved in sales negotiations.

intrinsic value   The underlying value of a product or service from the perspective of the buyer. In the analysis of an intrinsic value buyer, the product or service is considered a commodity with no fundamental quantitative or qualitative differences among the alternatives. In this scenario, the buyer will base his/her purchase decision on price.

investigating needs   Identifying the needs of a potential customer is the purpose of a first sales call of a multiple-call sales process. As a consultative salesperson, one's task is to first discover the needs and problems of the prospective buyer and then demonstrate how one might be able to help him/her solve them using the benefits of one's product or service. At the second appointment a proposal is presented based on the needs identified during the first sales call.

key accounts   A firm's most important, or key, accounts that are singled out for special attention because of their enormous buying power. Firms generally assign their most senior salespeople to these key accounts for relationship management and development purposes.

legal jurisdiction and arbitration clauses   From time to time, it should be expected that disagreements will arise among buyers and sellers after a service has been provided. It is wise to include in sales contracts the legal jurisdiction (state or municipality) where disputes can be settled through the courts and, if agreeable, to seek alternative means to resolve those disputes outside the court system.

letter of agreement   A signed and official letter of agreement outlines the basic understanding between the buyer and the seller for an economic transaction and represents a legally binding contract. Such a letter often contains nonperformance clauses, insurance and indemnification clauses, legal jurisdiction clauses, and arbitration clauses.

limited choice close   A close that uses a series of increasingly narrow product or service choices offered to the prospective buyer as a way of helping the buyer make a decision. This closing technique is often used when a prospect seems unable to decide but the salesperson knows that the benefits have already been accepted or sold to the buyer. The following describes a way to implement this method: (1) allow the prospect to examine several different "choice packages" and try to assess the degree of interest; (2) cease showing new choices when it appears that the prospect has been given ample selection; (3) remove products in which the prospect seems uninterested; (4) concentrate on products in which the prospect seems to be definitely interested.

matching statements   Buyers have needs to be fulfilled while sellers have products/services that can fulfill these needs; therefore, sellers communicate this ability by making statements that first acknowledge the need followed by indications of how the product/service fulfills the need–the buyers' need is verbally matched with a seller's product/service benefit.

means   This term refers to anything which can facilitate or make happen something else; specifically, this refers to the financial ability to make the sales exchange take place—the money to make it happen.

micromarketing   This term means that the salesperson in a B2B context performs all of the functions of traditional marketing in creating awareness, interest, desire, and ultimately action on the part of the organizational buyer. In this context, traditional marketing plays an overall supporting role for the salesperson as micromarketer. Instead of focusing on categories of customers traditionally called market segments, micromarketers focus on very specific business-to-business (B2B) customers who desire customized products and services.

minor closing   Also called *trial close,* it is a closing attempt made at an opportune time during the sales presentation to encourage the buyer to reveal readiness or unwillingness to buy. The minor close is most appropriate after obtaining sufficient agreements to buy *and* getting "buying signals."

monopoly   A term from economics describing a market in which there are many buyers but only one seller. When you have a monopoly, a salesperson can ask any price he/she likes.

motivation   The drive or compelling force that energizes people to do what they do in a given situation.

multiple channel selling strategy   A channel refers to a specific linkage between a selling company and a buyer; therefore if a company sells its products/services only through salespeople, this is a single-channel strategy. When other selling channels are added (Internet, direct mail, etc.) along with the single-channel (salesperson) the selling company is now using a multiple-channel selling strategy.

need-payoff questions   One of the four types of questions as coined by Neil Rackham whereby the seller encourages and actually guides the buyer into selling him- or herself. This occurs when the buyer begins making such statements as, "This meeting room will be perfect for my attendees" or "I can envision the wonderful experience that my attendees will have as they relax on the resort grounds."

needs   A need is usually viewed from the buyer's perspective and indicates a want, desire, required specification, problem to be solved, and so forth. It is the basis upon which all sales and exchanges are made; buyers seek solutions (products/services) that solve their problems or needs.

negotiations   Communications between two or more parties towards the development and maintenance of a contractual relationship. Advantage in negotiations generally extends to the party who is most prepared and knowledgeable in the negotiations process.

nonperformance clauses   This is a legal addition into a contract that specifies the penalties if either party to the signed contract fail to abide by the contract or Letter of Agreement terms.

oligopoly   A term from economics describing a market characterized by a small number of producers who often act together to control the supply of a particular good and its market price. An oligopoly exists when a few companies dominate an industry. This concentration often leads to collusion among suppliers, so that prices are set by agreement rather than by the operation of the supply-and-demand mechanism. For an oligopoly to exist, the few companies do not need to control all the production or sale of a particular product or service. They only need to control a significant share of the total production or sales. As in a monopoly, an oligopoly can persist only if there are significant barriers to entry to new competitors. Obviously, the presence of relatively few firms in an industry does not negate the existence of competition. The existing few firms may still act independently even while they collude on prices.

perfect competition   A term used to describe a competitive environment in which there are many suppliers of a product or service in the marketplace and the customer has access to considerable information about these offerings. Access to information available on the Internet is moving most sectors of the hospitality industry toward a state of perfect competition in which buyers no longer need salespeople for their product or service knowledge.

PLC   Product life cycle represents the stages a product or service theoretically goes through in the market, including introduction, rapid growth, maturity, and decline. The role of sales in each of these stages is fundamentally different.

PMS   An acronym that stands for a hotel's property management system.

PONS TEST   The Profile of Nonverbal Sensitivity test is a personality test that measures people's ability to read emotional cues of others in social situations. Research has shown that people with higher PONS scores tend to be more successful in their work and relationships; children who score well are more popular and successful in school, even when their IQs are quite average.

portals   Used in e-commerce, portals provide customers a single access point and information interface to a company, both inside and outside the firewall.

POS   An acronym that stands for a food and beverage point-of-sale system.

probing questions   Sellers are at their best when they ask the buyer many questions to discover all of the buyers needs. Sometimes, buyers give vague or incomplete answers. A probing question is a follow-up question to further discover the meaning underlying vague and incomplete buyer answers. For example, "Could you clarify what you mean by the word 'success'?"

problem questions   One of the four types of questions as coined by Neil Rackham whereby the seller asks the buyer about his/her emotional needs to be fulfilled in the buyer/seller exchange. It may be that the buyer does not want to make the purchase of an unsuccessful product/service because of the impact on his/her job or for other emotionally based reasons. This contrasts with Rackham's first and least sophisticated question, Situation Questions which ask about Physical Needs.

proof devices   Evidence that demonstrates and reinforces the product or service feature and benefits to a potential buyer. For example, it's powerful to demonstrate your food service by having a meeting planner eat a meal at the property or spend a (complimentary) night at your hotel, then do a site tour. Or, if you are presenting in the prospect's office, demonstrate your hotel's capabilities and quality by showing brochures or displays on your laptop computer, or thank-you letters from former clients.

proposal   A plan or suggestion, in this case, of how the salesperson's product or service can satisfy the potential buyer's needs. It is based on the needs discovered in the first appointment of a sales call and can be very detailed. A proposal signed by both the buyer and seller is generally considered to be a legally binding contract.

prospect   A prequalified *potential* buyer that has a high probability of eventually becoming an *actual* buyer (customer). The buyer has generally been prequalified as having the need for and ability to pay for the product or service the salesperson offers. Prospects (as opposed to suspects) are middle- to high-range-probability potential buyers—50 percent to 89 percent.

qualifications   Factors that can be discovered that indicate the probability of a prospect eventually becoming a customer. They can include the potential buyer's need for, interest in, and ability to purchase one's product or service. Increased qualification information can also lead to either a higher or lower probability of eventual purchase.

reciprocity   In the hospitality industry, a firm can be both a buyer and seller in its relationship with other firms. When these relationships evolve to the form of alliances, the firm may establish a rule that customers should be given preferential consideration when it comes to buying. However, the practice can get out of hand when a salesperson hints "If you do not buy from me, we will not buy from you." The recipient of this statement will interpret it as a form of commercial blackmail, and it will likely backfire on the salesperson. The FTC has been known to issue cease-and-desist orders to stop the practice. The perpetrating salesperson and firm can also be prosecuted under the Clayton Act if the practice serves to impact competition significantly.

referrals   A sales task designed to extend and develop more *internal* business from the initial buyer's organization and to obtain *external* referral business to industry associates and friends of the initial buyer.

relationship exchanges   This term indicates that the trust between buyer and seller is increasingly more important today than the price and other traditional selling terms. In other words, a trusting relationship needs to be established between buyer and seller, especially in complex sales, because all complexities cannot fully be understood by a buyer and he/she relies on the seller to ensure that the seller will not take advantage of him/her. So, exchange of trust and a relationship is an unspoken part of the selling exchange.

relationship management   Often described as account maintenance, relationship management is a sales task designed to continue nurturing an *initial* buyer through relationship strengthening while attempting to generate repeat business and referral business.

relationship selling   A sales strategy or mode targeted to *strategic partnership* with a high potential for repeat and referral business. *Relationship selling strategies* are designed to form deep cooperative relationships with buyers and suppliers in exclusive and quasi-exclusive arrangements.

REVPAR   Short for revenue per available room, REVPAR is another commonly used metric used by hotel and resort companies to gauge their success in generating returns on investment. It is calculated as: Revenue Realized ÷ Rooms Available = REVPAR.

RFP   An acronym that stands for a request for proposal forwarded by the buyer to potential suppliers.

rule of law   A standard of ethics in which the law defines what is right and wrong and where the line is from a salesperson's perceptive.

sales automation technologies   Sales automation is a use of information technologies to increase sales productivity and enhance customer and guest communication. Companies have generally experienced significant increases in a sales force's productivity by investing in such technology.

sales presentations/proposals   A proposal is the seller's written specification outlining all of the components of the product/service that will fulfill the buyer's stated needs. Often, this written document is used when the seller is in the sales process phase, "presenting" or "demonstrating" capability, and used as a visual aid when the seller is verbally telling the buyer how his/her product/service can satisfy the buyer's needs. Should the buyer agree that the proposal does not need any changes or adjustments, and then is signed by the buyer, the proposal becomes a legal contract. So, when a seller is making a *presentation* he/she is also making a *proposal*.

selective channel coverage   A form of channel mix in which a firm intentionally assigns an individual channel to one specific market without overlap or integration with the other channels.

simple goods and services   Product and services requiring little customization to satisfying a customer. They are often considered to be commodities.

single-problem close   A close that deals with a single concern or objection that stands in the way of gaining commitment from the prospective buyer. The buyer himself/herself comes to the conclusion that there is only one concern left. For example, a salesperson using the technique might say, "Mr. Prospect, it seems that you like all of the benefits that we have discussed except this one. Is that right? If I could take care of this, would you sign the letter of agreement?"

situation questions   One of the four types of questions as coined by Neil Rackham and is the first series of questions whereby the seller asks the buyer about his/her physical needs or problems to be fulfilled in the buyer/seller exchange. For example when selling meetings and conferences: "How many attendees, how many rooms, dates, budget range, etc?"

situational negotiation strategies or tactics   Situational or contingency refers to the wisdom of adjusting your actions based upon the circumstances in which you find yourself. So, some buyers are interested in price and therefore the seller should not focus on building relationships. In other cases, relationships are more important, thus a smart seller adapts and adjusts his/her selling strategies and tactics based upon the buyers situation–the buyer's situation should govern how the seller adjusts his/her strategies and tactics.

situational selling   A practice that represents a seller's strategic abilities to adapt and apply the correct selling process based on the buyer's perception of value. Transactional selling appropriately pairs up with intrinsic value buyers, consultative selling with extrinsic value buyers, and alliance selling with strategic value buyers.

special concession close   A minor closing technique whereby the salesperson offers the buyer something extra for acting immediately.

strategic partnerships   Long-term business-to-business relationship where firms recognize their common ground in a shared interest in capturing new sales or reducing both their costs. They begin working together creatively and cooperatively to improve the profitability of both firms. These relationships are generally characterized as win-win relationships.

strategic value   The value to a buyer of having access to the seller's total organizational resources and competencies. Such buyers are looking to form an alliance or partnership with the selling organization and are willing to radically restructure themselves to accomplish this. They are looking for a strategic alliance, where both the buyer company and the seller company recognize key complementary competencies about each other. Strategically, both buyers and sellers who enter into such alliances hope to reduce costs and to gain other operational efficiencies. A strategic alliance is a relationship between business equals who are working together to create an extraordinary level of new value that neither could create alone.

suspect   A prequalified *potential* buyer who has a high probability of eventually becoming an *actual* buyer (customer). Suspects fall into the category of low- to medium-probability-potential buyers—10 percent to 49 percent probability. Salespeople systematically attempt to convert suspects to prospects to customers.

Technology Acceptance Model   Arguably the best theory to explain why some companies and salespeople readily accept technology whereas others do not. According to TAM, the acceptance of software aids is determined by two beliefs: the perceived usefulness (that is, the extent to which the company and/or salesperson believes the system will improve his/her job performance) and perceived ease of use.

Total Quality Management   During the 1980s, the United States faced a threat from the Japanese in their ability to produce high-quality products. This was often referred to as the "Toyota Phenomenon." Americans were buying foreign high-quality products and US manufacturers were losing market share. W. Edward Deming is associated with this movement which stressed that the entire manufacturing and support systems must continuously be reexamined and readjusted to incrementally improve overall or total quality. This term is also known as Continuous Quality Improvement.

transaction   The basic event of an exchange between a buyer and seller. After a transaction takes place, there is no promise that the B2B relationship will occur again.

transactional selling   A sales strategy or mode in which competitive products are relatively simple and of comparable quality. Here, price is the principal issue for the customer, and the salesperson adds little value in the exchange process.

translation words   Translation words are useful to demonstrate capabilities to potential buyers. They are words that convert a *feature* into a *benefit* in the minds of buyers. A benefit is the value of a feature to the prospect—what the feature can accomplish for the prospect. People only buy results or solutions to problems. Salespeople must ensure that the prospect clearly understands the benefit. Translation words such as, "what this means to you," "thus," and "so," along with other words act as translations of features into benefits.

tying arrangements   When a seller conditions a sale of a product on the agreement that the buyer will purchase another product or service produced or distributed by the seller, an illegal tying arrangement results. Tying arrangements may be illegal particularly if it can be shown that the arrangement is for the purpose of reducing competition. A tying arrangement requires that in order to receive an order the seller must be willing to buy further products or services from the purchasing organization.

value   At its simplest definition, *Value = Benefits − Costs*. This term represents the benefits exchanged between buyers and sellers in an economic exchange that satisfies both parties' needs. Value to the buyer is usually found in the product or service but is increasingly found in the ease of the acquisition process itself. Value for the seller is usually found in the money or revenue received but can also include long-term repeat and referral business.

vortal   Used in e-commerce, vortals provide customers a single access point and information interface to a company, both inside and outside the firewall.

yield   A commonly used metric used by hospitality organizations to gauge their success in generating returns on investment. In a hotel sales context, yield is calculated through the following formula: *Revenue Realized ÷ Revenue Potential = Yield*. It is often tracked on a daily, weekly, monthly, and annual basis.

Index